LAST
NIGHTSHIFT
IN SAVAR

The Story of the Spectrum
Sweater Factory Collapse

DOUG MILLER

Published by McNidder & Grace
4 Chapel Lane, Alnwick, NE66 1XT

First Published 2012

A catalogue record for this work is available from the British Library.

ISBN: 978-0-85716-039-3

Designed by Obsidian Design

Printed and bound in Great Britain by Martins The Printers,
Berwick-upon-Tweed, Northumberland

This book is dedicated to the memory of
the sixty-two victims
of the Spectrum Sweater Factory Collapse.

Contents

Acknowledgements

My special thanks are due to the following people.

Khorshed Alam, Noor E Alam, Z.M. Kamrul Anam, Roy Ramesh
Chandra, Badruddoza Nizam, Caroline Bayley, Carole Crabbé,
Ineke Zeldenrust, Lynda Yanz, Catia Gregoratti,
Aleix Gonzalez Busquets, Neil Kearney, Runa Khan,
Javier Chercolés, Shirin Akter, Patrick Itschert,
Razaul Karim Bhuiyan, Jenneke Arens, Maggie Burns,
Klaus Priegnitz, Shahriyar Hossain, Maren Böhm,
Farjana Godhuly Khan, Shehab Uddin, Steve Grinter,
Ashling Seely, Laura Carter, Veerle Planckaert, Lesley Crofton,
Fanny Gallois, Carlos Piñeiro Aneiros, Dietrich Weinbrenner,
Asif Saleh, Silvana Cappuccio, Felix Poza Pena,
Antonio Abril Abadin, Eva Kreisler, Mic Porter, Sylvain Macé,
Kamal Uddin, Deborah Rotsaert, Lakshmi Bhatia, Evelyn Bahn,
Mahabubur Rahman, Jafrul Hasan Sharif, Jahangir Alam,
Jenefa Jabbar, Raja Gopal, Simon Walvin, Jennifer Moore,
Rory O'Neill, Repon Chowdury, Lizzie Dutton and Dan Rees.

Figures and Tables

Figures

Figure 1: Artist's impression of construction phases of Shahriyar Fabrics 1997, Spectrum Sweaters Phase 1, Spectrum Sweaters Phase 2. Courtesy: Lizzie Dutton.

Figure 2: Bangladesh Exports in Knitwear and Markets 1991 2008. Source: BKMEA.

Figure 3: Annual average price change in ex-factory (FOB) prices for wovens and knitwear calculated as total export value/total export volume. Source: (Uddin, 2006:63).

Figure 4: Geographical origins of the Spectrum workers. Courtesy: INCIDIN.

Figure 5: Small Diameter Circular Knitting Machines. Photo courtesy: Hamidul Islam.

Figure 6: Knitting operators. Photo courtesy: Sonia Sweaters.

Figure 7: Collapsed factory. Photo courtesy: Clean Clothes Campaign.

Figure 8: A rescuer searches inside the collapsed floors. Photo: Shehab Uddin.

Figure 9: Buckled Columns. Photo courtesy: Spectrum owners.

Figure 10: NGWF demonstration in support of the Spectrum victims in Dhaka. Photo courtesy: CCC.

Figure 11: Noor-e-Alam and Jahangir Alam on their European tour organised by Clean Clothes Campaign. Photo courtesy: CCC.

Figure 12: Friendship's economic classification of the families of the victims. Courtesy: Friendship.

Figure 13: Distribution of forms of assistance to Spectrum families under the Friendship Phase 2 initiative. Courtesy: Friendship.

Figure 14: Neil Kearney (ITGLWF) and Javier Chercolés (Inditex). Photo: Caroline Bayley, courtesy: BBC.

Figure 15: Distribution of cheques to the families of the deceased at the BGMEA headquarters, August 2010. Photo courtesy: Inditex.

Figure 16: Shafiqul Islam in his new job at the reception of the Inditex sourcing office in Dhaka. Photo: author.

Figure 17: The new facility on the site of the old Spectrum factory. Photo: author.

Tables

Table 1: The Structure of the RMG Sector 2005.

Table 2: The Relative Export Performance of Different Apparel Items for the RMG sector during the life of the Spectrum Sweater Factory, (in Million USD).

Table 3: Accidents in RMG Factories 1990–2005.

Table 4: Companies implicated in the disaster based on labels discovered in the rubble or submitted by Spectrum workers, and other sources of information, May 2005

Table 5: The Spectrum Voluntary Relief Scheme Estimated Value.

Table 6: Cases filed regarding Dowry under Suppression of Violence against Women and Children Tribunal (2008–2009). Source: BNWLA.

Foreword

I am delighted to have been asked to introduce this book which takes us inside the global textile and clothing sector. Doug Miller has a long association with the Bureau for Workers' Activities (ACTRAV) particularly through his work as multinationals coordinator and research officer with the International Textile Garment and Leather Workers' Federation. The multinationals work of the International Labour Organisation has focussed on a greater promotion and follow-up of the Tripartite Declaration of Principles concerning Multinational Enterprises and Social Policy (MNE Declaration) – a key tool for promoting labour standards and principles in the corporate world. It is vital that we pay more attention to the globalization of industrial relations as a response to the internationalization of company operations and to the role that the ILO and its constituents should play in shaping it. However, to do this requires a deep understanding of the processes at work in the value chains operating in each industrial sector. This book does precisely this, lifting the lid on the workings of the global fashion industry, and taking us through what is a harrowing account of the social impact of an industrial disaster in a developing country where insurance coverage for health and safety remains pitifully poor.

The strength of Doug Miller's book lies in its breadth, and as the story unfolds we are given insights into the historical beginnings of a manufacturing sector which became wayward at its very inception, fuelled by latter day sourcing practices which fostered the 'race to the bottom' in textile and clothing workers' conditions, which are a feature of the industry today. It is the mandate of the Bureau for Workers' Activities to strengthen representative, independent and democratic trade unions in all countries, to enable them to play their role effectively in protecting workers' rights and working conditions. Bangladesh, however, is a country where trade unions are compromised in providing effective services to their members at the workplace by a dogged resistance on the part of the employers to prevent workers from exercising their rights to freedom of association and collective bargaining. What is remarkable in this account is the way in which the affiliates of the International Textile Garment and Leather Workers' Federation, led by its late General Secretary Neil Kearney, were able to work – at times under extremely difficult conditions – to mobilise international support and to pressurise those multinationals sourcing from the factory to provide additional support for the families of the deceased and the injured. The particular 'rights based' initiative developed by the Global Union in conjunction with the Spanish multinational Inditex to provide enhanced compensation and a pension for the victims was an unprecedented move and merits particular attention in the book.

As ACTRAV continues to promote the Decent Work agenda, the account contained in this book draws important lessons for our four strategic objectives of employment, social protection, social dialogue and tripartism, and international labour standards and fundamental rights at work, and above all points to the importance of collective and individual human agency in the achievement of these goals. Doug Miller has done us all a service in reminding us of that fact and I thank him for this valuable contribution.

Dan Cunniah
Director, Bureau for Workers' Activities (ACTRAV)
International Labour Organisation
Geneva
Switzerland

Preface

This book started out as a request made by Javier Chercolés, head of corporate social responsibility at Inditex SA, the Spanish multinational fashion retailer and owner of the ZARA brand, to write up a business case study focusing on the Spectrum Sweater factory disaster which occurred in 2005 in Bangladesh. Inditex had been one of the buyers sourcing from the factory in Palashbari, Savar, which collapsed on April 11th killing 62 workers and injuring – in some cases seriously – a further 84 workers. He was particularly keen to place in the public domain the details of the relief scheme which had been developed in conjunction with the International, Textile Garment and Leather Workers' Federation (ITGLWF) to assist the families of the deceased and the injured, and which was still very much in the process of being implemented.

At the time of the collapse, I was seconded from the University of Northumbria to the International Textile Garment and Leather Workers' Federation (ITGLWF) coordinating, amongst other things, research on multinationals. Whilst I was aware of the case, this was not something I became directly concerned with, although this clearly became an important piece of solidarity action for the Global Union, in which the late Neil Kearney, its General Secretary, became personally very involved. The subsequent cooperation between the ITGLWF and Inditex SA in developing a relief scheme for the victims ultimately resulted in the signing of a global framework agreement on international labour standards between the two parties in October 2007. This new relationship led to the creation of, amongst other things, a jointly sponsored post in worker rights in fashion, which I held at the University of Northumbria between 2008 and 2012.

After conferring, Inditex and the ITGLWF decided that this relief initiative merited not just a case study, but a book, since this was a much bigger story involving concerted international solidarity action, new roles for trade unions on the ground, the response of the Bangladesh government and the Ready Made Garment industry itself, at a time when the sector was in the throes of becoming exposed to a newly liberalised global apparel trading regime. Moreover, as in every industrial disaster, there were inevitably questions of causality and culpability, which would normally be the subject of a public or official inquiry, which to date has not taken place.

Trying to do justice to a story from the recent past and which, for a number of the parties, was and is still 'live', has been a challenge. The task has resembled the piecing together of a giant jigsaw puzzle. In seeking to minimise gaps in the overall picture, I have endeavoured to maintain as much critical distance as possible in this process. This said, I am grateful to Inditex and the ITGLWF for financially supporting a number of visits to Brussels, Amsterdam and not the least four field trips to Bangladesh, as well as providing access to relevant documentation, and meetings with the families of the deceased and injured.

I was able to construct a skeleton and chronology from news coverage, a process facilitated by the existence of the on line archives of two main English speaking Bangladeshi newspapers in particular – the Daily Star, and New Age. Inevitably, in the media frenzy immediately after the collapse, all manner of explanations for the disaster circulated and the many necessary references to the news media gives a sense of the 'noise,' selective reporting and downright falsehoods surrounding the issue. The piecing together of events was augmented by access to email correspondence between the ITGLWF and the buyers at the factory and the extensive urgent appeal documentation and email correspondence of the International Secretariat of the Clean Clothes Campaign (CCC) in Amsterdam. For this I am grateful to Veerle Planckaert and Ashling Seely at the ITGLWF offices in Brussels for their assistance, and to Ineke Zeldenrust for granting me an interview and access to the Spectrum files at the CCC, as well as the national CCC co-ordinators, in Belgium, France, Spain, Germany, the Netherlands, and Sweden whom are too numerous to mention. Additionally, I was able to get detailed accounts from the two main initiators of the Inditex/ITGLWF Relief Scheme: Javier Chercoles – former Director of Corporate Social Responsibility at Inditex SA and the late Neil Kearney, General Secretary of the ITGLWF, and Runa Khan, the director of the Friendship initiatives sponsored by

Carrefour and subsequently by KarstadtQuelle and Cotton Group.

I am grateful to CCC and the Alternative Movement for Resources and Freedom Society, who conducted interviews with survivors, former employees and the families of the deceased within weeks of the collapse. Some of these testimonies particularly in relation to industrial relations in the Spectrum factory could not be verified. Reference is, however, made to the relevant source material in the endnotes. I am particularly indebted to Razaul Karim Buiyan, of Inditex Bangladesh, and the officers of the Bangladesh National Textile and Garment Workers Council (BNC) of the 9 union federations affiliated to the ITGLWF, in particular, Roy Ramesh Chandra, Kamrul Anam, Badruddoza Nizam, Noorul Islam, and Amirul Haque Amin for their assistance. The field trips enabled me to meet with a number of the injured workers and family members. Where victims gave their permission, their names have been used in full in the interests of making this a living account of events. Thanks are also due to Mtr. Mahabubur Rahaman, Director of production and planning at Sonia and Sweaters Ltd. for providing me access to their premises in my efforts to understand the processes involved in sweater manufacture.

Finally, I wish to thank Mr. Shahriyar Hossain for granting me access to the new factory which has been built on the same site, and for providing a frank account of the development of his business, and, crucially, his efforts to establish the real cause of the catastrophe. I was the first and only individual to date to have approached the owner about facts regarding the disaster, despite the publication of numerous allegations made both in and by the media, and the selective reporting of unofficial investigations by civil engineering bodies. For his critical review of my draft I am deeply grateful.

Spectrum was probably one of the worst disasters experienced so far in the Bangladesh Ready Made Garment sector. It was not just felt across the whole of the country it also reverberated around the world and particularly Europe, where some 27 brands were alleged to have been sourcing from the factory either in the recent past or at the time of the disaster. Consequently, the story of the collapse needs to be rooted and understood within the broader context of the country's position in the global market for apparel, and the position of Bangladeshi workers in the Ready Made Garments Industry. From a historical perspective in terms of its impact on the industry, Spectrum arguably ranks with the Triangle Shirtwaist Factory Fire in New York in 1911 where 146 young female immigrant seamstresses perished in a New York tenement factory. It has been argued that the Triangle disaster 'sparked a reform effort that in 4 years made New York into the model of a progressive state'[1] since it brought home the need for a rigorous implementation by government and industry of the industry wide agreement which had been signed a year earlier as a 'Protocol of Peace' between the New York Apparel Employers' Association and between the shirtwaist workers and cloak makers unions – the International Ladies Garment Workers Union (ILGWU) and the Amalgamated Clothing Workers Union (ACWU). It did not, however, take long for the gains made under 'Protocolism,' and subsequently the New Deal, to be undermined by the emergence of the so-called 'outside' shops,[2] heralding a transfer of production from New York into unorganised states, a pattern which was to take on a globalised form later in the century.

Almost 100 years later, many commentators saw Spectrum as a wake-up call for the industry and the Bangladeshi government in particular, and the opportunity for reform once again emerged, particularly against a backdrop of change in the global textile trading regime. Only now new actors were on the scene – the social compliance teams of those multinational brand-owners and retailers who had outsourced their production to footloose manufacturers in LDCs under the quota system and, in addition to an internationalised trade union movement, a growing band of NGO activists determined to expose and campaign around the abuses of worker rights which such outsourcing tended to breed. Spectrum did not lead to a Peace Protocol – if anything it was seen as another case over which the ongoing industrial struggle between employers and organised labour in the sector could be played out. Nevertheless, a reform agenda most certainly emerged from the tangled mass of rubble and bodies at Palashbari, and seven years later, as this book goes to press, following the satisfactory completion of the Inditex/ITGLWF relief scheme in 2011, a new agreement has been reached between Bangladeshi and international labour rights groups and trade unions and US-based apparel company PVH (owner of Tommy Hilfiger and Calvin Klein brands) to improve safety at their supplier factories in Bangladesh. The agreement provides for a new programme for independent building inspections, worker rights training, public disclosure of inspection reports, and a long-overdue review of safety standards[3]. Other multinational buyers are being urged to sign up to the protocol.

The Spectrum initiative seriously called into question the existing boundaries of corporate social responsibility in relation to the limits to buyer accountability in outsourced production, and the extent to which multinationals should engage in poverty alleviation initiatives. Consequently, it has proved necessary to unpick the different positions taken on the part of multinational retailers and the joint retailer programme known as the Business Social Compliance Initiative (BSCI) in this case. I am grateful therefore to Javier Chercolés, former Director of Corporate Social Responsibility at Inditex, Alexandre Hildebrandt and Maren Böhm, former employees of KarstadtQuelle/ Arcandor (which went into liquidation in 2009), Carole de Montgolfier of Carrefour, David Sienaart and Deborah Rotsaert of Cotton Group, and Stephanie Luong of the BSCI for their assistance on some of these questions.

Fairly early on, it became clear that in addition to the Inditex/ITGLWF relief scheme, a number of other organisations and companies sought to assist the injured workers and the families of the deceased and that these initiatives too would require detailing. I am grateful to Runa Khan, Enamul Haque and staff at Friendship Bangladesh for providing access to the documentation of the Carrefour and subsequent Karstadt/Cotton Group initiatives. Thanks are also due to Jahangir Alam, who assisted with a small impact assessment of the Friendship initiative, K Masud Ali at the NGO INCIDIN, Shirin Akter at Karmojibi Nari and Khorshed Alam at the Alternative Movement for Resources and Freedom Society, and to Asif Saleh and Farjana Khan Godhuly of Drishtipat.

In Chapter One, which provides a brief historical explanation of the phenomenon of the 'sweating of labour', the argument is made that the core elements of the particular system of production which still dominates many sections of the global garment industry today were established in the first half of the 19th Century. In essence these have remained unscathed and if anything have intensified under the process of internationalisation, itself fuelled very much by contradictory tendencies in the global textile and apparel trading system. Greater demands have, however, been made of this production system with the rise of 'fast fashion' as a marketing tool and consequently a new pattern of consumer behaviour. The expansion of the Spectrum Sweater factory has to be seen within the context of this buyer-driven apparel value chain, changes in the terms of trade, and a period of overconsumption. However, it must also be considered against the backdrop of weak state regulation and worker protection in an effort to make the Ready Made Garment sector attractive to the buying nations of the world.

Chapter 2 describes the fateful night and of the efforts to rescue the workers, and the wider human damage left in the wake of the disaster. Chapter 3 presents an analysis of the causes of the collapse and the inadequacies of the existing state and buyer systems of factory inspection in respect of occupational health and safety. The Spectrum disaster led to widespread mobilisation of Civil Society, both at national and international level, and these are dealt with in Chapter 4 and 5. Chapter 5 also details the reaction of those multinational retailers which had been sourcing from the factory. The pressure brought to bear by Civil Society, particularly at the international level, produced 2 quite distinct responses on the part of the buyers – on the one hand a fast track relief scheme aimed at bringing immediate relief to the victims' families, on the other an attempt to develop an exemplary compensation scheme which would establish for the first time the concept of a periodic benefit for manual workers in Bangladesh. Both these approaches merit some detail which is the focus of Chapter 6. By the beginning of 2009, the consensus amongst all stakeholders in Bangladesh was that the scheme developed by Inditex and the ITGLWF should be brought to a close with a lump sum payment. By this time other factors – specifically a need to undertake a risk assessment of the vulnerability of the Spectrum widows and their children, a spate of further fires in the RMG during 2010, and emerging prospects for an industry wide protocol on industrial injury compensation – now had to be factored into the story. Late in 2009 matters were complicated by the sudden death of Neil Kearney – one of the prime movers of the Spectrum scheme. Moreover, in September 2010 Javier Chercolés resigned his post at Inditex. Both their respective successors set about diligently familiarising themselves with the scheme in all its complexity and achieving satisfactory closure in April 2011 and driving multi-stakeholder dialogue in Bangladesh on the issues of accident prevention and compensation. These issues are considered in Chapter 7 which reflects upon the overall success of the campaigns mounted at national and international level by analysing responses on the part of the employers, and the government in Bangladesh, as well as the international buyers. The final chapter critically deals with the limits of corporate social responsibility, questions of proportionality of response, and the replicability both at national and international level of relief schemes of this nature.

This book is about a global industry which has long been out of control and the story of the iniquities of unfettered, outsourced commodity production, compounded by lax public administration at a national level. It is the story of failures in social protection and the lessons which have been learned and not yet learned by the authorities in Bangladesh, and it is the story of what can be achieved through sustained national and international campaign pressure by trade unions and labour rights organisations. It is also an account of the emergence of two quite different but replicable approaches to the provision of relief for workers in such calamitous circumstances, which hopefully sheds light on some of the contradictions of corporate social responsibility in the globalised economy in which we live today.

I have endeavoured to report facts and opinion as accurately as possible and accept responsibility for any factual errors in this account. Whilst in Bangladesh in my meetings with the various parties I found myself repeatedly using the phrase 'wanting to do justice' to all those, including the factory owners, whom I met in my efforts to piece together the story of an incident which so horribly robbed 62 families of their children, their spouses and their livelihoods, and impacted on hundreds, if not thousands of others. In my meetings with the family members and some of the injured, I was left in no doubt about the depth of their appreciation for the humanitarian efforts of those trades unionists, NGO activists and CSR managers who to this day refuse to let the victims of the Spectrum collapse be forgotten. I hope that this book, which I dedicate to the memory of the 62 victims, will in some small way serve as a testimony to that fact.

Doug Miller

Newcastle, March 2012

Abbreviations

AMRF	Alternative Movement for Resources and Freedom Society
ASK	Ain O Salish Kendra (ASK), the Legal Aid and Human Rights Organisation
BDT	Bangladesh Taka
BGMEA	Bangladesh Garment Manufacturers and Exporters Association
BILS	Bangladesh Institute of Labour Studies
BLAST	Bangladesh Legal Aid and Services Trust
BKMEA	Bangladesh Knitwear Manufacturers and Exporters Association
BNC	Bangladesh National Council (of ITGLWF affiliates)
BNWLA	Bangladesh National Woman Lawyers' Association
BUET	Bangladesh University of Engineering and Technology
CCC	Clean Clothes Campaign
CIFE	Chief Inspectorate for Factories and Establishments
CMT	Cut make and Trim
CPD	Centre for Policy Dialogue
Crore	one crore is equal to 100 lakh or 10,000,000
Drishtipat	a non-profit, expatriate Bangladeshi organization for human rights in Bangladesh
EBA	Everything But Arms Initiative
EU	European Union

FAA	Fatal Accidents Act 1855
FOB	Freight or Free on Board – the ex factory price
GSP	Generalised System of Preferences
IEB	Institute of Engineers of Bangladesh
IGA	Income Generation Activity
ITGLWF	International Textile, Garment and Leather Workers' Federation
Karmojibi Nari	Working Women's Initiative Bangladesh
Lakh	a unit of 100,000
LDC	Less Developed Country
MFA	Multi Fibre Arrangement
Naripokkho	'For Women' NGO
NGWF	National Garment Workers Federation
RAJUK	Rajdhani Unnayan Kartripakkha – Bangladesh Capital Development Trust
RMG	Ready Made Garments
ROO	Rules of Origin
SETEM	a network of 10 Spanish NGOs working on international issues Which coordinates the Spanish CCC Campaña Ropa Limpia
SKOP	Sramik Karmachari Oikka Parishad or Alliance of National Trade Union Confederations in Bangladesh
Sromik Nirapotta	Workers' Safety Forum
Uttorshori	means [progeny, posterity] an internet based discussion forum
UNCTAD	United Nations Conference on Trade and Development
UNDP	United Nations Development Programme
WCA	Workmen's Compensation Act 1923

CHAPTER 1

'Sweaters' and 'Sweating' in Bangladesh

It perhaps comes as no surprise that the word 'sweater' has no equivalent in the Bengali language, having been adopted as a loan word for these knitted outer garments which gradually replaced or were worn along with the woollen *chadar* or *shawl*, both traditional in the region of South East Asia. In the English language however, the word 'sweater' can have an entirely different meaning denoting a type of employer with whom many workers in the Bangladeshi Ready-Made Garment (RMG) industry, would be familiar. For this curious English/American term of 'sweater' has long been associated with the 'needle trades' (Bythell, 1978; Blackburn, 2007; Stein, 1977; Ross, 2004), and those employers, – frequently the 'middlemen' – deemed responsible for the exploitation of workers in terms of pay, excessive overtime and inhuman working conditions. In the early phase of mass clothing production 'sweated' labour tended to denote the experience of women working at home under 'sub-contract' (Blackburn, 2002). However, new production systems which pre-dated the emergence of the factory system in clothing in the second half of the Nineteenth Century began to establish a *modus operandi* which has shaped, in quite a fundamental way, the means by which the conduct of business and the sweating phenomenon continue to prevail in the clothing industry today.

A classic early example of this can be found in a new socio-economic production hierarchy spawned by the invention of the Jacquard loom at the turn of the Nineteenth Century and its widespread application in silk manufacture with its epicentre in Lyon, France, in the 1830s.

Here:

> Four hundred silk manufacturers formed the top layer of the
> Lyon system known as the *'fabrique'*... They were capitalists
> without factories and without a direct workforce... Most of
> their capital was locked up in silk and in the punch-cards
> that held their designs. The next layer down was the 8,000
> master craftsmen who owned their workshops and two to
> six looms. The typical set up was for the master and his wife
> to weave... While the rest of the looms would be worked
> by journeymen weavers and apprentices, numbering about
> 20,000... sitting for twelve to fourteen hours at the loom,
> powering it with a treadle, taking a light blow to the stomach
> up to 30,000 times a day (Mason 2007: 30).

In London two decades later, the tailors were reeling from the
impact of a similar production hierarchy in their own trade, which
had created a rift between the 'honourable' bespoke outfitters and
the 'dishonourable' trade of the 'show' shops' and 'slop' shops,
where people would buy their 'cheap and nasty clothes', and, where
'sweating' had a much wider meaning:

> For at the honourable shops, the master deals directly with his
> workmen; while at the dishonourable ones, the greater part of
> the work, if not the whole, is let out to contractors, or middle
> men – *'sweaters'*, as their victims significantly call them – who,
> in their turn, let it out again, sometimes to the workmen,
> sometimes to fresh middlemen; so that out of the price paid for
> labour on each article, not only the workmen, but the sweater,
> and perhaps the sweater's sweater, and a third, and a fourth,
> and a fifth, have to draw their profit (Kingsley, 1850: vii).

When the treadle operated lockstitch sewing machine heralded the
onset of mass garment production in the latter half of the Nineteenth
Century (Brandon, 1977; Hausen, 1978), the factory system came
to be viewed – erroneously – as the antidote to the problem of the
sweated home or 'outworker'(Olberg 1896). In the factory:

> ... the manufacturer employs his own workmen... who
> can be seen by the factory inspectors and where they
> can organise to develop a common understanding (J.R.
> Commons, 1901, in Stein, 1977: 45).

However, it did not take long for the production system, which Kingsley had so despised, to take root in the factory system too. By the end of the first quarter of the Twentieth Century garment manufacture in the USA and Germany, for example, had a pyramid shape, at the top of which sat the so-called 'jobbers' who drew up the designs and in some cases developed their own manufacturing capacity but increasingly relied on middlemen (the new 'sweaters') whose business strategy consisted in extracting the most labour they could at the lowest price possible from manufacturing units with the most vulnerable workers that could be found (Hausen 1978; Wolensky 2002; Bair, 2009). For 'sweating' to develop, according to Blackburn, two primary inter-related conditions were necessary: 'an over-supply of labour and a lack of trade union organisation amongst the workforce', underpinned by secondary factors such as trade swings, seasonality of demand for a product and lack of good management (2007: 3 & 7).

Fast forward to the last quarter of the Twentieth Century where the sweating phenomenon was well into the throes of internationalising itself into a complex global 'buyer-driven' supply chain, in which the clothing manufacturer with some notable exceptions was beginning to cede market power to the brand owner or large retailer (Gereffi, 1994), and where improvements in quality now meant that clothes were no longer necessarily 'nasty' but where buying departments were ensuring that they could come in cheap. There are interesting parallels between the silk 'manufacturers' of the first half of the Nineteenth Century, the 'jobbers' of New York and Chicago in the early Twentieth Century, and the branded marketers who emerged on the crest of the 'new economy'[1] era of the 1990's in Europe and the USA. Uninterested in the business of owning production facilities, these new buyers were keen to promote their brand identity and domestic market share on the back of quality garments sourced directly from supply factories ideally in developing countries. For here labour could come cheap and/or through a network of intermediaries – arguably Kingsley's new 'sweaters' – who could source from subcontractors they had on their books. Towards the end of 1990s, the brand marketers and fashion retailers were joined by the *value* retailers – the new kids on the block – who were keen to expand into apparel with their own 'private label' clothing ranges and to take a slice out of the high street fashion retail market. Like their competitors, they too needed to outsource the production of these soft goods to countries where costs could be kept low and, in line with their business strategy, driven down.

However, the system had its own internal contradiction that was exposed by the onset of international outsourcing to the less developed countries. Sections of the industry, particularly textile and clothing manufacturers in the developed economies, became very vulnerable and began to question the premises of the free trade regime which had been established under the terms of the General Agreement on Tariffs and Trade (GATT) in 1948. GATT had provided a framework for the gradual reduction in tariffs (import duties) on industrial goods and the prohibition of quantitative restrictions on imports and subsidies. Exceptions to these global rules could be made, and so the industrialised countries pushed through the so-called Multi-Fibre Agreement (MFA) in 1974, which had as its long term goal the progressive liberalisation of the textile and clothing trade but which at the same time sought to provide some breathing space for their domestic manufacturers via a 'quota system' designed to limit the imports of categories of certain garments (cf. Ferenschild and Wick 2004).

More than any other factor, it was quota which led to the rapid internationalisation of production in the industry. As manufacturers tried to circumvent the quantitative restrictions on their product, one of their principal strategies was to relocate their manufacturing capacity to a country which had quota for a particular product category and retailers and brand marketers began to procure their product from a country with quota, able to supply the right product, at the right quality, at the right price. The upshot of this new trading regime in textiles and clothing was that some 160 producing countries now vied with each other for business from the three key markets – the USA, Japan and the then EEC.

Bangladesh entrepreneurs entered this global production system modestly at first in the 1970s, positioning their industry along with a number of other developing countries as a source of low cost woven garment assembly with a workforce which soon came to be seen as the cheapest in the world (Joshi, 2002: 14). The gains which organised labour had made in social protection and working conditions for the textile, garment and footwear workers in the so-called developed economies would soon be nullified as the displaced production called for a new emergent working class in these sectors in the LDCs which would have to begin that struggle again. At the turn of the Twentieth Century, *Justice*, the British weekly newspaper of the Social Democratic Federation, had viewed 'sweating' as the 'real basis of capitalism and source of modern riches' with its roots in:

> … unrestrained and furious competition among propertyless men and women for starvation wages, accepted only because they can keep body and soul together in no other way[2].

Some 70 years later the garment workers of Dhaka and Chittagong found themselves in precisely the same situation even though working and living in the RMG sector constituted several notches up from the grinding poverty back in their home villages in rural Bangladesh. Most had found work in what is known as 'cut, make and trim' (CMT) in the so-called apparel value chain. Cut, make and trim is the end phase of a quite complex manufacturing process which requires relatively small investment at the outset, since essentially the prerequisites are floor space, some cutting tables and sewing machines and, depending on the contractor's requirements, finishing equipment such as ironing presses and packaging facilities. Cut, make and trim operations began to flourish on the floors of existing buildings in the middle of Dhaka, the capital of Bangladesh. Such operations remained and remain, however, essentially low value added because of the historical valuation of labour in the sector and because woven fabric had to be imported into Bangladesh. This meant that a relatively small proportion of any export earnings would be retained by the sector, since fabric was the largest cost element and had to be paid on to a foreign supplier. For branded marketers, fashion retailers and value stores in the buying countries, Bangladesh was an attractive sourcing proposition as far as *basic* garments were concerned – that is standard apparel items generally not subject to fashion trend. As one industry source has put it:

> Earlier, Bangladesh was simply like … a tailor's shop – I have 100 machines – you give me everything and I will stitch for you[3].

Not content with rock bottom prices for labour, importers from Bangladesh were also concerned about the most favourable terms of trade too. Clothing consignments which were free of an import tax (duty) and/or restriction on the volume of goods (quota) which could be shipped, were crucial factors for buyers and traders. Bangladesh, the EU and the USA had been signatories to the Multi-Fibre Arrangement also known as the Agreement on Textiles and Clothing (Rashid, 2006: 12–13). However, both the EU and the USA had recognised Bangladesh's Least Developed Country (LDC) status and exempted the country from any quota restrictions. While the US still imposed duties on ready-made garment imports from Bangladesh, the European market suddenly became much more attractive for Bangladeshi entrepreneurs as the country qualified under the EU Generalised System of Preferences[4] (GSP) granting Bangladesh exporters tariff free status on their products.

By the mid-1990s, the Bangladesh Ready Made Garment (RMG) business was booming, accounting for fifty per cent of all manufacturing exports[5]. Up until the mid-1990's, the Bangladesh government had issued manufacturers the so-called Utilisation Declaration (UD) necessary for approving the duty free import of any raw materials used in apparels manufacturing. In 1994, they handed over this authority to the Bangladesh Garment Exporters and Manufacturers' Association (BGMEA), the employers association which had established itself at the end of the 1970s. This gave it enormous power over its member firms[6], which at that time encompassed some 2,353 units with 1.29 million workers[7]. Under GSP, however, exporters had to demonstrate under the EU's 'rules of origin' (ROO) that a substantial proportion of the value was added to the garment in country. Looking to seize this opportunity, a small group of eighteen Bangladeshi knitwear entrepreneurs realised the strategic necessity to move away from simple, low value added, cut make and trim (CMT) operations evident in the woven sector, towards the establishment of upstream manufacturing processes including dyeing and knitting inside the country. In 1996 they established the Bangladesh Knitwear Manufacturers & Exporters Association (BKMEA) which set about creating a critical mass for the sector resulting in an expansion of investment and membership of their organisation to 914 member firms by 2005, and a trebling in the share of knitted exports from a 1990 figure of 7.64 per cent[8]. (cf Siddiqi 2004)

Garment Category	Number of Firms (adjusted)	Share (%)	Employment
Woven	1673	47	836500
Knitwear	1495	42	747500
Sweaters	392	11	337120
Total	3560	100	1921120

Source: The World Bank, Bangladesh Developments Series, Paper 2, December 2005.

Table 1: Structure of the RMG Industry 2005.

This type of expansion had enormous impact on urban growth in Bangladesh, particularly in and around Dhaka and Chittagong. In 1972, Dhaka was a city of about one million inhabitants but by 2005 its population had grown to about fourteen million, swollen by a great influx of rural migrants looking for work in a booming sector. Growth in the industry had resulted in a shortage of land for industrial expansion with property prices in parts of Dhaka comparable to those in London (Fairwear Foundation, 2006:7). In response, investors opted either to expand their factories upwards or relocate to the outskirts of the capital and the low-lying wetlands (Rahman, Bhattacharya and Moazzem, 2007:5) Reclamation continued at a pace as canals, paddy fields and waterways were dredged and/or hastily filled up with soil and sand.

In 1997, when the owners opened the Shahriyar Fabrics factory specialising in knitted T shirts at Palashbari outside of the Savar Export Processing Zone, their first two main clients were the Belgian Cotton Group – a major promotional T shirt supplier – and the German private label Multiline Group. All signs for their business were pointing in two directions, towards on the one hand 'backward linkage', i.e. investment in some of the processes 'upstream' in the manufacturing chain from CMT (namely fabric manufacture and dyeing), and on the other towards the cultivation of more buyer contacts in Europe. Soon the company had orders from Carrefour,

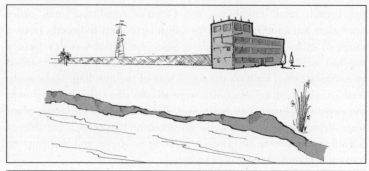

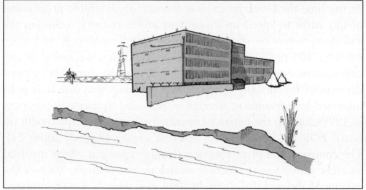

*Figure 1: Shahriyar Fabrics 1997, Spectrum Sweaters Phase 1,
Spectrum Sweaters Phase 2. Courtesy: Lizzie Dutton.*

the French retail chain and the German retail and mail order operation KarstadtQuelle and its subsidiaries and indirectly from a range of other European retailers. Since the initial 4 storey factory was too small to accommodate dyeing machines, these were installed in a separate shed built on the south side of the building. Some multi feed circular knitting machines were also in this shed, but such was the expansion in the knit business it would not be long before plans were being drawn up to build an adjacent bigger unit capable of housing more dyeing and circular knitting machines and also running a sweater manufacturing operation.

At the time the Government was offering an extensive programme of incentives to speed up investment in the country, including tax and duty exemption on the import of capital machinery and spare parts for 100 per cent export oriented industries, a removal of any ceiling on investment, and tax holidays of up to 10 years. The owners' decision to 'functionally upgrade', as it is known, may also have been informed by government sweeteners provided to garment exporters in 1999–2000 to the extent of twenty-five per cent of the freight on board FOB (ex-factory price) value of export (Rashid, 2006: 21). The company had plans for considerable expansion which involved an eight storey Sweater factory stretching out from the back of the existing Shahriyar Fabrics unit. In 2000, they were, however, informed by the district Cantonment[9] Board – in this case Savar – that in line with normal practice, the first stage of the build should be up to five storeys[10]. Plans were submitted for a four storey factory on top of the ground floor which included in the design reinforced concrete cement piling and RCC foundations to a depth of nearly 60 feet which would support a further four floors. The owners' plans were to exercise this option at a later stage.

With an average seventy per cent value addition, the trend in knitwear was certainly to go large, since retention of export earnings could be secured by in house dyeing and fabric manufacture. Such was the eagerness to proceed, construction of the new factory commenced two years before the plans were approved. This was considered to be the average length of time between a planning application and approval being granted. For factory owners eager to meet the upsurge in demand with factory extensions or new-build, such a delay could seriously impact on return on investment. Premature construction prior to the granting of approval was allegedly a not uncommon occurrence at the time. As the build commenced towards the end of 2000, knitwear exports to the EU began to surge, as can be seen in Figure 2. Confidence in the sector was boosted by the launch in Brussels of the EU 'Everything But Arms initiative' (EBA) in 2001 which assured the continuation of GSP for an indefinite period for all LDCs. Sweater and T shirt production began to ride the crest of this wave, and European buyers were quick to seize on this sourcing opportunity for the T shirt and sweater market in particular, accounting for eighty-three per cent (US$ 1,780.57 /€1,424.45 million) of total knitwear exports in FY 2003–2004 followed by the USA (11%, i.e. US$ 236.79/ € 189 million) (Uddin, 2006). Typically as the RMG sector expanded, so too did its structure and hierarchy. By 2002 there was a tier of some 907 agents or middlemen in Bangladesh acting on behalf of multinational buyers and/or themselves in the RMG sector.[11]

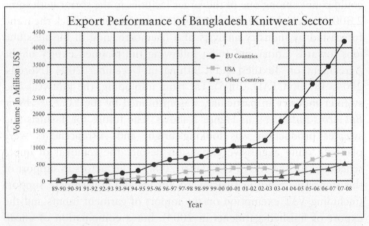

Figure 2: Bangladesh Exports in Knitwear and markets 1991–2008.

By 2003 the owners were ready to expand Spectrum Sweaters again, and since they had sunk RCC piling and foundations for an 8 storey building at the outset, submitted plans for an upward extension by a further four floors to the Cantonment Board for which they received a receipt. However, such was the desire to respond to the soaring demand from the European buyers and to maximise their return on investment, they commenced building upwards, despite an absence of planning approval, while partial production continued apace on the floors below. According to a survey conducted in 2006, sweater units had been increasing their capacity by on average twenty-six per cent (Rahman *et al.*, 2007: 7). Although the factory was not completed by the time of the collapse, the aim was to have a capacity of upwards of 116,000 sweaters per month after completion of the build[12]. Annisul Huq, President of the Bangladesh Garment Manufacturers and Exporters Association, and owner himself of an 800 machine sweater factory with 2,000 workers, boasted at the time that the number of sweater factories with over 1,000 machines had reached a hundred and that some giant operators had twice this number (Fairwear Foundation, 2006: 9). Workforce size in sweater factories averaged 1,000–1,200 workers. Although Spectrum was listed with a workforce of 1,016[13], by the time the extension was built and the workforce expanded, the combined Spectrum/Shariyar Fabrics factory complex could count among one of the larger facilities in the sector with some 2,300 workers. Unpredictably, Bangladesh was able to buck the trend forecasted by industry analysts of a haemorrhaging of business and jobs towards China and India following the planned expiry of the Agreement on Textiles and Clothing in December 2004 (Nordås, 2004: 38; UNCTAD, 2005). Far from imploding, the knitwear and sweater industry in particular, was cushioned by the EU *Everything But Arms initiative*[14] as Figure 2 shows. The future for T shirts and sweater production was looking bright and entrepreneurs were planning quite aggressive expansion despite the removal of quota scheduled for the end of December 2004.[15] The factors in support of this stance were not just backward linkage and government support (including VAT exemption on the import of garment inputs and the export of finished garments in 2004), but a combination of cheap labour (Uddin, 2006), price competitiveness, and a rising level of productivity (Kee, 2005; Bakhta, Salimullaha, Yamagatab and Yunusa, 2008). Moreover, by early 2005, the Bangladesh RMG was enjoying a reversal of fortune since both the EU and the USA felt compelled to impose the so-called 'China safeguards' in the wake of the expiry of the Agreement on Textiles and Clothing. China's accession agreement to the World Trade Organization (WTO) in 2001 allowed WTO members to impose quantitative restrictions, or 'safeguards', on imports of any Chinese textile or apparel product if these imports threatened severe disruption in the home market. As hundreds of retailers began switching production to China from 1 January 2005, imports of garment categories (including knitwear) began to soar in Europe, in some cases by up to 1,200 per cent. Whilst this clearly had an impact on jobs in South East Asia, it was only when factories in Italy and France began shutting that the EU acted, re-imposing quotas on ten categories of garments coming from China. Retailers were thus forced to switch their sourcing back to competitor countries with Bangladesh and Cambodia in particular benefitting from a market which was re-jigged for a further 4 years until 2009[16].

The boost in export performance of certain garment categories can be seen in Table 2 and in 2005 the share of knit garments in total apparel exports from Bangladesh stood at forty-three per cent with, it was claimed, a new knitwear factory being added every day[17].

Year	Shirt	Jackets	T-Shirt	Trousers	Sweater
2000–01	1067.22	570.33	593.87	652.44	474.04
2001–02	871.22	412.34	546.28	636.61	517.83
2002–03	1019.88	464.51	642.62	643.66	578.38
2003–04	1116.57	364.78	1062.11	1334.85	616.31
2004–05	1053.34	430.28	1349.71	1667.72	893.12
2005–06	1056.87	408.97	1781.51	2165.25	1042.61

Source: Export Promotion Bureau in Ahmed and Hossain (2006: 4).

Table 2: Relative Export Performance of Different Apparel Items for the RMG sector during the life of the Spectrum Sweater Factory (in Million USD).

Sweating in the RMG

Such expansion however, came at a cost for manufacturers and the buyers were complicit in this, demanding an ever lower FOB or freight on board (ex-factory) price (Uddin, 2006: 61–66). At the retail end,

FOB prices negotiated between a buyer and a supplier remain highly confidential, but at the supply end there is less sensitivity about such data. At the time of the collapse, ex-factory prices for Sweaters at Spectrum were averaging between $3 and $4 per piece. Basic polo shirts would cost a buyer/agent $2 to $2.50 while the FOB prices for T shirts ranged between $1 and $1.50.[18] Although printing was subcontracted at Spectrum, with on-site dyeing and fabric knitting, much of the value could be retained, but in terms of the whole *'value chain'*, the manufacturing cost remained a small proportion of the retail price (Miller & Williams 2009) and had been falling (see Figure 3).

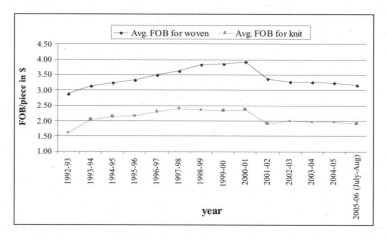

Figure 3: Annual average price change in ex-factory (FOB) prices for wovens and knitwear Calculated as total export value/total export volume. Source: Uddin, 2006: 63.

Managing such price deflation against rising costs in other areas usually has implications for working conditions. One way in which buyers extract a lower FOB is by negotiating a discount on an increase in the volume of the order placed, or offering a better than average payment schedule. For suppliers, faced with rising overhead costs, finding ways to maintain the bottom line might involve the practice of not paying overtime and requiring workers to stay to complete the target. An additional course of action would of course be sub-contracting:

> What happens is in the bigger factory I have 100,000 units to be shipped by 1 month's time, but the price I get if I produce the entire quantity... I won't have a profit margin... Then obviously I will try and take some to a subcontractor ... the retailer or agent doesn't know... A lot (of subcontracting) comes from contacts with other factories in the vicinity[19].

Most of this unauthorised sub-contracting is normally cash business and lies at the heart of the 'sweating' phenomenon which Charles Kingsley was describing back in the middle of the 19th Century. Spectrum was no exception here, taking on subcontracted work during its start-up phase allocated either from fellow entrepreneurs or from buyer's agents.

> In sweaters there are approximately 5 gauges: 1.5, 3, 5, 7, and 12 gauge – these are usual. Say you have got 100 machines of 3 gauge but you have an order where you need at least 300 3 gauge machines. So what do you do – you do 100 here and go to 2 other factories. People were saying we are a new factory so they were giving us a lot of subcontract orders[20].

Little is known about the extent of labour cost engineering undertaken by the buyers (when negotiating an order), and even less is known where subcontracting is involved when such agreements are made between factory owners (Miller, 2010). Suppliers in Bangladesh were also forced to grapple with a new demand from buyers – the result of changes in fashion marketing/consumer behaviour on the high streets of Europe. Known as 'fast fashion', and associated with a business model pioneered by the lead brand team (Zara) at the Spanish multinational Inditex S.A. (one of the buyers at Spectrum) this approach relied heavily on 'Quick Response' management methods, the aim being constantly to create new designs and fresh products in an attempt to lure consumers back into their stores for repeated visits (Bruce and Daly, 2006). By shortening the lead time between design and production, new mini collections could be launched effectively every two months (Pfeifer, 2007: 14). Traditionally, fashion buying cycles had been based on long term forecasts made one year to six months before the season (Bruce and Daly, *op.cit.*). Fast fashion ruptured the notion of seasons in high street fashion and changed the way that supply chains were to be managed. Inditex, not untypically as far as Spectrum was concerned, was one of the buyers which were unaware that an order for Zara Kids sweaters for the South American market had come through an Indian agent[21]. Generally such non fashion items or 'basics' as they were known, could be produced with a longer lead time and Bangladesh was becoming a favoured source for such items. But even basics could require quick replenishment if they sold well. Moreover, the fast fashion concept had permeated most segments of the fashion market, where it simply meant 'lean retailing' (Abernathy *et.al.*, 1999) or 'continuous flexible flow' (Watson, 2009)[22]. In the run up to the expiry of the Agreement on Textiles and Clothing (end of 2004) commentators were already remarking on the need for suppliers in Bangladesh to reduce their lead times down from 90–120 to 60–90 days (Kahn, 2004) and the industry was itself reporting a decrease in delivery times and a corresponding impact on overtime levels (Hurley and Faiz, *op.cit.*). Lead times at Spectrum were between 60–90 days.[23]

As Figure 4 shows, the pattern of labour force participation in a number of Asian economies, is for young women and men to leave or be lured from the rural hinterlands to newly emerging and, for Bangladesh, expanding garment industries as a means of trying to lift their families out of the depths of rural poverty (Afsar, 2003). Since the 1990s the RMG sector has absorbed more than 1.5 million workers of which ninety per cent are rural migrants. Most are young adults, both male and female, between the ages of fifteen and thirty-four, able to find work with relative ease but forced to live in slums or squat on public land (Afsar *op.cit.*). With eighty per cent of workers in the RMG sector female, wage rates in the industry have tended to reflect the way in which women and assembly work in the industry are viewed. This quote from a Bangladesh factory owner is symptomatic of these attitudes:

> All the female workers are from the rural area. The work is new for them, they can neither read nor write and have no skill, and therefore their productivity is very low. In the village they were just doing some housework. In the factory the work is different. We are getting criticized from Western countries but they just do not understand that the salaries are corresponding with the work these women

perform, we cannot pay more. And you have to control them much more than in other places because they are not used to work, without control they would sit around chatting the whole day (Petra Dan quoted in Fairwear Foundation, *op.cit.*: 42).

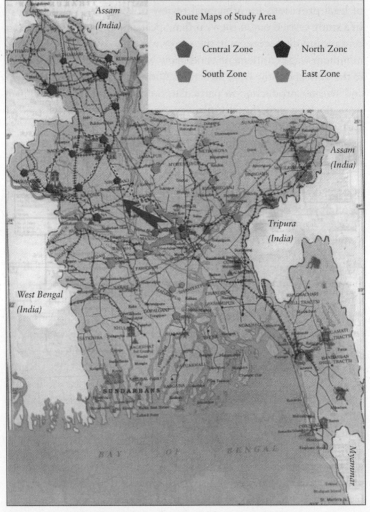

Figure 4: Geographical origins of the Spectrum workers.

With the minimum wage at BDT 930 (US$ 15) for a grade seven entry level helper after training and BDT 4,500 for grade one as at 2005, these rates were not only low, compared to wage levels in competitor countries in the Asia region, they were pegged at rates which were low relative to other industries in Bangladesh. Moreover, they had not moved for the ten years prior to the Spectrum disaster, in spite of legal provisions for a biennial review of wages by a Wage Board. In a study carried out in the year that Spectrum opened, over fifty per cent of unskilled workers in the sector were not aware of their exact minimum wage entitlement[24] and many women were reportedly kept in the dark about the wage structure. With the emergence of knitwear and sweater production in particular, however, more and more men were flocking into the industry – a situation consistent with other parts of the world, where women were losing out as manufacturing processes became more capital and skill intensive and where earnings are higher (Barrientos, Kabeer and Hossain, 2003). The male-female ratio had been changing slowly in favour of men in knitwear (Zohir, 2001; 2003) because of the possibility of achieving higher earnings through piece work.

Working at Spectrum[25]

Although separately registered companies, both the Shahriyar Fabrics and the Spectrum factories worked closely together since the circular knitting machines and the dyeing machines located on the ground floor and housed also in the Spectrum building were exclusively used for T shirt production in the Shahriyar Fabrics facility. When the factory collapsed, it was the middle of the sweater production season which runs from February to mid-August in the Bangladesh Ready Made Garments (RMG) industry. Most of the orders for sweaters and T shirts were coming through agents and buying houses acting on behalf of Spectrum's European clients, but like many companies in the Bangladesh Garment Manufacturers' Export Association (BGMEA), a good proportion of the work was undertaken on a subcontract basis work for other colleagues who were incapable of meeting a delivery schedule, or a specific volume or perhaps even a price. Much of this type of work would be carried out at times without the knowledge of the traders and multinational buyers who originated the order.

With rising demand for sweaters, the labour market position for young and strong sweater operators had never been better and their piece rate earnings with production bonus could take them to well beyond what their supervisors would be earning. But of course, such work is seasonal and physically demanding, requiring repetitive pulling of the carriage handle back and forth along the length of the knitting machine. Although the effort is probably no different from that expended by a female hand loom weaver, operating knitting machines had become an almost exclusively male preserve. Such was their new found bargaining power it was not unknown for operators to go back to their villages for a few days after pay day in the full knowledge that they would have a job open for them when they came back. Some workers had done precisely that on the evening of the collapse.

Consequently at Spectrum, there was a much higher male ratio because of the sweater and dyeing operations. Sweater machine operators – could sometimes earn much more than 5,000 BDT if they were able to meet the production target. Workers who earned over 3,000 BDT a month would receive a production bonus. There were, of course, different piecework prices for different items – ranging between BDT 8 and 100 per piece. Although at the top end of the earnings league in the sector, sweater operators worked seasonally and averaged out over a year their pay was more modest and many still reported debts on average of 6,300 BDT – mainly for medical treatment either for themselves or for family members (Rahman *et.al.*, *op.cit.*: 13).

For women in the factory, employed in the lower grades as helpers, stitchers, linkers and finishers, the starting rate was the government minimum of 930 BDT. Linking operators on assembly were on piecework, and their production targets varied. Inspectors and finishers were on a flat rate (Alam, 2005: 3; CCC, 2005b; Rahman *et al.*, *op.cit.*: 13). Workers whose attendance record for the previous three months had been unblemished received a bonus of BDT 100. Operators who were on production bonus did not earn overtime, but it was claimed that targets were often excessive (Alam, 2005). Wages were calculated on the 20th of every month and paid on the 10th of the next which meant that 20 days wage always in arrears. It has been suggested that it was the norm in industry for workers not to know exactly when they were going to be paid (Fairwear Foundation, 2006:

45), but at Spectrum, workers' wages were normally paid on the 10th.

Following 10 years of wage stagnation and wanton disregard by employers of the 1961 Minimum Wages law and the Wage Ordinance of 1994 (Pratima, 1998), pressure had been building up in the RMG workforce for an increase in the minimum wage to address the issue of cost of living. Given the cost of basic items in 2005 – oil was BDT 60 per kilo, rice BDT 20 and rents varied between BDT 800 and 1,500 per month (CCC, 2005b), living wage estimates at the time varied between BDT 1,800 and 3,000 per month for the starter wage. Consequently, it comes as no surprise that overtime levels were excessive across the industry (Fairwear Foundation, 2006: 46; Chowdury and Ahmed, 2005; Berik and van der Meulen, Rodgers, 2008), since maintaining a poverty wage (less than the UN definition of a $1 per day) inevitably encouraged a long hours culture (Paratian and Torres, 2001) as this would be the only means by which workers could get anywhere near a living wage. While twelve to 16 hour days/6 day weeks were the general norm for export factories in full production, Spectrum was in partial production at the time. As one Spectrum worker commented:

> I do inspection work, my basic salary is 3000 BDT per month plus about 400 BDT bonuses... Overtime pays 10 BDT per hour. For the night shift we get 30 BDT extra. On night shifts, we often have to work till three a.m. in the morning, then we go home and then have to start again at 8 a.m. For lunch we get one hour. I go home for lunch because I live near the factory. At night if we have to work overtime we only get a little snack, two bananas, a piece of cake and an egg. We get it from the factory at around seven p.m. There is no canteen in the factory. The earliest we are ever allowed to go home from work is 7 p.m[26] (CCCb, 2005).

At Spectrum, a (male) helper in the dyeing section earned more at 1,800 BDT per month. Here workers were on two shifts – a 12 hour day shift from eight in the morning until eight in the evening and a night shift from eight in the evening until eight in the morning one week on, one week off. The overtime rate for the day shift was double time on the basic rate (exclusive of the housing and medical allowance as per national minimum wage agreement), but there was no separate overtime rate for the night-shift except on Friday, the Muslim day of rest. The worker who provided this information claimed he had nothing left at the end of the month to remit to his family back home[27].

Unionisation at Spectrum was low and had not yet reached the critical mass necessary to invoke the statutory recognition procedure. As a member of the BGMEA, management at Spectrum was expected to hold the Association's line that trade unions were to be resisted at all costs at factory level (Fairwear Foundation, 2006: 38–40; Muqtada, Singh and Rashid, 2002). This disregard for the core ILO conventions[28] which addressed freedom of association and collective bargaining, (and which were to be found restated as core principles in the supplier codes of conduct of all the main buyers at Spectrum and Shahriyar Fabrics) meant that the workers had no collective voice in the factory – the general norm in the RMG – a crucial factor if the pressure created by the sweating system was at all to be minimised. In the competitive world of apparel production at the lowest cost, labour standards enforcement could be all too readily jettisoned in an effort to achieve some profit. Moreover, 'sweating' was now dictated by the lean retailing policies of Northern buyers, and abetted by a Government as part of its export orientated industrialisation policy (Wells, 2009: 569–570). However, for the workers who turned up for work at Spectrum on that fateful night, 'sweating' was something far removed from their minds.

CHAPTER 2

Zero Fifty Hours in Palashbari[1]

The evening of 10 April 2005 could have been like any other at the eight storey Spectrum Sweater factory in Palashbari, in the district of Savar, Dhaka. It was the middle of the sweater production season which runs from February to mid August in the Bangladesh Ready Made Garments (RMG) industry. The floor doors were open, but all the windows were closed to prevent the mosquitoes getting in. It was very stuffy. The main gate outside was locked. Somewhere between 200 and perhaps 240 workers were in the factory[2]. The eight storey Spectrum Sweaters had only been in partial production for about seven months. Its sister factory, the adjacent Shahriyar Fabrics building had closed for the night. This last year had seen the addition of another final storey to the sweater factory although building works were still incomplete. The build during the last 5 years had been relentless but in stages – a floor at a time as and when funds from the bank had permitted.

Business was booming both for staple T shirts and the more seasonal sweaters. Sweater production was well under way for the coming autumn season in Europe. In February, work had been slack and some workers had been laid off, but during March, a number of night shifts had been run. On this evening the only night shifts which were running were the seven gauge knitting machines on the sixth floor and the small diameter circular knitting machines on the third and ground floors (producing jersey for the T shirts). As per usual, the dyeing machines on the ground floor were operating round the clock for Shahriyar Fabrics. Some twenty dyeing machine operators had commenced the nightshift at 8 p.m. where temperatures were as usual sweltering, since the boiler which feeds the dyeing machines was located here too, There was no finishing work scheduled that night, so this floor was deserted. The second floor was also deserted. This was one of the floors which connected through to the adjacent Shahriyar Fabrics factory. Production on this floor, often earmarked for this sister factory, would normally be undertaken by some 330 sewers in two sections, but the largest section of workers had not turned in for the night shift[3].

Figure 5: Small diameter circular knitting machine.
Photo: Courtesy Hamidul Islam.

22

Figure 6: Knitting operators. Photo: author. Courtesy: Sonia Sweaters.

Floors four (linking) and five (five gauge knitting machines) were deserted. The sixth floor[4] housed approximately 200 manually operated seven and three gauge sweater machines and had around 100 knitting operators in on this evening. Half the shift – those working on the three gauge machines had left at 9 p.m. after receiving their pay (CCC, 2005a)[5]. The 10th of the month was usually pay day and a number of night shift operators had come in early to get their wages. Other workers, concerned that they might get robbed on the way back home to the tin shacks littered between the many garment factories in Palashbari, had elected to come back during daytime on the 11th to collect their pay. The owners who usually stayed back to check that everything was running smoothly, had decided to leave at about 11 p.m.

Conditions were quite cramped between the machines as some maintenance fitters were undertaking repairs on this floor alongside those operators who had clocked in. Among them were best friends and neighbours Noor Alam and Jahangir Alam. Both were in their early twenties. Another work colleague was Shafiqul Islam, a 17 year old who had only been working in the factory for 8 months. He had just handed a stack of 12 sweaters to the production controller to book in for his piecework earnings and was heading back to his machine where he worked 13 hours a day, six days a week. It was nearly 1 am and snack time: there was no canteen in the factory but night shift workers were normally given some fruit, a piece of cake, and an egg. As the workers waited for the supervisor to return with their food, one of the knitters felt a funny sensation, as though someone had just pushed him in the back. As the whole floor swayed, suddenly it began to sink almost as if the workers were in a lift. Everything was plunged into darkness and as the power tripped there was a 'big bang like thunder' (CCC, *op.cit.*). Some workers thought it was an earthquake. But it was no tremor – in the north east corner of the factory, the reinforced concrete pillars had failed creating a 'hinge' as the concrete flat slab first floor gave way, pulling all the other storeys over like a pack of cards in that direction. There was little hope for those workers trapped in between these floors.

A young helper in the dyeing section described the situation:

'... about 100 could escape during and after the collapse. The doors of my floor were open, but the main gate on the road side was locked. The key was with one of the Ansars (guards) who didn't want to open the gate. He only did so after a security man came and forced him to open it. I and some others took out about 30 people from the collapsed building, We tried to stop cars on the road to take the wounded to the

Figure 7: Collapsed factory. Photo Courtesy: Clean Clothes Campaign.

hospital, but cars didn't stop. Then we made a roadblock, we put all bricks on the road and so forced cars to stop.' (*Ibid.*)

As the dust settled, the eight storey Spectrum building had been reduced to a three storey high pile of debris. The adjacent four storey Shahriyar Fabrics building was, however, still standing. The floors had collapsed in such a way that the height between them in places was less than one foot. These huge flat slabs of approximately eleven inch thick concrete were now a tangled mass of thick rod steel, broken concrete and machinery festooned with sweaters and T shirts from the finishing floors. As some family members and workmates were woken in the middle of the night by their cell phones, they had to make the chilling realisation that the gasping voice at the other end belonged to a husband or workmate trapped in the rubble (Daily Star, 2005a). Hearing the screams for help, fire-fighters at many points made holes in the concrete and supplied oxygen and light inside to save the trapped from dying of suffocation.

Police, fire-fighters, army, the Rapid Action Battalion and locals rushed to the scene but remained helpless without the necessary equipment. Noticing their plight, fellow workers and local residents frantically joined them burrowing with their bare hands in the debris in search of survivors in the darkness. Milon Howladar, one of the knitting operators trapped under the debris, had cried out and his voice had been recognised by his father and brother who battled all night to try to reach him. When the army arrived in the morning they tried to eject them from the site, but his father grabbed a plank of wood and retaliated as the soldiers tried to force him off the site. One of the journalists on the scene intervened and they were allowed to continue their burrowing until they were finally able to reach their relative. He had severe internal injuries.

Some workers were lucky:

'I was next to a window with a grill when the factory collapsed. That saved my life. I came out of the building only ten minutes after the collapse. I know because I looked at my watch when I came out, it showed 1.04 a.m.' (CCC, *op.cit.*)

One of the knitting supervisors was also one of the fortunate. Trapped in what was, he felt, like a tomb with 6 other workers, he suddenly saw a small torchlight appear signalling a way out. Like a snake the 7 men crawled holding each other's legs until some 20 minutes later they were dragged out through a hole (Daily Star, 2005b). Unfortunately they had to leave Noor e Alam who was unable to crawl with them. Noor was still holding the machine handle when the collapse occurred and his hand and arm had become horribly entangled in the rubble and what remained of his knitting machine (Daily Star, 2005a). Although only 3 yards away from the exit hole, rescuers were unable to drag him out, despite his calls to lift the machine to allow him to pull out what was left of his arm. The rescue team and medics contemplated amputation to release him. Fearing the worst, he begged his brother in law to fetch his three-year-old son to the site so that he could see his little boy for the last time (Daily Star 2005b). At 4pm in the afternoon of the 11th, Noor was finally freed with his arm still intact but it was in a horrible state.

By dawn a full scale rescue operation was underway, and a team of rescuers from the Army Engineering Corps and the Fire Brigade began a round the clock operation. The authorities called in reinforcements from the police, army and paramilitary troops (Rapid Action Battalion) and by noon a small crane was on site, but it was unable to approach the sections which needed to be removed first. By now the number of rescuers had swelled to over 1,000, but many were ill equipped to deal with the task in hand (Daily Star, 2005c). The rescue task was a difficult one. In order to reach the trapped workers, it was necessary to remove one slab after another beginning at the top. The heavy weight and bulk of each floor slab and their reinforcement connections made it difficult to separate each one and pull them out, since the slightest movement could trigger an imbalance and change in the whole shape of the pile of rubble jeopardising the lives of any remaining survivors (Disaster Database, 2005). A decision was taken to cut through to the ground floor and to use search lights at each level to search for survivors. Around 400 trained rescuers from the Army, and Fire Service and Civil Defence now worked round the clock on six-hour shifts aided by some 100 day-labourers with shovels and baskets. It took the team some 38 hours to open a five foot by four foot wide hole in what was left of the top floor (Daily Star, 2005a). By now thousands had gathered to view the tragedy, many having waded through the paddy fields beyond the canal. They could only look on helplessly, cordoned off by the authorities to prevent them from hampering the rescue effort. The Prime Minister, Khaleda Zia and the State Minister for Home Affairs, visited the site and instructed the concerned officials to intensify the rescue operation and ensure proper medical treatment of the survivors. As the rescue effort continued apace and bodies were brought out, confusion reigned as to the number of workers who may have been in the factory at the time and could still be buried under the rubble. Some of the recovered corpses were badly disfigured and decomposed, and could only be identified by their clothes, jewellery and mobile phones they had in their pockets (Daily Star 2005d).

Figure 8: A rescuer searches inside the collapsed factory.
Courtesy: Shehab Uddin.

Representatives of the Bangladesh Garment Manufacturers and Exporters Association appeared on site to confirm the identity of the bodies as they were handed over and then to deliver them to their relatives with an amount to cover the carriage costs of the coffin back to their home village. On the 19 April, 8 days into the rescue operation, the team finally called off the search. The official figure of the numbers of dead workers was declared to be sixty-two and those rescued around 100. Of the dead, five still remained unidentified at this time (Disaster Database, *op.cit.*). However, an unspecified number had been able to escape the building at the point of collapse.

After eight days the site had been completely cleared and the district administration had sealed off the area around the factory, deploying about 100 police, two platoons of armed soldiers and a further twenty-two security guards to look after the recovered goods (Daily Star 2005e).

It is difficult to comprehend the full scale of the human damage wrought by a disaster of this magnitude. Some of the details would not become clear until a year later following the two fact finding missions set up by Bangladesh NGOs Friendship and INCIDIN. Of the sixty-two dead, two were women, one of whom was 7 months pregnant[6]. Twenty-one of the deceased were aged between 17 and 21 years, and eighty per cent had been with the company less than a year (Bangladesh National Council of ITGLWF affiliated Unions, BGMEA, INCIDIN, 2006). Of the fifty-four workers classed as seriously injured, fifty-five per cent of these were under the age of twenty-five[7]. In total, some thirty-eight workers were deemed critically injured (INCIDIN, 2006: 13). Eighteen of the injured were treated at the Apollo Hospital, a private clinic, and released within days. Others were admitted to the Cantonment Military Hospital (CMH) but it was difficult for friends and relatives to determine their wellbeing since no visiting was allowed there (Sramik Nirapotta Forum, 2005). Of those who were severely injured, a number were eventually transferred to the Orthopaedics Hospital in Dhaka.

Some workers needed blood transfusions and constant dressings, which were paid for by the owners through the BGMEA but they appeared to be insufficient and there were reports of orderlies demanding payment after dressing wounds (SNF, 2005). This led to altercations at the hospital (Farazi 2005). Members of Sramik Nirapotta – the Workers Safety Forum – volunteered to donate blood and provide support for the seriously injured, but when they turned up at the hospital, they became concerned about the conditions of the victims[8]. The human damage reached well beyond the confines of the hospital wards and out into the Bangladesh countryside where the extended families of the victims lived, but it would be some time before efforts could be made to fully identify the immediate family members and account for their economic circumstances. Of the dead, almost half were married with dependants and children less than five years of age. Among the fifty-four injured, thirty were married, the majority of whom were under the age of twenty-five. Eighty per cent of the wives had no income, and their dependent children were, understandably, very young (Arens, 2005: 15-17). Moreover, the victims were all from extended families. For the dead, in addition to the immediate spouse and children, a total of 118 additional dependent relatives would eventually be identified – the majority of whom were unemployed, living in rural poverty with no alternative sources of income (INCIDIN: 2). Nearly seventy per cent of these were female. Twenty-seven were over the age of sixty and half were living off the assistance of others (Arens, *op.cit.*: 22). A similar picture emerged for the injured, for whom 125 dependants of roughly equal gender were identified. Of these, eighty-one had no source of income and thirty-three were aged fifty and over. The average monthly income of those who were in gainful employment was approximately BDT 1,444 (€18)[9]. Because of acute poverty and physical conditions, it soon transpired that they had been unable to approach any of the authorities or unions or NGOs for help[10]. Collectively and individually, the lack of earning capacity in the families of both the dead and injured placed the dependants in a dire poverty situation, compounded further by an unwritten ban on women engaging in any economic activity outside of their home and there was next to no access to any agricultural work which might be available. Many had both dependent parents in law and children to take care of on no income. There was the very high probability that without some intervention, those rendered disabled would 'be reduced to penury – with most ending up as roadside petty traders or beggars'.[11]

Beyond these victims were the hundreds of workers who had now been forcibly unemployed by the events. Because the factory records had been allegedly destroyed, the BGMEA at the request of the local unions, set up a makeshift office to establish a precise number of workers. Some of the local unions and labour rights organisations claimed a figure of 5,000 (Arens: *op.cit.*: 6), against a figure of 2,700 (combined Shahriyar Fabrics 1,500 and Spectrum Sweaters 1,200)[12]. Those who had registered on the BGMEA list had not yet been paid their outstanding wages for the shifts worked in the month preceding the collapse. For these workers, the reality of hardship now began to hit home. Less than a week after the collapse, grocers in Palashbari had stopped providing credit to the workers. Some workers had to resort to lying that they had managed to get a job at a neighbouring factory as a way of squeezing more credit from their grocer (Daily Star 2005a). A number of workers who could afford the bus fare had returned home. Others had, however, opted to stay in Palashbari and surrounding villages and turn up for their outstanding wages. Many were now horribly caught between two stools – some owed money back in their home villages and dared not return. Others had fled in the night because of the debts they owed to local grocers, landlords and neighbours. By now many of the unemployed Spectrum workers, official and casual, had had no other option, but to begin to seek employment at some of the surrounding sweater factories (Daily Star, 2005f).

The survivors and families of the deceased were now preoccupied with day to day survival, given the woeful level of industrial accident protection for workers and their families in Bangladesh based on laws enacted during the days of the British colonial rule. The statutory entitlement for the families of the deceased derived from an out-dated piece of Workmen's Compensation legislation passed in 1923 under British colonial rule. A worker's family could expect a miserly lump sum BDT 21,000 (€254). Any further lump sum amounts would be based on the good will of the owner and whatever supplementary amount was deemed appropriate by his employers' association. Because of the spate of factory fires in the sector, leading to considerable loss of life, the BGMEA had introduced a mandatory group insurance scheme in 2002 and established a supplementary payout of a further BDT 79,000 (€956)[13] to round the total 'compensation' sum up to 100,000. For those amongst the fifty-four workers who had been hospitalised some of whom suffered injuries which threatened their capacity to ever work again, there was no state medical provision to cover their medical costs. Compensation for incapacity was based on the same legislation and determined purely on the basis of loss of earnings calculated by a percentage factor as per the severity of the injury (as assessed by a qualified medical practitioner). It was in any event not intended to exceed sixty per cent of monthly earnings, and in the case of temporary disablement (whether total or partial), a worker would receive a half-monthly instalment equal to twenty-five per cent of the monthly wages, for the period of disablement or 5 years, whichever was shorter[14]. Although the owner acting through the BGMEA had covered the workers' immediate medical costs, based on existing industrial practice, the fear was that the legal provisions covering worker incapacity due to an industrial accident might not be implemented. Moreover, for those rendered unemployed by the collapse, whilst technically they may have been entitled to a redundancy payment, no such payments were forthcoming and they could look forward to no unemployment benefit.

As the nation mourned and tried to recover from a state of shock, a public debate once again ensued about the state of occupational health and safety and the enforcement of building regulations in the RMG sector.

CHAPTER 3

A Disaster Waiting to Happen...

Astonishingly, within a day of the collapse reports appeared in the media of a case being filed at the Savar police station implicating the owners of the factory for causing death due to negligence (Daily Star, 2005f). This was to prove symptomatic of a media frenzy surrounding the efforts to establish cause and apportion blame, most of which focussed on the owners. The owners had wanted to come to the factory immediately:

> The moment we received the call... we thought about immediately coming to the factory because this is our industry, this is like our family, our children, but people around the area – the officers – said it was better that you don't come here now... a lot of people were agitated[1].

Although the owners had gone to ground, they immediately issued a press release that they would provide immediate cash assistance to the victims and they also took out an advert in the press on the 13 April in which they expressed their willingness to compensate the families of the dead whilst leaving it to the BGMEA to determine the rate (Juberee and Farazi, 2005) and stressed that 'one hundred percent standard had been ensured at every phase of the construction'. The advertisement also stated that the structural design of the building had been undertaken by experienced graduate engineers of the BUET (Daily Star, 2005g).

Establishing cause

A five member investigative committee was set up swiftly and tasked by the *RAJUK (Rajdhani Unnayan Kartripakkha)* – the Capital City Development and Planning Authority2 – to submit a report within 3 days. Having carried out an initial inspection of the site, the committee requested sight of the planning documents from the Spectrum owner, but these had been destroyed in the collapse and therefore were not forthcoming. Realising the enormity of the task before them, they enlisted the support of six technical experts from the Bangladesh University of Engineering and Technology (BUET). The Chair of the RAJUK informed the media that they would 'go for action against the violators' (New Age, 2005a) and his sentiment was echoed by the State Minister for Home Affairs, when he visited the site, declaring 'No one responsible for the incident will be spared' (Azad, 2005).

When the rescue effort was finally abandoned eight days after the collapse, the RAJUK committee had still not concluded its preliminary investigation. Unfounded allegations continued to circulate in the media, leading to a number of rash judgments. As early as 24 April the parliamentary standing committee in the Ministry of Labour and Employment held the Spectrum owners responsible for the unauthorised design of the collapsed building (*Daily Star*, 2005h). While the RAJUK continued its investigation, the BGMEA also formed a fifteen member committee including experts from the BUET under the chairmanship of the BGMEA's standing committee on safety measures. The RAJUK report did not surface until 27 April. The Chairman of the RAJUK forwarded it to the Ministry of Housing and Public Works. The report was not made public but some of its findings announced in a press conference, fuelling once again a premature and ill-informed impression of the cause of the disaster and the four owners, and the three engineers were named as the parties responsible for the construction of the doomed factory.

The majority of the factories in the Dhaka division of the Chief Inspectorate for Factories and Establishments (CIFE) tend to be housed in buildings constructed neither for industrial/commercial purposes nor located in industrial/commercial locations. Spectrum on the other hand had been purpose built outside of Dhaka. Following soil tests conducted by a recognised civil engineering company, the owners had submitted plans for a four storey factory on top of the ground floor but had included in the design reinforced concrete cement piling and foundations to a depth of nearly 60 feet suitable for an eight storey building. They had hoped to exercise this option at a later stage when planning approval might be forthcoming. Such developments do, of course, require planning permission, but at the time of construction there appears to have been confusion over jurisdiction for this, authorisation either being required from the *RAJUK* or the district Cantonment Board. Building construction was originally regulated by the Building Construction Act of 1953, but efforts were made given the risk of earthquake and flooding to unify and update all norms regarding building safety into a National Building Code in 1993. Although the Government had provided funding to coordinate the preparation of the code, it had never been made law, nor incorporated into other existing building legislation and experts were reportedly of the opinion that the code elements were being routinely flouted by architects and construction engineers particularly where high rise construction was concerned (Alam, 2005).

The owners commenced the build of the Spectrum Sweater factory at the end of 2000 before they received approval for the first phase which was finally issued in 2002. In their initial enquiries at the Savar Cantonment Board, they were informed that the plans should be for a five storey building in the first instance[3]. Since their plans had always been for a higher 8 storey structure, their design provided for three or four twenty/twenty four inch diameter RCC cast in situ piles to be sunk to a depth of sixty-five feet under each RCC column which would accommodate this and they instructed the engineers to sink foundations to this depth according to the design provided by the BUET engineers. Construction work commenced on a plot measuring 9,374 square feet. However, the local authorities including the RAJUK and the Housing and Public Works Ministry did not have the human resource to monitor whether buildings had been constructed according to approved design or if piling had been properly carried out. It is a debatable point whether building inspectors, would have been assigned the task of scrutinising Spectrum in any event during the preliminary phase of the build, and whether an inspector would have been in a position to assess the quality of the concrete in the base columns when such pillars were in fact beneath ground level.

In 2003, the management decided to expand the factory upwards with the addition of a further four floors, and maintained partial production while the concreting of the additional floors was underway. In their first interview with the media, which did not take place until November 2005, the management stated that they had originally applied to the Cantonment Board for permission for a five-storey building (including a ground floor) as a first stage and filed plans for approval for a four storey extension in 2003 for which they had received a receipt from the authorities but that this had been destroyed along with other paperwork in the factory collapse. During the summer of 2005 after the rubble had been removed from the site, an independent and unofficial investigation was undertaken by a group of members of the Institute of Bangladesh Engineers, (IEB). This report did not appear until October 2007, some two and half years after the disaster and the unpublished RAJUK investigation report.

Clearing away residual debris and digging down on the Eastern side of where the factory had stood they found the pile caps completely intact, thus quashing the theory of foundation failure. Many of the theories which had circulated in the media in the wake of the collapse – that there had been a boiler explosion, that the foundations had given way, and that the building had been constructed on soft soil and in the ditch/canal – were rejected. Other theories were all given more rigorous consideration[4]. The IEB conducted tests on the construction materials, soil and the design adequacy of the foundations they had examined. These did not categorically point to cause of failure. Whilst considerable variation in concrete strength was found from tests conducted on random samples from columns and slabs cast with aggregate including both on brick chips and stone chips as specified by the designer, the engineers' report noted that some strength deterioration could have been associated with the collapse[5]. In addition the quality and strength of the construction materials were tested by the BUET on at least three occasions during 2005/6. They confirmed that the materials were within a satisfactory level even though the materials submitted for test were 'disturbed samples' of concrete submitted following the accident[6]. The IEB report drew attention to a more credible explanation of the cause of the collapse – discernible from the north easterly direction in which the floors collapsed. What was found here suggests a compelling explanation of the 'trigger' of the disaster:

Figure 9: Buckled Columns. Courtesy: Spectrum Owners.

> For about 2 feet of the column above the pile cap, the column reinforcement (was) buckled and twisted. The concrete at this portion was very weak and contained clay and other deleterious particles. The concrete was so soft that aggregates would easily be pulled out with bare finger... There were twelve [actually sixteen – owner's note] twenty-five millimetre diameter high yield reinforcement bars that perhaps carried the load of the building but due to sustained creep these ultimately buckled... that led to the collapse of the whole building[7].

In May/June 2006, as construction work was about to commence to rebuild the factory on the former site, a team of BUET engineers acting on behalf of the owners who were desperate to understand the cause of this catastrophe which had so horribly changed their lives, undertook a further investigation. On clearing the remaining debris in the North East corner of the factory site and locating the existing pile caps and grade beams, they discovered a further column, which bore a striking resemblance to the column described in the IEB report (See Appendix 4 and Figure 9). When poked, the reinforced 'concrete' crumbled opening up the possibility that either no or insufficient cement had been added into an RCC mix prepared for two base sections of these adjacent pillars, or, that in each case, soil and rainwater had filled the base of the shuttering which had been prepared for an RCC mix and this had not been removed before the pour. It was this fundamental weakness at the base which provided little support for the rods in these two columns which began to buckle. Once the columns had buckled, the slab/column connections became 'hinge-like' on the upper floors causing them to sway in an east, north easterly direction. These storeys then gave way with tremendous vertical impact on the floors below, because every individual floor was a single 'flat slab' unit roof by itself. The entire building lost its equilibrium causing it to collapse like a pack of cards.

If this was indeed the point of failure in the building, then no vibrations (as were claimed) could have caused the Reinforced Cement Concrete (RCC) mix to degrade since there were no upper floors and no heavy machinery at the time that these two base sections of the ground floor pillars were being put in place. Of course subsequent vibrations common in most factories would probably have caused a weakening of the degraded 'concrete' casing surrounding the rods in these two base pillars. Whilst both possible causes point to potential supervisory failure on the part of the construction company rather than a failing of technical competence, they also raise questions about building inspection and oversight on the part of the Cantonment Board. As has been established above, since construction commenced prematurely, i.e. before the granting of planning approval, no initial inspection of the first phase of the build, could have been carried out anyway.

Overall the evidence would appear to suggest that the collapse was caused by systemic failure rather than negligence on the part of the owners. As the IEB report concluded:

> The lessons learned from the Spectrum Sweater factory building failure strongly emphasize the need for the implementation of [a] Quality Management System in our organizations, and... quality assured structures and services for the building industry. This also requires [the Government] to critically review and evaluate weakness in our present system of building planning, design and construction regulations, the need for training individuals at all levels of work and bringing commitment to it. Of course this needs commitment of all concerned including the top level of governance. Political will of the democratic Government is a must to achieve it[8].

Occupational health and safety in the RMG

The IEB report focussed in the main on construction management but Spectrum also raised serious questions about the level of oversight of occupational health and safety in the ready-made garment sector in Bangladesh. It is the office of the Chief Inspectorate of Factories and Establishments (CIFE) whose responsibility it is to enforce the Factories Act of 1965 and the Factories Rules of 1979[9]. Organised into four divisional offices – Dhaka, Chittagong, Khulna and Rajshahi, the CIFE has a total establishment of 110 staff but thirty vacant inspector positions (BOSHE and Centre for Corporate Accountability, 2006: 5). Nationally, of some eighty officers just thirteen field inspectors had jurisdiction for safety legislation in over 24,229 registered factories, some three million shops and establishments and two ports. A further nine enforced – quite separately – health and welfare legislation (BOSHE and Centre for Corporate Accountability, 2006). For the Dhaka division, which covers Savar and the Spectrum Sweater factory, a mere four inspectors were responsible for policing factory safety. Spectrum would have had a one in 729 chance of ever receiving both a health and safety and welfare inspection (*op. cit.*: 20), a situation not uncommon in developed economies today[10]. Section 39 of the Factories Act regulates building safety, and under subsection 2, inspectors are authorised to serve an order prohibiting further use of any building deemed to be in a condition dangerous to human life. Rigorous enforcement of the legislation was not, it would appear the way in which inspectors were going about their business. Unannounced inspections, whilst permissible, were not part of their practice (*op.cit.*: 23), and fines for non-remediated breaches of the safety law amounted to a derisory maximum of BDT 1,000 (€11). Even more worrying than the absence of punitive fines, was the unethical professional practice of accepting bribes (Transparency International Bangladesh, 2005; New Age, 2005b)[11]. Attention had been drawn to this unacceptable state of affairs on numerous occasions in representations to the ILO Committee of Experts on the Bangladesh Government's Compliance with Labour Inspection Convention 81 (BOSHE and Centre for Corporate Accountability, *op.cit.* cf. also ILO 2006) but the Government response to the Committee's recommendations had been to plead poverty, despite an

Year	Name & Location of Factory	Fatalities
1990	Saraka Garments, Section 10, Mirpur Dhaka	27
1995	5 Poster Industries Ltd, Pallabi, Mirpur, Dhaka	10
1996	Trimud / Suntex, Pallabi, Mirpur, Dhaka	11
1996	Lusaka Garments, Ibrahimpur, Kafrul, Dhaka	9
1996	Navelli Garments, Mohakhali, Dhaka	5
1996	Tamanna Garments, Mirpur, Dhaka	27
1996	Tohidul Fashion, Shewrapara, Mirpur, Dhaka	14
1997	Rahman & Rahman, Mirpur, Dhaka	22
1997	Shanghai & Zahanara Garments	24
1998	Phoenix Garments, Dhaka	10
1999	Rose Garments, Gazipur	5
2000	Globe Knitting, Banani, Dhaka	12
2000	Dora Garments, Gulshan, Dhaka	12
2000	Chowdhury Knitwears, Shivpur, Narsingdi	53
2001	Miko Sweaters, Mirpur, Dhaka	24
2004	Omega & Shifa Apparels, Mirpur, Dhaka	8
2005	Sun Knitting & Processing, Siddhihrganj, Narayanganj	23
2005	Spectrum Sweaters, Savar, Dhaka	62

Source: Fairwear Foundation, 2006.

Table 3: Accidents in RMG Factories 1990–2005.

alarming catalogue of accidents in garment factories leading to 300 fatalities and 2,510 injuries in the fifteen years leading up to Spectrum as can be seen from Table 3.

The compliance efforts of the buyers

In numerous apparel sourcing countries, including Bangladesh, labour administration provision is effectively subsidised by, a privatised factory inspection service in the form of teams of social auditors who undertake, amongst other checks, safety audits on behalf of the multinational buyers. Such checks are normally conducted as part of a broader investigation of a supplier facility. Social auditing, is used by a number of leading brand owners and retailers in the sector first and foremost as a risk assessment and 'reputation management' tool. This information gathering process is intended to demonstrate to their customer base and the wider society (usually in their annual sustainability reports) that buyers are acting as 'global citizens' and upholding fundamental workers' rights in their supply chains. However, many buyers in the sector do not invest in social compliance[12], either because they are too small, too blinkered, or because they are able to 'piggy back' on the programmes of those compliance conscious buyers who are sourcing from the same factories.

A social audit seeks to determine the extent to which a supplier is meeting a series of expectations laid down in the buyer's code of conduct. These expectations derive in the main from employment standards based on International Labour Organisation Conventions which have been ratified by member governments of the ILO and implemented into their national (labour) law. Although the Bangladesh government has ratified all the main ILO Conventions[13], the track record of the RMG on labour rights up to 2005 had not been good (Kabeer and Mahmood, 2006; Choudhury and Hussein M., 2005; Murshid *et al.*, 2003; Morshed, 2007).

Some buying companies had opted for establishing their own in house teams to monitor the adherence to employment standards, but inevitably, in order to satisfy the calls for independent verification of internally conducted compliance activities, some turned to the use of external 'auditing' in varying degrees as a backstop (Ascoly and

Zeldenrust, 2003). The majority of those buyer firms with a social compliance function have tended, however, to rely on social auditing firms to inspect their supplier facilities. This has spawned a whole compliance industry and some audit companies such as Intertek and SGS have become multinationals in their own right with local offices in Bangladesh and other key sourcing locations.

Prior to business being contracted, general audit practice requires prospective suppliers to complete a supplier self-assessment form and submit this to the buyer before a full audit is commissioned. The social audit procedure has become fairly standardised and buyers and their auditors have adopted agreed guidelines, amongst other things, for the duration of audit per factory workforce size, pre audit information gathering, the number of worker interviews per workforce size and formats for what are known as corrective action plans – or CAPs (Sedex, 2009; BSCI, 2007; SAI, 2004). To audit a factory the size of Spectrum would have normally required two auditor days. (Sedex, *op.cit.*:12 see also SAI, *op.cit.*) Although audit procedure has become standardised, there can be wide variations in auditing practice, leading many to question the role of auditors and the value of this activity as a credible tool for social compliance (Pruett, 2005; Harney, 2008; O'Rourke, 2002; Locke *et al.*, 2007). Since auditing is a privatised commercial activity paid for by the supplier or the buyer, depending on the perspective of the latter, pressure obviously exists to curtail the number of audit days and for the auditor(s) to gather all the necessary information in the time allocated. Consequently the quality of audit practice can vary enormously with audits often repeated in the same facility by audit companies acting on behalf of different buyers. Suppliers view such inspections, understandably, as a waste of their time, an intrusion and an unnecessary constraint on their right to manage. For the buyers, audits constitute an immensely bureaucratic, time consuming yet necessary cost. For auditing companies this is a steady source of business. For workers who have not received prior coaching, an audit interview or focus group is not a place to jeopardise one's job.

In a move to address some of these problems, a number of the retailers led by the German Foreign Trade Association (Aussenhandelsvereinigung) had pushed the formation of the so-called Business Social Compliance Initiative in November 2002.

The BSCI was conceived as a sector wide solution for retail, providing a common auditing platform for its member companies[14]. It included at the time three companies sourcing from Spectrum: the German retail group KarstadtQuelle (later renamed Arcandor), the Belgian Cotton Group, and Inditex, the Spanish fashion retailer. Ninety-five per cent of the audits under the BSCI system had to be organized and paid for by the supplier, not the buyer. Being able to fall back on a reliable management information system on conditions in supplier factories would be vital for member firms, should they wish to place business with a particular supplier and/or stand accused in the media of a worker rights violation. Despite existing weaknesses in social auditing as a means of gathering data on some key compliance issues, health and safety is generally regarded as an issue where a factory inspector or auditor with a 'trained eye' can detect areas for action since the physical presence of hazards or absence of precautionary measures are clearly observable and detectable from an audit methodology point of view (Pruett, *op.cit.*).

During its period of operation Spectrum had not been subjected to a social audit. The factory had been in a state of constant build and was taking on subcontract work during much of this time[15]. As would later transpire, many of the buyers were oblivious to the fact that they had production in the factory, a not uncommon state of affairs in the global apparel industry. Indeed only one buyer claimed to have audited the facility back in 2002 but this was probably the Shahriyar Fabrics building since little of the Spectrum factory had been constructed by then, and since no audit findings had been made public from this inspection, it is not known whether the company had a clear set of regulations and procedures regarding occupational health and safety in line with ILO convention 155 and ILO recommendation 164 (as specified under the BSCI Code of Conduct[16]) for dealing with accident prevention[17].

It is fair to say that until that fateful night structural safety, although covered by the Factories Act, had not figured either on the inspection schedules of the factory inspectorate, nor the social auditors, who had become preoccupied with the issue of fire safety in the wake of the Sun Knitting and Processing disaster at Narayanganj. Here, three months prior to the Spectrum collapse, some twenty-three workers had perished in the flames of a fire in which scores of others had been injured, unable to escape because many of the exits were blocked and fire extinguishers inoperable (Daily Star, 2005i). In response, the Parliamentary Standing Committee on Occupational Health & Safety had directed the CIFE to conduct a random survey on factory safety in the RMG sector, and a team of four inspectors had visited some 100 factories. In their report submitted just days before the Spectrum collapse, forty-eight of the 100 factories were found to be operating without basic safety arrangements. However, the report went on to say that manpower shortages within the CIFE prevented any legal action being taken against the establishment owners (Daily Star, 2005j).

Was Spectrum a disaster waiting to happen? The evidence would appear to suggest a serious structural defect progressively deteriorating underground over a period of five years, apparently caused by shoddy workmanship and lax management on the part of the construction company. Would this have happened had plans been approved in a timely manner and the first phase of the build been scrutinised by the Buildings Inspectorate? Given that the faulty base columns were under the ground and beneath eye level and could only be viewed from above, this may have proved difficult for an inspector. Moreover there was inconclusive evidence relating to the issue of gaps and cracks between the free standing Spectrum and Shahriyar units[18]. Consequently the central questions relating to responsibility remain perhaps unanswerable. However, as far as Bangladesh civil society and the media in particular were concerned, the Spectrum factory collapse was one disaster too many and it was time to go on the offensive. The Spectrum owners were now about to be thrust into the gathering storm.

CHAPTER 4

Bangladesh Civil Society Mobilises

The whole nation was shocked by the events in Palashbari. The shock extended to the thousands of Bangladeshi expatriates all over the world. For some time a number had been organised in two online communities of mainly professionals and academics – Drishtipat[1] and Uttorshuri[2], where they had engaged in online awareness raising about the state of human rights abuses in their homeland. Asif Saleh, an executive director at the UK branch of Goldman Sachs, had established Drishtipat through a group of fellow bloggers leading to the formation of a critical writers' collective in 2001[3]. One member of the collective, Farjana Godhuly, a well-respected freelance photographer who was working in Bangladesh at the time, was one of the first to visit the rescue operation and document the human suffering of those relatives and friends who agonisingly waited for news at the factory site. The harrowing images were posted in an online exhibition[4] as part of a global effort to raise money for relief of the victims. As of 11 June their efforts, together with Uttorshuri, had raised $15,407. Drishtipat was able to arrange relief payments via Ain O Salish Kendra (ASK), the Legal Aid and Human Rights Organisation and Sromik Nirapotta, the Workers Safety Forum[5] to cover the medical expenses of those severely injured and hospitalised workers and to arrange visits to their dependants whom they assisted with payments to make some longer term provision for income generation. Fifteen victims received initial assistance by this means.

The Workers Safety Forum was an umbrella for a number of Bangladesh Civil Society groups – trade unions, NGOs, rights and women organisations which soon took to the streets in defence of the victims of the collapse. Feelings were running high – within two days of the disaster, a series of rallies were held at which exemplary punishment was demanded both of the owner and the senior officials in the government bodies deemed to have been involved in the approval of the construction of the factory. At a rally at Muktangan in Dhaka, Aminul Haque Faruq, leader of Sramik Karmachari Oikya Parishad (SKOP) the umbrella trade union organisation in Bangladesh[6] expressed grave concern over the slow process of the rescue operation and called on the government to enlist international assistance if the necessary equipment for such a rescue operation was not available. The National Garment Workers' Federation, one of many garment unions in the sector, was amongst the first unions to take a lead demanding BDT 200,000 compensation for each of the victims' families. Established in 1984, the NGWF claimed a membership of 20,000 with only one quarter of these dues paying, spread across twenty-eight registered factory based unions and over 1,000 factory committees[7]. It had an office presence in Savar and some thirty-nine members at Spectrum, five of whom were among the dead and a further twelve of whom were injured[8]. The union's first priority was to see to it that the bodies were returned to their families. Its second was to take care of the injured, and its third was to protest:

> Today 22 April NGWF organized a 'country-wide Protest And Condolence Day' in Dhaka, in which more than 500 workers participated. Participants carried RED and Black Flag... the sign of protest and sorrow. Some of the... leaders and other trade union leaders also present to express their solidarity[9].

Outside Dhaka, similar types of action were organised in Chittagong, Savar, Narayangong and Gazipur. The plan was to step up action with a series of demonstrations in front of the offices of the authorities which now had a role to play in ensuring that adequate compensation and relief would be distributed to the victims/families. The NGWF joined forces with the Bangladesh Garment Industry Workers' Federation and together they arranged for thousands of leaflets to be printed and distributed with photographs of the dead and a clear statement on behalf of the workers. Together the unions formulated seven demands:

1. The arrest of the owners.

2. The establishment of a Committee of Inquiry with the participation of trade unions.

3. Payment of BDT 200,000 compensation to each family of the dead.

4. Proper treatment for the injured.

5. Payment of outstanding payment of monthly wage of March and April and overtime payment of February, March and April.

6. Job security with wages or compensations according to the Law for the whole workforce.

7. The establishment of a tripartite committee to inspect safety precautions and working conditions in every RMG factory[10].

The trade union situation in Bangladesh continued to be a messy one at this time in the RMG. A key factor here, still prevalent to this day, was the dogged refusal on the part of the employers to accept the core employment standards of freedom of association and collective bargaining at the workplace as enshrined in ILO Conventions 87, 135 and 98 respectively and the Government's complicity in this. These core conventions can be found in every code of conduct of those buyers serious enough at least to issue a statement of the principles to which they expect their suppliers to adhere. Although ratified by the Bangladesh government, the International Trade Union Confederation felt compelled to report:

> The right to form and join unions is not respected in practice, despite numerous ILO criticisms. The right to strike is not recognised by law and workers are regularly sacked, beaten or subjected to false charges for being active in union activities. Export processing zones fall under a special labour legislation whereby basic rights are not permitted. Recent attempts to change the law to permit freedom of association in the zones have been the subject of numerous proposed amendments from the ILO to bring the draft law into compliance with international core labour conventions 87 and 98, which have yet to be acknowledged by the government of Bangladesh (ITUC, 2006).

Because the garment employers had succeeded in keeping most unions outside of the factories (Rahman et al., 2007: 12), on the industrial front they continued and continue to remain weak and fragmented. To act as a *bona fide* union organisation, a trade union federation must undergo a process of registration with the Directorate of Labour. At the time the NGWF was one of forty-three trade union federations in the RMG. Each federation would normally consist of a number of factory unions but under Bangladesh labour law, for a factory union to gain recognition, union organisers had to collect the signatures of thirty per cent of the workforce before activating registration. This would be often carried out clandestinely, with the owners only discovering the presence of the union upon receipt of the notification from the Directorate of Labour, and then moving to victimise or sack those workers who have signed up. At Spectrum, it had obviously proved difficult for the NGWF to achieve the thirty per cent target.

With a union density of approximately five per cent in the RMG (ITUC, 2006:1), the absence of an organic trade union movement had at least two impacts. Firstly, most union activity had been confined to campaigning on the streets and/or to providing some medical facilities and training to members. As campaigning organisations, unions had at times served the purposes of the political parties with which they are aligned[11]. In this respect, however, the NGWF was one of a number of trade union federations which had remained independent. Secondly and crucially, union leadership was not representative of the vast majority of women who make up the ranks of workers and the union membership in the RMG with many male leaders emerging from former and current political activists (Khan, 2002: 189–190).

Despite this union fragmentation and weakness, some alliances had nevertheless been possible: the Bangladesh Garments Workers Unity Council, the Bangladesh Garment Workers and Employees Unity Council and the Bangladesh National Council of Textile Garment and Leather Workers Federations (BNC). The latter consisted at the time of eight (now nine) unions which had affiliated to the International Textile Garment and Leather Workers' Federation (ITGLWF) – the Global Union for the sector. At the time of the collapse, the NGWF was not an affiliate, although the Federation had an application pending which was subsequently accepted. The low union density and absence of extensive women's organisation and leadership in unions is paralleled by the presence of a large number of NGOs in Bangladesh focusing on labour rights and women's rights in particular, many of which now became engaged in support of the workers at Spectrum: the women's rights organisation – Karmojibi Nari, the Legal Aid and Human Rights Organisation – Ain O Salish Kendra (ASK), the Bangladesh National Women Lawyers' Association, *Ubinig* (Policy Research for Development Alternatives), Oxfam Bangladesh, *Odhikar* – a Bangla word meaning 'Rights'; the Bangladesh Society for the Enforcement of Human Rights, Sammilita Nari Samaj (the United Women's Front), Nijera Kori (We do it ourselves), Sammilita Samajik Andolon (a platform of professionals) and the Bangladesh Legal Aid Trust. A number held mourning rallies at Muktangan at which they demanded the arrest of the company owners and a national day of remembrance for the victims. They all called upon the government to conduct an immediate structural audit of RMG factories and to shut down those which constituted a building hazard to workers (Daily Star, 2005k). On 17 April, representatives of these organisations called a press conference at the National Press Club. Representatives of *Sammilita Nari Samaj, Nijera Kori, Sammilita Samajik Andolon* and the Bangladesh Legal Aid Trust were also in attendance. They demanded that the persons and the authorities responsible for the tragedy be brought to book for their negligence, and that the Government make public a full list of the victims and ensure that their families were paid adequate compensation to the tune of BDT 700,000 (€8,400). They further called for a full investigation and report from the Chief Inspector of Factories and the publication of the planning and approval documents. (Daily Star, 2005l).

On the 19 April, the day on which the rescue operation was terminated, trade unions belonging to the BNC called a press conference at which the same demands were reiterated. A seven point list of demands was tabled which included a similar compensation to the family of each victim who had perished; the establishment of a national workers' compensation commission, a review of factory safety procedures by a fully representative investigation commission, the trial of the owners, along with an authoritative list of workers at the factory. They further called for a national day of mourning. Pressure was kept up on the 20 April as members of the Bangladesh Paribesh Andolon (BAPA), a community environmental group, formed a human chain in front of the RAJUK. Between the 21 and 25 April, the Sromik Nirapotta Forum (SNF) the coalition of fourteen human rights, labour, environmental

49

and civil rights organisations met to draw up a Charter of Concerns which they submitted to the BGMEA on the 25 April. In their charter they called on the employers to:

1. expedite a prompt and public report by its five member investigation committee into the actual reason for the collapse, the ownership of the land, the legality of the construction and the liability of the owners to compensate the victims;

2. take any necessary action, including expulsion from the BGMEA, against the owners ; pay appropriate compensation, over and above the promised 100,000 sum to the bereaved families, the short term and long term medical care and hospitalisation costs for those injured (including replacement of limbs) and to re-employ those workers of both Shahriyar Fabrics and Spectrum Sweater Industries Ltd., who have lost their jobs due to the building collapse;

3. assess the number of workers who have lost their jobs by obtaining all necessary documents and files from the owner, including placing advertisements in all papers for workers to present their IDs, punch cards or some form of worker identity;

4. make available the Association's rules and criteria for membership of the BGMEA;

5. set up a neutral, independent body to monitor the safety policies and procedures of its members' factories and a joint body together with representatives of the Worker's Safety Forum to apprehend the accused owner' (Daily Star, 2005m).

Three days later they served legal notice on the authorities of their intention to deposit a writ. This was followed up by a public announcement by Amirul Haque Amin of the NGWF of his union's intention along with the Bangladesh Garment and Industrial Workers Federation to lay siege on the Home Ministry on 28th to demand the arrest of the owners.

Figure 10: NGWF demonstration in support of the Spectrum victims in Dhaka.

The battle over compensation

Compensation was a critical issue for the unions and labour rights organisations. The relevant international standards relating to the circumstances of the victims derive from ILO Convention 121 concerning Benefits in the Case of Employment Injury (1964). For the deceased two benefits would normally be required – a funeral benefit covering all the costs and for the families of the deceased a periodic payment to the beneficiary equivalent to at least fifty per cent of either the deceased's prior earnings or a standard wage of an ordinary adult male labourer[12]. Less developed countries without adequate administrative facilities could pay the benefit as a lump sum. Under Article Nine a standard is established with respect to the provision of medical care and cash benefits (in the form of a periodical payment) to the injured. Convention 121 had not been ratified by successive governments in Bangladesh and as detailed in Chapter Two the existing legal provision in respect of worker compensation was archaic, based on two pieces of British Colonial legislation enacted under the Raj

– the Fatal Accidents Act (FAA) of 1855[13] (as amended 1955) and the Workers' Compensation Act of 1923 – and complicated by the absence of a system of direct employer liability insurance. Whereas worker compensation law in Europe and the USA generally establishes a system of employer liability insurance, indemnifying victims of industrial disasters in return for the employee waiving their right to sue their employer for negligence, section 1A of the FAA provided for family members or their representatives to sue for compensation if the death was occasioned by actionable wrong. Most, if not all cases, had been dealt with under the Workmen's Compensation Act of 1923 which made provision for a woefully inadequate lump sum of BDT 21,000 for the family of each deceased (rounded up in the RMG to 100,000 by the employer under a BGMEA rule). In the case of temporary disablement, compensation would be paid for the period of incapacity or for one year, whichever period was shorter. 100 per cent of the wage was only paid in the first two months, while in the subsequent months, two thirds of monthly wages would be paid.

On 16 April, the Government Chief Inspectorate for Factories and Establishments (CIFE) duly filed a compensation suit with Dhaka's first Labour Court, citing paragraph ten of the WCA, and claiming BDT 21,000 (US$352 as at April 2005) for each of the forty-four dead workers who had been recovered up to that point. This amount was of course seen by the unions and NGOs as derisory and within a week of the collapse, (Karmojibi Nari – the Working Women's Initiative in Bangladesh had put forward a compensation figure for the families of the dead of seven lakh[14] (BDT 700,000) (approx €8,471.52 as at April 2005) (Ahsan, 2005a). On 20 April a judge ordered the owners to deposit BDT 21,000 for each of the forty-four families who had petitioned the court. Some legal commentators argued that the compensation suit should have been brought under the provisions of the FAA under which a court could rule that compensation to the dependants of a dead worker should equal the worker's total income of her/his entire remaining service life.

The BGMEA had established an employer's group insurance scheme in 1997 but had made this mandatory in 2002 and fixed a new amount of BDT 79,000 (€956) to round the payout off to BDT 100,000, as mentioned above. Since the workers were not in the employ of the BGMEA, some lawyers termed this additional payout a humanitarian donation, rather than compensation. Either way it was the owners who paid the full BDT 100,000 to each family in the end (Juberee and Farazi, 2005)[15]. Even the majority owner did not recognise the term compensation but for a different reason:

> For myself I never said 'compensation' because even if you lose a finger it cannot be compensated by the world's wealth...I called it 'cash assistance'.[16]

As the unions consulted with the authorities about the upcoming May Day Rally at Muktangaon in Dhaka, where more than 15,000 garment workers were expected to take part, the BGMEA arranged for a ceremony to disburse their 'compensation payments' (79,000) to the families of the victims on 3 May. They were at pains to stress that this additional amount had been paid by the owners. However, the burden of proof was placed on the families of the deceased to come forward to attest their relationship to the deceased at the BGMEA offices rather than be placed on the owners to provide these details (Daily Star, 2005n). Some nineteen of the twenty-four families received the amount paid by the owners. Five families identified failed to show. A further sixteen families were compensated again by the owners through the BGMEA at their offices at a meeting attended by the Minister of Labour and Employment.

In early May, some two weeks after its deadline, the BGMEA investigation submitted its report highlighting structural weakness as the main cause. On 8 May, almost 1 month after the tragedy, two of the owners finally appeared before the District and Sessions Court in Dhaka with their lawyers to petition for bail. The Dhaka District Public Prosecutor, moved for a rejection, and after hearing both sides, the judge rejected the initial bail petition, setting 12 May for the formal hearing and the two men were sent to the Dhaka Central Jail (Daily Star, 2005o).

On the day of the petition hearing, Garment Sramik and Shilpa Rakkha Jatiya Mancha submitted a memorandum to the deputy commissioner demanding BDT 500,000 as compensation for each of the families of the dead, dismissing the BDT 100,000 sums which had been handed over to twenty families as derisory. A lump sum figure of BDT 300,000 was also demanded for each worker rendered disabled by the collapse and BDT 100,000 for each of the remaining injured workers. The main demands had now crystallised and were articulated at each worker demonstration: punishment for the factory owners, increased compensation for the victims of the collapse, a major overhaul of health and safety in the RMG sector, and jobs for those workers unemployed by the disaster.

On the morning of the 12 May, the day of the trial, a hundred garment workers organized by Jatiya Garments Sramik Jote and the Bangladesh Garments and Industrial Workers Federation, marched on the court. They arrived at noon to find the building cordoned off by a large police contingent. (Daily Star, 2005p) By this time the court had been in session for ninety minutes, and the police inspector assigned to the case submitted a petition for taking the accused into remand which was rejected by the court, and the bail petition made by the lawyers acting on behalf of the defendants, was once again rejected by the court. This was indeed encouraging to the unions and labour rights organisations since there had been little trust in the judiciary which in Bangladesh at this time operated under the management of the state executive in Bangladesh. This lack of independence could of course lead to a politicisation of legal judgement. As one commentator remarked:

> Such a captive judiciary is incapable of providing a neutral arena for protecting the interests of the populace. Those with the greatest influence obtain favourable rulings regardless of the rule of law (Downey, 2007: 45).

Some 12 days later on the 24 May when the owners were released on bail, a writ petition was filed with the High Court by four injured workers and nine labour rights organizations seeking a judicial resolution of these demands and directions to the authorities to prevent further such disasters in future. This so-called public interest litigation, or PIL, was a relatively new form of class action suit based on section 102(1) of the Bangladesh Constitution under which organisations or individuals could seek a legal remedy from the High Court on behalf of a class or group of people where there had been a breach of fundamental rights. PIL started back in the early 1990s in Bangladesh and the number of such writs had been rising. A PIL can be filed generally where 'public interest' at large is affected and since the application to the Court could be made by an 'aggrieved person,' and this term had been interpreted quite widely, the way was open for such a writ to be submitted. The writ cited (and still cites) the respective Secretaries of the Home Office, the Labour and Employment Ministry, the Ministry for Industry, and the respective Ministries for Food and Disaster, Land, Environment and Forest, Chief Inspector of Factories, the RAJUK, the Chief Executive Officer of Savar Cantonment Board, the Fire Service, the President of the Bangladesh Garment Manufacturers and Exporters Association, BGMEA and the three directors of Spectrum Sweater Industries Ltd.

During May the NGWF sent a memorandum regarding the payment of outstanding wages owing to some fifty Spectrum workers to the Chief Inspector of Factories and Establishments (CIFE) who had filed a case at the Labour Court. The Court dismissed the case on the grounds that the outstanding wages had been paid. At the end of the month the union rallied hundreds of garment workers from the Savar district together with their colleagues from the Spectrum factory and their families, to a sit-down demonstration at the site of the Spectrum factory. Relatives of the dead and injured workers spoke at the rally about their desperate plight. It was an emotional gathering. Work colleagues who had not seen each other for over six weeks, embraced each other and the family members of the victims. A number of workers had distressing tales to tell of how they had been evicted by their landlords and now had no food. All but the seriously injured who were still in the Orthopaedics Clinic had no money for medicines or treatment. Some alleged that unscrupulous traders had made inflated demands for debt payments from the victims' dependants and that many grocers had ceased providing credit. The workers served notice that if their demands were not met within fifteen days they would be stepping up their action.[17]

Spectrum and the wider demands for change in the RMG

The Spectrum factory collapse was a catalytic moment for the Bangladesh labour movement. Pressure had been building up for years amongst the workforce over pay and health and safety in particular. The time had come for Civil Society to go on the offensive to bring about more systemic change in the management of health and safety in the RMG sector. The demands included the establishment of a tripartite committee to undertake an urgent structural review of all multi-storey buildings currently in use as garment production units and an inspection of safety precautions and working conditions in every RMG factory, specifically access and exit routes and evacuation procedures[18]. Furthermore should any unauthorized buildings be found without adequate safety measures, the authorities were called upon to take firm action against the owners particularly in the RMG centres of production in greater Dhaka, Narayanganj and Chittagong. Throughout much of 2005 and 2006, the Government and the employers were on the back foot as an alliance between Bangladesh Civil Society and their international counterparts, particularly in Europe, brought the issue of social compliance to the attention of the buyers. Some changes in the law and voluntary measures on the part of the RMG employers were going to be necessary if the RMG was to remain in the marketplace post MFA phase out – at least with those buyers who considered themselves to be socially responsible. A number of high level international conferences and roundtables took place during the summer of 2005 at which the trade unions in particular were able to voice their concerns and demands. Such meetings were of course relatively easy to manage and create a sense of constructive dialogue but out in the industry things were beginning to get out of control.

2006 got off to a particularly bad start for industrial relations in the RMG sector. Panna, a worker at the Titanic Productions factory in Mirpur was reportedly beaten to death by security guards for wearing a T shirt worth BDT 60 (€0.64 cents) without permission. It was alleged that his body had been hung up to make it look like a suicide. As the news of his death spread, hundreds of agitated workers gathered in front of the factory. Those inside went berserk, locked the doors and beat up one of the security guards (Daily Star, 2005q). This had become for many workers the last straw in a catalogue of issues – with allegations of frequent beatings and abuse by management and the withholding of wages if workers protested. Four months' overtime payments and one month's pay were claimed to be still outstanding (Daily Star, 2005q). This prompted a sit in by the Jatiyo Garment Sromik o Shilpo Rokkha Moncho (JGSSRM) outside the offices of the BGMEA to press home five demands: an increase in the minimum wage, enforcement of the ban on night work for women workers, the issue of appointment letters to all employees, the entitlement to week-long holidays and a full investigation into Panna's death.

By the end of February – on the 23 February to be precise – new concerns had emerged about the state of health and safety compliance in the RMG sector with the news that fifty-four workers had been killed and sixty injured in a fire allegedly caused by an electrical short circuit at the KTS Textile Industries in the port city of Chittagong. At the time of the fire (7 p.m. in the evening) over 1,000 workers had reportedly been in the building and, according to worker testimonies, the exits had been locked. On this occasion US buyers were in the frame (National Labour Committee, 2006). Within 2 days of what some labour rights organisations were calling the worst tragedy in the history of the RMG garment sector, there was another 'factory' collapse. On the morning of the 25 February, a five storey building owned by Phoenix Garments, but housing a number of factories and offices, gave way in the city's Tejgaon industrial area causing twenty-two deaths and injury to fifty workers. The upper floors of the building were undergoing unauthorised renovations into a 500 bed private hospital (Saha and Farazi, 2006). The pattern was chillingly similar to Spectrum – the owner of the building, who was also chairman of the City Bank of Bangladesh, was unable to be located and Phoenix Garments had been exporting clothing mainly to Europe (Daily Star, 2006a). On the same day of the Phoenix Building collapse, in Chittagong, fifty-seven workers were injured in a stampede when a transformer exploded at the Imam Group of Industries (reportedly housing the Moon Fashion Limited, Imam Fashion, Moon Textile, Leading Fashion and Bimon Inda garment factories). Fearing a subsequent fire the workers tried to escape through a narrow exit. As a result of the stampede four were reportedly in a critical condition[19].

There was thus a new poignancy to the first anniversary of the Spectrum Sweater factory collapse on 11 April 2006. Carrying red flags and banners, several hundred workers observed a token hunger strike on the 11 April at the Central Shaheed Minaret in Dhaka. Both the BNC and the National Garment Workers Federation declared the day as the Annual Health and Safety day for Garment Workers (Daily Star, 2006b). In a subsequent Round-table organised by the BNC, the unions called for the creation of a tripartite committee of experts to identify factories with faulty construction, reiterated their demand for increased compensation (BDT 700,000) and for the establishment of a trust fund for the victims and a dedicated industrial enclave for garment factories (Daily Star, 2006c).

So far there had been little joined up action on the part of the numerous trade union groupings but a number of factory incidents during May combined to propel the unions in the RMG sector to form a common platform. On 8th May, about fifty workers were injured in an attack by thugs allegedly engaged by the owners of Scandex BD Ltd at Savar. Faced with a sudden announcement that the piece rates for sweaters were to be reduced from BDT 25 to BDT 9.30, the operators had blockaded a main road for two hours. On the 11th May, workers of the New General Apparels factory in Gazipur engaged in a work stoppage in demand for outstanding pay and a wage increase. Some windows and machinery in the factory were damaged. Several days later, FS Sweater Factory of SQ Group in Sripur, Gazipur, stopped work in support of their demands for back wages and overtime. Although an agreement appeared to have been reached, police arrested three workers. In protest, their fellow workers blockaded a highway and disrupted traffic. As tension mounted, the police opened fire on the workers' demonstration leaving one dead and eleven injured. When the management filed charges against the three workers and a further eighty workers, the lid blew off the sector (Rahmann 2007).

By 22 May, eight garment factories had been ransacked and set on fire in Savar and the Savar Export Processing Zone (SEPZ). Many vehicles were also damaged and the disturbances resulted in a further worker fatality. The SEPZ Authority felt compelled to close a further sixty-seven factories claiming a loss of BDT 4,000 million as a result of these incidents. On 22 and 23 May, leaders and members of the BGMEA took to the streets in protest at the lack of Government response to the unrest. Following the Government's assurance about meeting workers' demands and the formation of a Minimum Wage Board, the workers lifted their blockade (Islam, 2006). However, this did not resolve matters. The worker outbursts were described by the president of the International Chamber of Commerce Bangladesh (ICCB), as being far from spontaneous and more as part of a calculated conspiracy against a growing garments industry. This was soon echoed in numerous quarters of the Bangladesh establishment with India, an arch industrial competitor country, seen as the culprit (Kumar, 2006).

At the end of month the Bangladesh Institute of Labour Studies and SKOP coordinated a meeting of some twenty-five trade union federations at which a ten point Charter of Demands was drawn up

(See Appendix 3). In amongst these demands were calls for a BDT 3,000 minimum wage, adherence to the forty-eight hour working week and on overhaul of compensation in the event of workplace accidents – BDT 500,000 to a nominated heir of the victim and BDT 700,000 for workers disabled by an accident. Moreover the Charter called for a ban on new multi storey factories and the relocation of multi storey production facilities to safer three-storey buildings (Islam K.A., 2006) (see Appendix 3).

Clearly shocked by the disturbances, the employers and the Government were forced into talks with the unions on the 11 and 12 June culminating in a Tripartite Agreement on the 12 June. In return for an immediate resumption of work, the agreement provided for the release of those workers arrested in clashes with the Rapid Action Battalion and police, the issue of employment letters and ID cards to all workers, a reaffirmation of respect for the national laws relating to overtime, holiday entitlement and maternity leave and the formation of a Minimum Wages Board to address outstanding wage demands in respect of a new national minimum (Islam, 2006a). There was however scepticism amongst the rank and file that these deals had been struck only to defuse the unrest and that the owners had no intention, with the exception of the reconvening of the Minimum Wages Board, of actually implementing any elements of the Workers Charter of Demands (Hasan, 2006).

The labour unrest became a platform for the Awami League, the main opposition party which was spearheading a campaign for political reform. The nineteen political parties in this League led by former Prime Minister Sheikh Hasina Wajed called for a 36 hour stoppage on the 13 and 14 June in support of the resignation of the Chief Electoral Commissioner and his two political appointees and to demonstrate against the excessive police force used during the clashes in Dhaka on the 11 June. When, in the autumn, the Bangladesh National Party stepped down at the end of its term, a caretaker government, designated by the Constitution to oversee the General election, usurped political control before the procedure for determining its composition had been exhausted, and the country was plunged into a political crisis. The elections which were scheduled for 22 January 2007 were boycotted by the Awami League on the grounds that the civil administration, election commission and the armed forces had become politicised. There was widespread violence and political rioting (Rahman, 2007) leading the President to resign as Chief Advisor, cancel the election, and appoint a new interim government in January 2007 which was intended to hold power for a limited period only until conditions could be stable enough to mount a fresh election. Although installed essentially by the army, the interim government was welcomed by many Bangladeshis and international observers as a necessary antidote to extensive corruption, widespread abuse of power and unrest. However, this came at a price. On the 25 January 2007 the caretaker government used the provisions laid down in Section 3 of the Emergency Powers Ordinance to issue a set of Emergency Power Rules (EPR). These suppressed opposition to the government and the freedoms of association, assembly and expression for a wide variety of groups including political activists, students, teachers, trade unions and other labour rights defenders, workers and journalists. Most of the trade union leadership, including officers of the BNC and the NGWF were forced to go into hiding as the enforcement of Section 3 of the Emergency Powers Ordinance prohibited processions, meetings and assemblies, and Section 4 outlawed industrial action and trade union activity with sentences of between 2 and 5 years imprisonment and fines possible. During this political crisis, which did not lift until elections were held in December 2008, it was difficult for the core group of trade unionists and NGOs who had made it their business to support the Spectrum victims to continue a pioneering new initiative which had emerged as a result of their efforts to internationalise their struggle. It is to this campaign initiative that we must now turn our attention.

CHAPTER 5

The International Solidarity Efforts and the Reactions of the Multinational Buyers

As the heads of corporate social responsibility of some of the more prominent European buyers from Spectrum woke up on the morning of the 11 April to the news of the collapse, they were oblivious to the fact that their companies had been sourcing from the factory or that they were about to become embroiled in one of the biggest national and international solidarity campaigns in the history of the clothing industry. Two global worker rights organisations now swung into action – the International Textile Garment and Leather Workers' Federation (ITGLWF) and the Clean Clothes Campaign (CCC). The ITGLWF[1] is a Global Union headquartered in Brussels representing some 230 affiliate organisations in the sector in some 110 countries. Its General Secretary, Neil Kearney, already had a reputation with the BGMEA for his dogged defence and promotion of garment workers' rights in Bangladesh. Although none of the ITGLWF affiliates which form the so-called Bangladesh National Council (BNC)[2] had members in the factory, for their leaders the Spectrum collapse was yet another example of the shambolic state of health and safety at work in the RMG and the chronic absence of adequate social protection for workers and their families in such industrial disasters like this. Within a day, a number of BNC unions and the secretary of the Bangladesh Garments Workers Unity Council (BGWUC) had notified the ITGLWF of the events in Palashbari. Since the ITGLWF is a Global Union representing manufacturing workers in the main, it had little organisational presence in the headquarters of European clothing retailers, although it had affiliates in each of the buying countries.

The CCC consists of a network of NGOs, labour rights organisations and a number of trade unions. The international secretariat of the CCC is headquartered in Amsterdam, and has national CCC networks in all the buying countries implicated in the collapse. The National Garment Workers' Federation (NGWF) in Bangladesh, which had membership amongst the dead and the injured at Spectrum, was part of the CCC network and Amirul Haque Amin, its President, maintained regular contact with staff at the Amsterdam office. Moreover, some of the CCC union partner organisations had representation on the works councils representing the employees at the headquarters of some of the major European buyers at Spectrum.

Establishing retailer involvement

Whilst strategically it was important not to lose sight of the principle that in the matter of reparation and justice for all those affected by the Spectrum factory collapse, answers would ultimately rest with local actors and national institutions, both the ITGLWF and the CCC knew that, from past campaigning experience, bringing pressure to bear on foreign buyers was of the utmost tactical importance. This they did as a matter of routine, by making particular reference to those codes of conduct which such multinational retailers and brand-owners had established to govern employer behaviour within their own supply chains. Past experience had also taught them that such external pressure was going to be necessary to achieve any concessions from the Government and the manufacturers' associations in Bangladesh. Matters were not helped by the plethora of textile and garment worker unions and women's, environmental and human and labour rights NGOs in the country. Relationships between unions and between NGOs and between unions and NGOs continued to be fractious at times. However, as is the case with disasters, such events have a tendency, at the outset at least, to bring potentially fragmented movements together.

On learning of the collapse in the early hours of the 11 April, the ITGLWF issued an immediate press release in which General Secretary Neil Kearney was quoted as saying:

> The tragedy is a combination of a desperate race for competitive advantage in a liberalised trade environment

and the inaction of the public authorities in ensuring safe
working conditions. The information available suggests
that firstly, the factory should never have been built in
such a location – and certainly not a nine (*author's note
eight*) - storey building – and secondly, workers should not
have been working at that time. Some would say this is
the inevitable consequence of the race to the bottom now
underway as a result of unregulated trade in textiles and
clothing... (ITGLWF, 2005a).

Requests for solidarity action from several concerned ITG affiliates
and non-affiliates began to arrive at ITGLWF headquarters. These
detailed a series of demands on behalf of the Spectrum workers[3].
The collapse for them had once again highlighted the parlous state
of factories in the RMG sector and yet another group of families of
the deceased and those workers maimed by the disaster now faced
a future of dire poverty. The official solidarity calls received by the
ITGLWF all contained the same four demands:

- Full and humanitarian compensation of all victims of the incident;
  including the survivors, injured (Including rehabilitation of those
  who have lost their limbs), and the family members of the victims.

- A National Probe Body to investigate the incident to include
  representatives of the trade Unions and other civil society actors.

- Expulsion of the owner from the BGMEA.

- A national Review of Health and Safety in the RMG involving
  Government, Trade Unions, BGMEA, civil society actors and the
  ILO[4].

The CCC, in a release on the same day, developed jointly with local
and international union and NGO partners, pledged to work to clarify
demands on next steps concerning full and independent investigation,
full disclosure of the workers and victims, appropriate compensation
and structural preventative measures[5]. On the 13 April, Neil Kearney
wrote to the Prime Minister of Bangladesh, urging her to commission
an immediate structural review of all multi-storey buildings currently
in use as garment production units; to launch an examination of all
plant and machinery and access and evacuation routes and to reform
the factory and wage inspectorate into a body capable of making
regular checks on workplace safety. He further called for adherence

to labour legislation, particularly relating to hours of work and made specific reference to the Government dispensation to the garment industry which had permitted four hours of overtime per day in breach of the terms of ILO Hours of Work Convention No. 1 and of almost every code of conduct adopted by brand names and retailers sourcing from Bangladesh (ITGLWF, 2005b)[6].

A critical variable in the ability to maximise the international pressure on the government and the Spectrum owners were those companies which had been sourcing from the factory. However garment supply chains remain notoriously complex and opaque. The labyrinthine nature of international apparel outsourcing helps maintain supply chain secrecy. Supplier locations are intended to be each buyer's and each buyer's agent's best kept secret. Suppliers too are often reluctant to disclose the whereabouts of their subcontractors. Other than the pressure brought to bear on the licensees of college apparel in the US to disclose their suppliers (Doorey, 2005), no multinational buyers had a policy of factory disclosure at this time. Some months later, the ITGLWF, along with other campaigning organisations, were finally able score a victory on this front with the sportswear giant Nike and a number of other companies soon followed suit (Miller, 2008). However, with private label retailers, supply chain transparency was a less likely prospect. Such is the level of high street competition retailers are loathe to give any competitor companies the slightest edge, so for buyers their sources of supply remained and remain a matter of strictest confidentiality. However since many suppliers are proud to trumpet the names of their clients on their websites, and buyers themselves are usually quite well informed about who is sourcing from whom, such confidentiality requirements remain specious.

For campaigners, establishing a picture of how a particular buyer has been sourcing has thus become somewhat of a fine art, requiring a combination of knowledge of company law and structure, brand awareness, up to date information on developments in the sector, an ability to burrow into a company's website (ITGLWF, 2006), and crucially, on the ground contact with workers at the particular factory in question. Both the ITGLWF and the CCC had developed expertise in this area and embarked on education programmes to sensitise trade unionists and unorganised workers in the sector of the importance of label and brand awareness. The only way that a brand or retailer could be unequivocally tied to a particular factory could be by the labels found in the facility, but even here labels might not directly lead a researcher to the brand owner which might operate under a different identity. Whilst not every garment worker or trade unionist in the sector appreciated the need to become label savvy, Amin had been encouraging newly recruited NGWF members to bring labels from their factories to his office where he could maintain a database[7]. This could prove risky for some workers where theft of labels could be construed as a dismissible offence.

The situation was somewhat different in the case of the Spectrum factory collapse since garments, labels and swing tags were strewn around the site and likely to remain so for quite some time. If confronted with labels, buyers could still deny a presence in the factory, arguing that they had ceased trading with the supplier in question or that they had simply requested samples, or that their involvement was time bound and not current at time of the particular violation or event. Sometimes their argument might be that their percentage of production had been insignificant or that they had outsourced the task of finding a factory to a third party i.e. an agent. Often labels could turn up because the factory in question had been engaged as a subcontractor without the knowledge and/or consent of the initial contractor.

Immediately, both the ITGLWF and CCC contacted their affiliates and partner organisations to establish which companies had been sourcing from the factory. The Bangladesh unions checked with some of the workers while at the same time a field representative from the American Centre for International Labour Solidarity based in Bangladesh, organised the retrieval of labels from the site. By April 15 the ITGLWF and CCC had established in the first instance, that several major European retailers were implicated in the collapse. In a statement to the press on the same day, CCC announced that:

> ... the Spanish-based Zara (Inditex group), French-based Carrefour, Belgian-based Cotton Group, the German companies Steilmann and Neckermann (Karstadt–Quelle), and the Dutch-based Scapino have produced their garments at Spectrum Sweater (CCC, 2005b).

On the morning of the 15 April Javier Chercolés, head of CSR at Inditex was woken at 7 a.m. by an irate Neil Kearney denouncing his company for its implication in the disaster[8]. The two agreed to meet in Brussels.

It would be some time before a more complete and accurate picture of the companies sourcing from Spectrum could be established. On the 3 May, a worker from the CCC visited Bangladesh as part of a two week fact finding mission for the Clean Clothes Campaign (Arens, 2005). She was able to establish first-hand accounts from some of the workers who survived the collapse and the surviving family members of the dead, as well as piece together a more detailed picture of the buyers involved in the collapse. This enabled the CCC to begin researching the brands and buyers behind each tag found, and compile a preliminary table of the buyers sourcing at the factory. Since Spectrum workers confirmed that, in effect, the Spectrum factory was linked to the adjacent Shahriyar Fabrics facility, both the ITGLWF and the CCC treated these as one and the same. Table 4 lists the companies implicated in the disaster on the basis of labels found at the site and information from other sources.

Some of these labels were untraceable at the time, and some still remain untraced. A number of other companies were implicated by various sources including quality audit documentation, and fellow buyers. When confronted, they confirmed that they had been sourcing there. Others denied any presence, ultimately threatened litigation and/or simply remained silent.

The buyers respond

Within a matter of days, the Business Social Compliance Initiative (BSCI), of which a number of the identified buyers were members, convened a meeting at its headquarters in Brussels. By now the CCC urgent appeals system had resulted in all 126 members of the BSCI receiving a letter and the ITGLWF had issued a strongly worded press statement. Although acknowledged as a step forward in seeking to reduce the wasteful duplication of factory auditing, the BSCI had drawn criticism from the ITGLWF and the CCC in particular for failing to establish itself as a multi-stakeholder body with labour and NGO involvement (Merk, 2004). Nevertheless the Belgian CCC which was headquartered in Brussels succeeded in attending

Label or brand	Company (owner of label/brand)	Location
Attention	Owner Unknown	U.K.
B & C	Cotton Group	Belgium
Concept EB Bluhm	Bluhm Köln GmbH	Germany
Grandes Superficies de Mexico SA	Not identified at the time But Carrefour	France (for Mexico)
Zara, Za Boy	Inditex	Spain
Kirsten Mode*	Miro Radici (formerly Steilmann)	Italy
Le Frog Sport	Neckermann/ KarstadtQuelle Not identified at the time	Germany
Thomas Lloyd	Owner still Unknown	Unknown
Harvest	New Wave Group	Sweden
ViceVersa GR	Owner still unknown	Unknown

*As reported by Jenneke Arens (2005: ix).

Source: Author, based on CCC (2005c) list posted with additional research.

Table 4: Companies implicated in the disaster based on labels discovered in the rubble or submitted by Spectrum workers, and other sources of information, May 2005.

the afternoon session of the BSCI meeting. At this early meeting the BSCI stressed the need to identify the exact causes of the collapse and declared their willingness to organise a mission to Bangladesh since they expected a lot from the Bangladeshi government, and the BGMEA. Following the meeting, Javier Chercolés, the then Director of Corporate Social Responsibility at Inditex used the opportunity to visit the offices of the ITGLWF where he met Neil Kearney for the first time. Inditex, the Spanish Fashion retailer, headquartered in La Coruna, is a company which for some time had resisted the urge to move production offshore having retained an extensive supply base in Spain and Portugal (Tokatli, 2008). However, it was now very much going global with its outsourcing, in line with the general trend throughout the industry. It had developed its own 'Tested to Wear' audit methodology[9] for the auditors it worked with, and had a relationship with both national unions for the sector – FITEQA[10] and UGT[11], both ITGLWF affiliates, which had membership in its domestic supplier factories and with SETEM – Secretaría Técnica Federación Setem a coalition of a number of NGOs which coordinates the Spanish CCC (Campaña Ropa Limpia). Chercolés, formerly with Price Waterhouse Coopers, knew his way around the world of actuarial calculations for insurance purposes, and in their exchange offered the ITGLWF his expertise in putting together a relief scheme for the victims, having remembered the lack of support for the victims of the Bhopal chemical disaster in India in 1984[12]. Kearney, a former head of the Information and Research Department of the British National Union of Tailors and Garment Workers[13], had been elected General Secretary at the ITGLWF's 6th World Congress in Tokyo in 1988 and had a compendious knowledge of the industry, amassed from over two decades of crisscrossing the world's industry in a tireless effort to defend and promote worker's rights. He was particularly respected by the unions in Bangladesh – which had always received his special attention as the country with the lowest labour costs – and was determined to work with his affiliates to bring about change. Both agreed to go to Bangladesh at the earliest opportunity and to involve other buyers in the visit.

This joint initiative certainly bucked the trend in the sector since international buyers had a tendency to co-opt NGOs into the remediation of code violations in their supply chains rather than seek

to work with the relevant Global Unions in the sector. The French
multinational Carrefour, the first international buyer to respond with
practical assistance for the Spectrum victims was no exception here
accepting a humanitarian call from Friendship, a Bangladesh NGO
which had a track record of disaster relief. Carrefour, which was
not a member of the BSCI, had been working with the Federation
Internationale des Droits Humaines (FIDH) since 1997 to monitor
its supply chains rather than turn to the ITGLWF for its soft goods
supply chain[14]. FIDH had assisted Carrefour in the development of a
Supplier Charter and formed a partnership with the company through
a joint monitoring body called INFANS. In addition to internal
control conducted by Carrefour's quality and commercial teams,
external controls of the supply chain were provided by professional
audit companies and then a third party random check provided by
INFANS. (Crabbé, Leroy and Caudron 2008: 15–24)[15]. Separate
to the FIDH in France is "Ethique sur L'Etiquette", – the French
Clean Clothes Campaign, whose namesake in the French speaking
part of Belgium is Campagne Vêtements Propres[16] with a Flemish
counterpart – Schone Kleren Campagne[17]. As a company operating
under the French model of workplace representation, Carrefour
Group and Carrefour Belgium had trade union representatives on
the respective works council structures in the company. These were
members of retail worker unions, some of which are affiliated to the
Union Network International (UNI).

In Germany, the CCC (Kampagne für säubere Kleidung) had
participated with KarstadtQuelle and a number of other retailers in
the Roundtable on Codes of Conduct (coc-runder-tisch), a multi-
stakeholder initiative bringing together trade unions, the private
sector, NGOs and representatives from the government. Similar to
the UK Ethical Trading Initiative, the round table was conceived as a
forum for dialogue and learning. The Unified Services Union (VerDi)
as well as the Metalworkers Union (IGMetall)[18] were also represented
within this body, which was an initiative of the Foreign Trade
Association of German Retailers (AVE). However the German CCC
had withdrawn from the Roundtable in 2004 over their perceived
lack of concrete progress in the initiative.

The CCC approached the works council at KarstadtQuelle to raise
the issue at the company council and supervisory board and was

responsible for much of the press coverage in the Spiegel magazine (Klawitter, 2005) and later in the Frankfurter Rundschau. Maren Böhm was responsible for CSR within KarstadtQuelle at this time and spent much of her time in the Far East Sourcing office in China. CCC also contacted Steilmann who confirmed having sourced from Spectrum in the past[19], but it was reported that the company made no initial overtures to provide any assistance to the workers. They had also targeted Kirstenmode GmbH, which Steilmann had sold in 2003 to the Italian company Miro Radici, which agreed to contribute €5000 since garments bearing its label were found at the site. It was reported that the sweater importer and owner of the Concept EB label found at the site, never responded to numerous calls from the German CCC while another small company threatened an injunction on CCC if it continued to associate its name with the Spectrum collapse.

When it comes to companies, the ITGLWF and the CCC have essentially different ways of working. For the NGOs, emphasis is placed on campaign work and conducting urgent appeals which may involve email actions and street activities in front of a retailer's high street store. Whilst both share an interest in improving workers' rights and working conditions in the sector, NGOs are not interested in a systematic on-going dialogue in the way that a trade union would be, since strategically on-going dialogue is seen as an inroad to future collective bargaining. However, since CCC is a network of NGOs and trade unions, it has a commitment to creating space for unions to organize and bargain at the workplace.

Since the late 1990s, the Global Unions have been pursuing so-called international framework agreements to establish such a dialogue with multinationals, but for the ITGLWF this had been a difficult process (Miller, 2004). Unlike other sectors, where global agreements on employment standards had been mediated via the headquarters trade union, the demise of trade unions in the buying countries in the garment sector meant that on the face of it there were few points of access (Miller, 2008). Moreover, industrial relations in garment manufacturing had had a particular chequered history and the gains which textile and garment worker unions had made in the buying countries had been virtually annulled as production had moved offshore. Trade union organisation and collective bargaining in garment manufacturing in particular had been stunted by the anti-trade union stance on the part of the new Asian manufacturing contractors (Appelbaum, 2005). Hence from a Global Union point of view, developing dialogue with MNCs in the form of so-called international framework agreements to implement their responsibilities *vis á vis* the core ILO conventions on freedom of association and collective bargaining enshrined in their corporate codes of conduct had become a central component of their programmes of action (Croucher and Cotton, 2009).

One Spectrum buyer – Carrefour – had such an international framework agreement, with Union Network International (UNI), the Global Union for Commerce Workers. This concise agreement, signed back in 2001, was perfectly understandable in terms of global union jurisdictions, since it was intended in the first instance to apply to shop workers throughout the company's global retail network. It did however provide a brief, if somewhat limited, statement of intent with respect to its supply chain[20]. In Carrefour's case, however, as indeed with a number of other so-called 'giant' retailers (Hearson, 2009), the company had to manage a number of product supply chains which reach out into metalworking, foodstuffs, wood and textile and apparels. Arguably the need for social dialogue with the Global Unions which organise in each these sectors was just as great.

There was, however, no agreement between Carrefour and the ITGLWF and, although a decision had been taken at the ninth World Congress at Istanbul in 2004[21] for the ITGLWF to explore the option of merging with UNI, there had been no communication from UNI to the ITGLWF regarding Spectrum and Carrefour[22]. One of the first overtures towards the buyers was made on 14 April by the Belgian CCC in respect of Carrefour Belgium. The initial response was reportedly negative, a spokesperson stating that the only possible intervention route would be via the Carrefour Foundation, which in this case was unlikely to do anything since it was not a natural disaster and not a country where the company had a retail presence[23]. When they responded to questions from the unions at Carrefour Belgium, – the CNE (Centrale Nationale des Employés) and Setca / BBTK (Syndicat des Employés, Techniciens et Cadres de Belgique) and the LBC (Landelijke Bediendencentrale) – they confirmed that Spectrum had been producing children's garments for Carrefour Belgium and had placed four orders for 8800 TEX basic items which were despatched 15 November 2004[24]. Under Belgian law the works council is entitled to invite experts to the meeting and in this capacity the Belgian CCCs began to work with the comité d'entreprise to formulate a series of probing questions for management[25]. In the case of the parent company, Carrefour Group, the French CCC, Ethique sur l'Etiquette asked FIDH to intervene. Carrefour Group informed FIDH that the last order at Spectrum had been in 2002 in which no specific safety problem was detected. Carrefour had a representative in Dhaka who was following the situation but had no initial budget or mission beyond information gathering[26].

Another Belgian company approached, was the Cotton Group which owns the B&C brand. The Cotton Group was at this time the most important promotional t-shirts retailer in Belgium. Labels marked B&C Europe had been found at the site. Although the company claimed that its production was from the adjacent factory, it eventually transpired that Cotton Group had indeed been sourcing from both units and that their orders were ready for shipment and stocked in the Spectrum factory at the time of the collapse. The company declared its readiness to take steps to help the workers and their families and pledged to use monies allocated for payment for received shipments to contribute towards compensation and outstanding wages to workers. They had a Belgian contact in Dhaka who reported efforts to contact the owner, and that further business with Shahriyar Fabrics was on hold pending a positive structural audit of the factory. A hastily organised audit of the adjacent standing unit took place within 2 months of the collapse and some forty frightened workers were viewed by the auditor in the finishing section, where this adjoined the previous Spectrum facility[27].

Late April and early May, the ITGLWF wrote to the respective CEOs of Carrefour, and Inditex SA, KarstadtQuelle, and B&C (Cotton Group). CCC continued to put pressure the brands via its Urgent Appeal system, having by now received more detailed demands developed by NGWF with workers locally. Neil Kearney urged the companies to:

- ensure that the survivors as well as the families of those that died received exemplary compensation, as well as the payment of any outstanding wages or benefits

- disclose their audit findings on Spectrum as well as their reasons for failing to uncover the hazards in the factory as well as breaches of their respective codes of conduct

- take urgent measures to ensure their code of conduct was properly implemented throughout their supply chain

- disclose full details of their supply chain so that trade unions and others in civil society could ensure that minimum conditions were being met, and

- undertake a structural review of all their production facilities, with particular attention to multi-storey buildings, to ensure the buildings were structurally sound, as well as a structural examination of all plant and machinery and evacuation procedures in the same[28].

The company responses to the ITGLWF and CCC urgent appeals began to arrive during the first week of May. Inditex SA, the owner of the Zara Boy label found at the site, was the first to reply to the ITGLWF, explaining that they were unaware that Spectrum was a supplier since the order had been placed by a trader in India[29]. They further explained that the blanket audit of their supply base outside of Europe was nearing completion and that corrective action plans would be put in place in due course. They had notified civil society groups in Spain including FiteQa – the trade union Federation which has membership in their factories in Spain – as well as the Spanish Red Cross and the NGO SETEM Secretaría Técnica Federación Setem which coordinates on behalf of the CCC in Spain (Campaña Ropa Limpia). (CRL) and were proposing to the BSCI the creation of a multi-stakeholder task force to address the issues raised by the collapse[30].

The Director of Sustainable Development at Carrefour Group was next to respond on 11 May on behalf of her company. She confirmed that Spectrum had supplied a one off order of 130,000 units in 2004, but that the factory had not been audited. She further informed the ITGLWF that 'as a humanitarian gesture' Carrefour had called upon the local NGOs 'Friendship' and Karmojibi Nari which specialised in emergency relief and women's rights to reach out to the workers in Savar[31]. One of the key issues for the victims in disasters like this is emergency relief but for the unions on the ground in Bangladesh, their demands signalled to the ITGLWF that it was time to make a real push for more systemic change in health and safety policies and to finally address the issue of worker compensation. 'Relief' in such circumstances is financial assistance to meet the immediate hardship and needs endured by the victims, compensation on the other hand is recompense in such situations for the drastically changed physical and economic circumstances which has befallen the victims. This needed to be formulated to provide medium to long term indemnification. For Neil Kearney this was an opportunity to push for something much more fundamental and far reaching, namely:

> ... a replicable intervention model to calculate future fair and ethical indemnities to mitigate the negative consequences of any accident in countries characterized with a lack of instruments to compensate victims and their relatives[32].

At the time of the collapse, compensation for industrial accidents was calculated in Bangladesh under the Workmen's Compensation Act, 1923 (WCA), as amended 1987. It was a 'strict liability' scheme which indemnifies workers for workplace injury or death irrespective of any wrongful action on the part of the employer/owner. Strict liability means that it is necessary to determine only that the employee was there at the place of work at the time of the accident and that the employee did not deliberately cause the accident. Suing for damages, however, requires that the families sue the owner under the Fatal Accidents Act 1855 and successfully demonstrate negligence on the owner's part. This would lead to individual determinations which could be substantially higher should the multinational buyers be 'joined' in such a case. Few cases had however been brought under this legislation. Section 4.1 of the WCA specified compensation amounts. In case of death, the worker's family received 'an amount equal to fifty per cent of the monthly wages of the deceased workman multiplied by the relevant factor' (4.1.a); in case of permanent total disablement, compensation was 'sixty per cent of the monthly wages of the injured workman multiplied by the relevant factor' (4.1.b). Moreover, under Schedule IV of the Act, the multiplier decreased as the age of the worker increased; the older the workers killed/ permanently disabled, therefore, the less compensation provided under the terms of the Act. Pursuing a compensation claim based on the FAA would take years, with no guarantee of success even before

the issue of multinational litigation could be factored in. Hence efforts
to establish a voluntary scheme involving the authorities, the owner,
the BGMEA, and the buyers were seen very much as the preferred
route. However, the politics of the situation and the limits of CSR
dictated that choice of words was going to be important in making
the scheme palatable to the Bangladesh authorities as well as the other
buyers. Although in essence the scheme constituted a compensation
package, the term 'relief scheme' was resorted to in order to keep
the buyers on board, since the term 'compensation' was not only a
measure which essentially was a matter for national regulation, it also
raised the spectre of 'joint responsibility'.

The Head of Social Affairs at Karstadt Quelle (KQ) the German
department store and on line retailer group later renamed
Arcandor[33], responded next on behalf of their CEO. The company
had placed a handful of trial orders with Spectrum early in
2004, but had then terminated its business relationship with the
company[34]. However the discovery of *le Frog* labels owned by the
Neckermann subsidiary of KarstadtQuelle at the site clearly negated
this assertion[35]. Moreover, it transpired subsequently that the Dutch
company Scapino and the German company Rehfeld were both
found to be sourcing from Spectrum via KarstadtQuelle[36]. A further
lobbying opportunity arose on 12 and 13 May on the occasion of
the fifth Annual Conference of the UK Ethical Trading Initiative
(ETI) a self-described multi-stakeholder alliance of companies, trade
unions, charities, and campaigning organisations working together
to improve working conditions in global supply chains. Over 350
representatives from businesses, unions, NGO's and governments,
including from the BSCI, the German Technical Cooperation Unit
– Gesellschaft für Technische Zusammenarbeit (GTZ), and the ILO
had gathered together in London. Shirin Ahkter from Karmojibi
Nari was scheduled to attend and the General Secretary of the
ITGLWF along with CCC representatives aimed to raise the issue
of Spectrum wherever they could in the workshops and plenary
sessions taking place during the conference. A keynote speaker was
Richard Howitt, member of the European Parliament and First Vice
Chair of the Foreign Affairs Committee Sub Committee on Human
Rights. Howitt had a special interest in ethical trade and spoke at
some length about the Spectrum case, reminding those present that

the ethical trade movement would ignore this at its peril, and calling upon European brands and retailers to make sure that the surviving workers and the families of the workers who died would receive their rightful compensation[37].

The relevance of this lobbying for the Ethical Trading Initiative was that many corporate members were sourcing from Bangladesh and that the news of the collapse had sent shock waves through their ranks. Acutely aware of the health and safety weaknesses in the RMG sector in the country, the corporate social responsibility departments of key buyers began to revisit their audit methodologies to include attestations from structural surveyors and sight of the factory plans, something which had not been part of audits up until this point. Lakshmi Bhatia, Gap Inc. Director of Global Partnerships was asked by the ETI to join the mission to Bangladesh now being organised by the ITGLWF and members of the BSCI.

Of all the buyer responses to the urgent appeals, Inditex was the only company to acknowledge a lack of awareness of its own supply chain. In a response to KarstadtQuelle, the ITGLWF drew attention to reports from Bangladesh which indicated that the buyer's product was issuing from the factory at the time of the collapse, and that this seemed to be an indication that orders were being placed indirectly by a trader or subcontracted by a first tier supplier without the company's knowledge. Moreover, on the matter of audit findings, the ITGLWF was keen to establish whether the company had been aware that Spectrum workers were required to work long hours when there were urgent orders. The national CCCs continued to pressure the brands based in their respective countries. At the KarstadtQuelle annual shareholders' meeting, the German CCC presented information about the Spectrum case. Whilst shareholders responded positively with requests to the KarstadtQuelle Supervisory Board for more background information, the German CCC reported that the company had failed to issue any statement indicating whether and how it was planning to help the workers in Bangladesh[38].

On 19 May the International Federation of Human Rights (FIDH) a French NGO issued a press statement on the response from Carrefour having tabled a number of questions concerning the company's sourcing activities from Spectrum. Carrefour's Belgian spokeswoman reiterated the company response to the ITGLWF and confirmed that an audit was carried out on their behalf in 2002 although not apparently at the facility at Palashbari. She offered to send a copy of the audit report on request but it never materialised (Campagne Vetements Propes, 2005). In line with Bangladeshi NGO requests, the retailer requested fresh audits of its suppliers in the RMG industry to include a systematic review of planning permissions and construction documents. Carrefour did not signal any intention to accompany the mission to Bangladesh. Those trades unions which are members of the Belgian CCC started a letter campaign towards Carrefour and placed the Spectrum issue on the agenda of a works council meeting with management scheduled for 9 June[39].

In the case of Scapino, the Dutch CCC contacted a senior buyer within two days of the collapse and learned that they were sourcing via KarstadtQuelle through an agent in Asia. Scapino confirmed that it followed KarstadtQuelle's code of conduct. A month later the company responded that it could not be held responsible for structural failures[40]. The Dutch CCC maintained pressure and arranged a meeting with the company on 30 May at the end of which Scapino acknowledged the unnecessary delays in compensating the workers and undertook to formally contact the BSCI in this respect as well as supporting the workers case for back pay and compensation for injured workers and their families as well as those families of the deceased. However, in this meeting, no actual amounts or concrete steps were discussed. Scapino did however undertake to ensure structural safety audits with its suppliers[41].

The first buyer's mission

The first mission of buyers set off for Bangladesh on June 4th, almost a month later than originally expected. In announcing the mission, the BSCI issued a press release on the 2nd June clearly concerned about some of the demands being made by the Clean Clothes Campaign in particular:

> It is legitimate to raise the question to which extent trading companies are obliged to take over the complete responsibility for the living conditions of the workers of their suppliers... Hidden faults in construction of facility building which endanger the physical integrity

of the workers and which could also lead to respective consequences for the families of the workers cannot be detected in the course of a social audit[42].

The delegation included Maren Böhm of KarstadtQuelle, Javier Chercolés Blazquez, of Inditex, Mr. Pierre Schmitz, of Cotton Group (B+C), Lorenz Berzau of the BSCI and was accompanied by Neil Kearney, Lakshmi Bhatia of GAP Inc representing the ETI, and Joaquín González Montadas, General Seceretary of FITEQA and representative of the Spanish Trade Union Confederation Commissiones Obreras. In an email to Badruddoza Nizam, General Secretary of the Bangladesh Garment Workers' League Neil Kearney announced:

> I will come to Bangladesh at the end of May and early June with some of the leading European retailers to establish what needs to be done to ensure adequate compensation for the families of the dead and missing and for the injured as well setting out measures to ensure that such a tragedy cannot happen again.

> You will know from the BNC that I have asked for meetings to be arranged with the BGMEA, BKMEA, the Prime Minister, Ministers of Labour, Commerce and Industry. The government need to be made aware that this is a top level delegation representing retailers who purchase nearly fifty per cent of Bangladesh's knit exports. One Belgian importer, the Cotton Group, alone takes seven per cent of total knit exports. These retailers will be demanding an urgent structural examination of all multi-storied factories as well as details of how the government and industry are going to ensure future compliance with all international labour standards as well as the labour and other laws of Bangladesh[43].

On day two of the mission, the delegation visited the Spectrum site. The local arrangements in Savar had been made by Amin (NGWF). The plan was for the delegation to visit the Spectrum site and meet with the injured and some of the families of the dead. A number of people had assembled at a centre in Savar. However anticipating that the group would go to the factory first, a number of injured workers

led by Amin had assembled at the site. However most of the buyers
arrived before the union group and went immediately into the still
standing Shahriyar Fabrics building. Neil Kearney takes up the story:

> When I arrived I went first to speak to the workers gathered
> at the factory. Amin was there and I was accompanied by
> Anam and others from the BNC. I think Lakshmi of Gap
> had also travelled with the BNC members. We talked to a
> number of the more seriously injured, including a couple
> who had lost limbs – Noor Alam was one.
>
> My abiding image of the day was of M who had been
> brought in a rickshaw and appeared like a dead body. He
> was the one whose flesh had been ripped from his arm and
> had lost three fingers. He was running a high fever and was
> literally as white as a sheet. He had had little treatment
> other than having the wounds dressed and was obviously
> in great pain. The buyers had simply walked past him lying
> there. You can imagine I was then in good humour!
>
> I remember then taking the steps two at a time and
> confronting the buyers group who appeared as if they were
> on a routine visit to a factory looking at the production
> that was still going on. I said something to the effect 'Have
> you seen what you have done?' and demanded to know
> why they had ignored the injured downstairs and insisting
> that they go out and talk them. It was at this stage that I
> decided I needed to take the lead... Otherwise it would be
> a bit like a tourist visit or buying trip.
>
> Afterwards we went to the Centre where the families of
> the dead – maybe twenty or more – and the injured had
> gathered. We spent some time talking individually to some
> of those there, taking notes, etc. Then when we were
> about to be a bit more formal, and tell those gathered
> why were there, etc. the BSCI part of the group suddenly
> said they couldn't stay as they had a meeting with officials
> at the Ministry of Commerce. I don't think that even
> related to Spectrum. I was pretty annoyed and said they
> had an obligation to those who had suffered and had,
> in many cases, travelled a long way to meet the group.

I even suggested that part of their group remain but they couldn't get away fast enough. It was pretty heartless. Only the Inditex people and Lakshmi of Gap remained. We spent a long time there listening as the injured told the meeting what they had experienced and as the families of the dead mourned their loss. Not all the dead had been identified at that time and a number of fathers and mothers simply brought and held a photo of their sons. It was a very moving and indeed horrible experience being in the midst of tragedy... with the relatives of those who had died horribly,... and in the presence of those who had cheated death and escaped[44].

From the meeting the delegation, accompanied by Lakshmi Bhatia, was taken to the homes of some of the injured. She was shaken by what she found:

We went first to this house of this boy whose entire lower body had been damaged as a result and he was lying in acute pain. He was in this really small room which would have been about eight foot by eight foot and his parents were there and some of the other worker families had come... He wasn't able to excrete properly and his body was getting poisoned. By the end of that meeting we had decided that M needed to be taken to hospital. We believe that... If we hadn't taken him to hospital he wouldn't have survived[45].

With the help of Anam and Amin, arrangements were made for him to be transported by rickshaw for treatment at the local hospital and money handed over to pay for the medical costs. During these days Lakshmi Bhatia, Neil Kearney and Javier Chercolés visited the other seriously injured workers in the public hospital in Dhaka. Neil Kearney in particular was horrified by what he found:

Around the world I have seen bad conditions but nothing as bad as in that hospital. At the time we said we would prefer to die rather than be admitted there. From what we could see patients received little treatment. Indeed they were usually cared for by family members who stayed with them

> sleeping on the floor by their beds. Everything was filthy.
> Cockroaches were having a field day. Javier arranged some
> clean bed linen including pillow covers.

It became clear that the injured were going to need immediate and better treatment.

A number of the injured had been administered some immediate treatment following the collapse and been discharged. This immediately alarmed Kearney and Chercolés who feared that without due care, some would remain disabled for the rest of their lives[46]. Some had received sums from the company accountant and a representative of the BGMEA but others had received nothing. On the phone to La Coruna in Spain where his company headquarters are situated, Javier Chercolés urged Inditex agreed to meet the medical costs of the badly injured victims and to pay their wages for the next 2 years. Inditex wired through €35,000 for immediate relief efforts. Anam knew of a newly opened Trauma Centre in the centre of Dhaka. A meeting was set up with the Director who arranged for the admission of as many of the injured as was required. Most of the twenty who were seriously injured could be moved there. For Shafiqul Islam, however, who was paralysed from the waist down, an official discharge was necessary, something which the duty registrar was not prepared to do. This would have to wait until their return in several weeks' time. Ensuring that the injured receive financial assistance for medical treatment and relief payments for the unemployed Spectrum workers necessitated a mechanism for transfer and disbursement. Kearney and Chercolés agreed to have these funds locally administered by the BNC, NGWF, INCIDIN and Oxfam Bangladesh.

On day three of the mission the delegation held a roundtable with Sheik Hasina, leader of the Awami League – the main opposition party. The meeting was arranged by the ITGLWF's affiliates, many of which supported the League. For Lakshmi Bhatia the meeting proved to be an important one:

> A handful of us were in the room with Sheik Hasina and
> her close advisers – it was such an intense meeting where
> (she) got emotional about how things had become so
> terrible in the country. As soon as we stepped out the entire
> press was there to interview us. Within a week Khaleda Zia

(the then prime minister) had announced the setting up of a compliance forum.

Members of the mission were disappointed that they had not been able to meet the Government. At the scheduled round tables, attended by legislators and major opinion leaders from education and the media, as well as the leading trade union organisations, opportunity was taken by Neil Kearney to berate the government for its poor factory inspectorate and lack of action to address the working conditions in the factories. The argument was made that the RMG in Bangladesh was risking business if the working environment in factories were not going to be improved (Daily Star, 2005r). To this end Javier Chercolés released the list of all seventy Inditex suppliers to the BNC unions in an effort to establish transparency for health and safety initiatives in relation to the Inditex supply chain[47]. Before leaving, the members of the mission succeeded in getting commitment to a series of measures to deal with the medium and longer term aspects of the tragedy. These included:

- the creation of an office on site to help compile an employee list and details on the dead, missing and injured

- an offer by Inditex to secure an independent assessment of appropriate compensation for the victims of the traged

- a demand for a structural survey of all multi-story garment factories, and

- a proposal for the creation of a tripartite Economic and Social Development Committee to develop and market the industry on the basis of respect for workers' rights, and

- the establishment of a trust fund for contributions from retailers, factory owners, the industry association and the Bangladeshi government.

The delegation served notice of its intention to return within three weeks. In its report of the mission released on 23 June, the BSCI sought to reassure the public that the Bangladesh Ministry of Labour would be revising and updating the labour law, and that the BGMEA had been asked to join a taskforce and to contribute to a trust fund to compensate the victims of the collapse. They were however eager to stress that BSCI audits were designed for 'transparency on social performance,' and that it was their function to check the quality of construction of a factory unit[48].

The second buyers' mission

The second mission to Bangladesh, as promised by the buyers, involved Maren Böhm of KarstadtQuelle, Javier Chercolés of Inditex, the local Bangladesh agent for the Cotton Group, Neil Kearney and Lakshmi Bhatia. No representative of the BSCI accompanied the group. Lakshmi Bhatia had been greatly moved by what she had witnessed in visiting the victims during the first mission:

> For me personally at that point in time, coming from the social sector – I used to work with street kids – and having entered the corporate environment, somewhere along the way you detach yourself from the reality of the workers' lives. I think this is a process of desensitisation which happens, so I was still very passionate but I wasn't feeling the pain, but this just broke open all of my barriers. Every single night I was breaking down. I was an emotional mess. In that period while I was there, I didn't know how to handle it. I was angry. I was so upset... It became like a personal mission[49].

There had been some discussion about her return to Bangladesh as part of this group particularly since the company had not been sourcing from Spectrum and there had been misgivings that Gap might end up guilty by association. However her second visit coincided with a conference in Dhaka hosted jointly by the United Nations Development Program (UNDP) and the Multi Fibre Agreement Forum. Set up in early 2004, the MFA Forum had been established as a multi-stakeholder network to improve the sustainability of those national industries rendered vulnerable by the expiry in January 2005 of the Agreement on Textiles and Clothing. Gap did have a supply base – still relatively small – in Bangladesh, but it was sufficiently concerned to undertake a structural review of its supplier facilities. Razaul Karim Buiyan was a vendor compliance officer for Gap in the country at the time and concerned about the corruption in construction approval and the fact that a factory load might not be able to withstand the levels of capacity which they were now requiring:

> After Spectrum we reviewed all the factories to check whether they had a commercial licence from the Rajuk and we found in some cases that although they had a

commercial licence, the factory was operating from a residential area. So we said that it was not enough to have a Rajuk licence... In one case where the factory had seven floors, we managed to convince the management to reduce the load on the upper floors by reducing from twenty-six to nineteen lines and we suggested moving the heavy fabric to the lower floors...[50].

The Dhaka MFA conference which took place on 27– 28 June was entitled, 'Forum for the Future: An Internationally Competitive Textile and Garment Industry'. It attracted around 150 delegates including the Ministry of Commerce, suppliers, civil society, buyers and the industry trade associations, and under the terms of the MFA Forum's Collaborative Framework all efforts were to be geared towards 'home-owned' and 'home grown' solutions (MFA Forum and UNDP, 2005). Despite all the predictions, Bangladesh did appear to be rising to the challenge of the so-called MFA phase out (i.e. the expiry of the Agreement on Textiles and Clothing). For the MFA Forum at least, the focus for the Conference was how the increasing orders – collectively the buyers in attendance accounted for some 90% of RMG production – could be translated into greater benefits for the workers in the sector[51]. Spectrum was clearly a talking point in side discussions at the event but the President of the BGMEA was at pains to counter the notion that the Spectrum collapse was a compliance issue in general. However, the Chair of the Board of the UK Ethical Trading Initiative, present at the event pointed out that the much-publicised factory collapse that killed more than sixty workers had brought Bangladesh's compliance issues afresh to the forefront (New Age, 2005c).

The INDITEX/ITGLWF relief scheme

Despite the sentiments of the Conference organisers, the victims of the factory collapse were at this time still without relief from either the BGMEA or the Government. During this second visit, Chercolés and Kearney met with some of the injured workers and their families. They found two of the more the seriously injured workers had not been moved to the Trauma Centre and were still languishing in the Orthopaedics hospital.

The BGMEA representatives had kept promising them that

they would be sent to India or Singapore for treatment but, they were warned not to accept aid from the unions or BGMEA would cease all responsibility for them. A BGMEA representative used to follow us around telling the injured workers afterwards that they shouldn't accept aid from the unions[52].

In their first meeting with the BGMEA to outline the Trust Fund proposal, Kearney felt forced to make a scene whereupon the Vice-President of the BGMEA who was chairing the meeting on the BGMEA side ordered one of their staff to accompany the ITGLWF General Secretary and the head of Inditex CSR and explain to the families of the two injured that they would be better treated in the Trauma Centre. It was that evening the transfer was made. However arranging the transfer for Shafiqul Islam proved problematic:

The staff nurse in charge said we would have to have an official discharge. This could only be signed by the Director of the hospital and he wasn't there. Only the threat of calling the Minister made her relent and I signed the discharge form. Then we had to hire an ambulance, a stretcher and two stretcher bearers. All these were found outside the hospital gates where they wait patiently for business. Then we had the problem of getting Shafiqul down to the ambulance. The stairways were narrow and steep so it was necessary to use the lift. But the lift was locked and the keys were said to be with the same Director who couldn't be found to sign the release. The stretcher bearers became impatient and insisted on stretchering down those treacherous stairs. And they did so carrying him head first. We watched in dread that after all the drama Shafiqul would slip off the stretcher and plunge head first down the stairs. Fortunately, he hung on. Without the transfer it is likely Shafiqul would have soon been dead. He was suffering from bad bed sores. Weeks without treatment probably contributed to his permanent disability[53].

The other pressing issue concerned the matter of financial support for the hundreds of Spectrum workers who were without a job. Inditex arranged for a first group of 191 workers to receive BDT 2000 each from the company as a relief payment. By July, Javier Chercolés and Neil Kearney had begun to discuss the logistics of establishing a relief scheme based on a Trust Fund into which the buyers would be invited to make voluntary contributions. Although a response to a single disaster, it was clear that if the mechanics of such a fund could be successfully worked out and implemented, then there would be the basis for a 'replicable intervention model' for use in other less developed countries. If it could constitute a standardized approach for international buyers then it would need to define

> ... commitments, and as closely as possible, the categories
> of beneficiaries to receive indemnities, the requirements for
> receiving such indemnities and the amount and possible
> payments to which the beneficiaries would be entitled[54].

For both instigators there was little doubt that if successful this would constitute a significant development in social protection and disaster management in all sectors and all those countries where such provisions were absent[55].

The management of assets by a group of persons or organisations for the benefit of the Spectrum victims' families and their disbursement in the form of a pension on the one hand would act as an embarrassing reminder to the Government of the necessary changes in labour law which this tragedy had now brought into sharp focus. On the other hand, going down this route could weaken any argument on the part of the local actors to invoke the Fatal Accidents Act *vis á vis* the Government. However, it appeared that the legal advice was that the Fatal Accidents Act was simply enabling legislation, which did not specify compensation in itself but allowed family members of the victim of a 'wrongful death' to bring a civil action in their name alleging that the employer was negligent and therefore responsible for the accident[56]. This of course could be used against the owner but it would be difficult to involve the buyers in any such litigation.

Setting worker compensation in the form of a trust fund in which the buyers would be asked to participate was going to be unprecedented and difficult. Although internationally recognised under the Hague Convention on the Law Applicable to Trusts and on their Recognition[57], any Trust Fund has to be governed by the terms of a trust document usually set out in the form of a deed which must be governed by local law. There are precedents for multi donor trust funds in Bangladesh but in matters like this they were going to require Government approval. If there was to be Government and employer 'buy-in', then the term 'compensation' would have to be avoided since this was a matter for regulation by national law. Since most of the existing funds had so far been tendered by Inditex, Javier Chercolés elected to have the Trust Fund drawn up under Spanish law. The Trust Fund was formally announced by the BNC at a press conference in mid-July in Bangladesh. Establishing the trust fund in Spain brought with it other problems. Fund management was one issue as was the problem of transferring substantial amounts of money into Bangladesh which would require government approval. Since Inditex did not have a trading account in the country, bank transfers would require special ministerial authorization. This was ultimately to prove to be a major obstacle to their whole initiative.

The international accounting and consultancy firm KPMG was commissioned by Inditex, at first with the support of KarstadtQuelle and Cotton Group, and in close collaboration with the International Textile, Garment and Leather Workers' Federation (ITGLWF), to undertake four tasks: defining those workers and dependents who are to be covered by the scheme, establishing criteria for eligibility, formulating terms of reference and finally calculating actuarial valuations. In terms of actuarial valuations KPMG were requested to calculate the following:

> … for the families of the deceased – full salary from 11 April 2005 till the date of payment of compensation; a lump-sum payment reflecting the wages and family composition of the victim; and a life-time pension based on the wages and family composition of the victim and adjusted annually for inflation; for those injured – full salary from 11 April 2005 till the date of payment of compensation; a lump-sum payment based on the age, injuries and wages of the victim; and a pension based on the level and duration of disability of the victim, his wages and family composition and adjusted annually for inflation[58].

There was precedent for calculating the former, but in the case of the injured, Chercolés set about developing a new actuarial table based on the Spanish road traffic accident insurance scheme.

The third buyers' mission

While KPMG was finalising its draft report, a third buyer mission was undertaken to Bangladesh during 9–11 September. The delegation met with the owner who informed them that he was unable to fully restart production at the adjacent facility. Some subcontract production was underway on the third floor of the building to keep 400 of the original workforce and senior management employed. Most of those workers rendered jobless appeared to have found employment but it was reported that about 100 were still without work at this time. Assurances had, however, been given by the owner that any member of the victims' families would be given the opportunity to train and have priority for employment at his new factory when it was completed[59]. Of the thirteen seriously injured patients who had been moved to the Trauma clinic, most had now been released pending fitting of artificial limbs. In two cases an offer had been made by Inditex to undertake further surgery at hospitals in Spain[60].

In her mission report, the Director of Social Affairs at KarstadtQuelle detailed her understanding of the proposed Fund, viewing it as:

- a one off measure to provide compensation and relief for the victims of the collapse

- not intended to be used as a global model in the event of any other factory disasters, although it may provide some guidance

- a proposal where compensation sums would be calculated on the basis of loss of lifetime earnings

- a proposal where the payment of contributions by the various stakeholders in the Fund (eg Government, trade union, BGMEA, BKMEA) would be one off, voluntary contributions

- and where the level of contribution would be a matter for each stakeholder – There was to be no minimum amount

- also where the distribution of payments to the workers would be in the form of a one off payment. There was to be no compensation formula

- an initiative in which Oxfam would take on the responsibility for distributing pension payments to the injured and families of the deceased.

In two key respects, KarstadtQuelle's interpretation of the Scheme differed from what had been originally proposed by Inditex and the ITGLWF – the fund was not seen as a replicable global model, and the indemnification to the victims was to be a one-off payment rather than a regular pension.

It was intended that a 'Spectrum task force oversight committee' would be established and that this would consist of five to nine local 'trustees,' the majority of whom would come from Oxfam with the remaining positions filled by a representative each from the unions, the BGMEA and a representative of the government. The committee would determine how the monies were to be disbursed[61]. Meanwhile, upon request of the NGWF and other local union and NGO partners, CCC had already decided to seek legal counsel on the proposed scheme and had approached the US based International Commission for Labour Rights and Richard Meeran, a legal counsel with experience in this area for their views. NGWF and CCC felt that relying solely on a commercial auditing firm (KPMG) was not a good strategy, and it wanted labour experts, also from outside Europe, to consider the draft. The ICLR responded with a number of recommendations. Whilst they found the Spanish lump sum payments favourable, they advised that European worker compensation schemes provided for 100 per cent replacement and recommended using purchasing power parity[62] rather than the ratio of minimum wages for determining the lump sum amounts. In addition they commented on the duration and value of the envisaged pension for the dependants of the deceased and disabled[63]. The response from Richard Meeran, was somewhat more circumspect and tactical. He had a track record of taking class actions on behalf of overseas workers against multinationals, most significant being the litigation against Cape Asbestos on behalf of South African workers (Meeran, 2001). His assessment was that if there was a realistic prospect of legal action outside Bangladesh against the European retailers, then the chances of improving the terms of settlement would be decidedly greater[64]. However, his experience had largely derived from proving the culpability of parent companies *vis á vis* workers employed by their subsidiaries. With outsourced production his law firm was going to require detailed information concerning the relationship between the retailers and the local factory

– particularly what the retailers knew or ought to have known about the relevant safety risks at the factory[65]. Moreover, there would be the issue of country of jurisdiction should the matter ever come to trial (Webb, 2003). The unions and NGOs in Bangladesh and the ITGLWF received this legal advice from CCC at the end of September. Although the NGWF was the main point of contact for the victims and the workers at Spectrum, Kearney saw the ITGLWF as the legitimate body for representing the workers in the negotiations with the brands to finalise the details of the scheme, although it was clear that on-going liaison was now going to be necessary with the NGWF which was not an ITGLWF affiliate at this point in time. Kearney had a tendency to follow the Anglo Saxon approach to industrial relations, giving precedence to negotiation rather than litigation. Whilst the unions in Bangladesh were happy for this route to be at least explored[66] the veiled threat of possible legal action in CCC letter to the companies on 30 September was intended to focus the minds of those buyers who were beginning to waver[67].

Meanwhile in Belgium the unions at Carrefour began to step up the pressure. The three commerce affiliates of UNI had written to the head of the Commerce section for UNI Europe, requesting that the Spectrum collapse be placed on the agenda of the Carrefour European Works Council[68]. European Works Councils are annual information and consultation meetings negotiated under the terms of an EU Directive dating back to 1994. In tabling the item to Carrefour management, he called on the company to increase its level of financial assistance on the ground and drew their attention to the need to address monitoring and controlling suppliers through a rigorous application of the SAI (Social Accountability International) SA 8000 standard. Carrefour persisted however with the Friendship approach and formally requested that CCC stop campaigning against the company. However, some of the unions in Belgium along with the Belgian CCC continued to campaign for Carrefour to support the Inditex/ITGLWF initiative.

In an email exchange between KarstadtQuelle and Javier Chercolés dated 19 October, it became apparent that the buyer had grown tired of the deferrals in producing a final version of the Trust Fund deed[69] and served notice of their intention to withdraw from the fund. Ostensibly, their complaint was that they were concerned about the delays which this would bring to the disbursement of funds but there appeared to be a position which had been taken in the BSCI that retailers should not be sucked into precedent setting compensation schemes of this nature and magnitude, since they could not be held responsible for the structural failures of a factory. This stance was reiterated in a press release issued on the eve of the first Anniversary of the collapse, when the Secretary General of the Foreign Trade Association announced:

> The Business Social Compliance Initiative (BSCI) regrets the tragedy which has killed and injured many people one year ago. Although the control of the construction of a factory building goes beyond the responsibilities of buyers and also the contents of social audits, BSCI members have increased their efforts to improve the situation[70].

In early December 2005, a delegation of six Belgian union members of the Carrefour works council and members of the Belgian CCC was accompanied by Amin and an officer from the NGWF in their visit to the factory site. The owner was not present but they were met by a member of middle management. The Spectrum site had been completely cleared and fenced off by now, but some dyeing machines were being stored under covers on the premises. Part of the sewing section of Shahriyar Fabrics had just commenced subcontracting and the product was for Tschibo – the German coffee chain which had long since expanded its retail portfolio and drawn criticism from German union VerDi and the German CCC for its sourcing policies on garments in particular (Burckhardt, 2006). One of the observations made by members of the delegation concerned the absence of fire extinguishers and evacuation signs (NGWF, 2005). At this time it was reported that a number of injured workers were still waiting for follow up medical treatment, outstanding overtime and severance pay. The delegation also agreed with NGWF that as early as possible, a list of unemployed workers should be drawn up and submitted to the Carrefour sourcing office in Bangladesh so that they may find them suitable employment (NGWF, 2005).

'Fast track' relief programme/garments rehabilitation project

By early December, a breakaway group of retailers had formed, and a meeting was arranged at the offices of INCIDIN in Dhaka to discuss the mechanics of an immediate or so-called 'Fast Track Relief Scheme'. The meeting was attended by the Head of Social Affairs of KarstadtQuelle acting also on behalf of Scapino, Steilmann and the Cotton Group. Members of Oxfam and INCIDIN attended this meeting but there were no union representatives present. It was resolved to use the amounts pledged by Cotton Group, Scapino, Steilmann and KarstadtQuelle for three purposes:

1. A lump sum payment of BDT one million for medical treatment allocated according to need ($US 16,000).

2. One off payments of BDT 50,000 to each of the twenty-eight seriously injured ($US 22,000) and the acquisition of six wheelchairs ($US 5,000).

3. 62 one off payments of BDT 10,000 to those families who lost their breadwinner (approx. $US 10,000)[71].

Whilst the minutes of the meeting pointed out that the 'Fast Track' was not conceived to 'substitute or compete with the Trust Fund' and was intended to bridge the gap until the Trust Fund was officially in place and up and running', Oxfam found themselves wrong-footed since apparently there was no mention in the meeting that the companies were abandoning the proposal of the trust fund[72]. Since no unions had been present at the meeting, nor were subsequently consulted about the decision to establish the Fast Track Relief Fund, the NGWF and the BNC continued to press all companies to engage in the Inditex/ITGLWF proposal. CCC and the ITGLWF perceived these company proposals as a poor substitute for the trust fund[73] and Oxfam withdrew from the Fast Track solution.

By the end of 2005 it had become clear to Javier Chercolés that Cotton Group and KarstadtQuelle had little intention of participating in the Inditex/ITGLWF proposal leaving him isolated within the BSCI. Early in 2006 both companies switched the funds they had allocated for the Fast Track Scheme to a second phase of the Savar Garments Rehabilitation Project run by the Friendship NGO. It was now becoming clear that the Spectrum buyers were split along four lines. There was the proposal by Inditex SA of Spain for the Voluntary

Relief Scheme which had the support of New Wave Group (Sweden) (and the French company Solo Invest which committed later in 2006). There was a second group of companies led by KarstadtQuelle (Cotton Group, Scapino, Steilmann) which had disengaged from this initiative in favour of a 'Fast Track Relief Scheme', aimed at meeting the immediate medical needs of the injured and support the families of the deceased and injured with one off payments for income generation activities. A third initiative was the solo effort still underway but about to conclude by Carrefour International which had elected to work through an NGO to focus on immediate relief for the families of the deceased and seriously injured. Finally, there was a group of companies which had either failed to respond at all or had denied any involvement with Spectrum – this involved a group of French, German and Italian buyers.

Spectrum workers' tour of European buyers

To maintain pressure on the buyers, the CCC organised a European tour for two Spectrum workers: Jahangir Alam and Noor Alam. Working with the NGWF and the Alternative Movement for Resources and Freedom in Society (AMRF), CCC aimed to raise awareness of the workers' plight by lobbying those companies which had thus far not committed to the Inditex/ITGLWF fund as well as get clarity and advance payments by the Inditex/ITGLWF fund. Jahangir Alam, was a knitting machine operator who had sustained back injuries in the collapse and had kidney and leg problems. His family had to begin selling off some of their assets and he was worried that his father, himself infirm, would have to take on more work to make ends meet. Noor Alam had lost his arm in the disaster and was left with two families to look after – one in Palashbari where he lived with his wife and child and the other in Madaripur where his own family lived. He longed to see the trust fund become a reality with as many companies participating as possible.

As the tour commenced in Belgium, Cotton Group declined to meet them, while Carrefour Belgium referred them to the company's international headquarters in Paris. However, they did have an opportunity to meet the Belgian retail unions. In France, a delegation of the French CCC (l'Ethique sur l'Ethiquette) accompanied the workers to a positive meeting with SOLO Invest, a women's, children's and

Figure 11. Noor Alam and Jahangir Alam on their European tour organised by CCC.

infants' clothing and accessories company, who agreed to contribute €5,000 to the fund and to engage in future discussions with the NGO on their code of conduct implementation. Later during their tour, the group returned to Carrefour International where they met with the Director of Sustainable Development, who appeared willing to discuss the trust fund proposal but had preconditions which included full participation by all companies and recognition that any prior contributions would need to be offset against any future financial contribution. In the Netherlands, the meeting with the management of Scapino was non-conclusive, although it was followed up by a lively public meeting attended by the company.

In Germany, the NGO lit candles outside of the main Berlin branch of KarstadtQuelle for each victim, which along with Steilmann had declined to meet the workers and their CCC companions. There was however widespread media interest in the story[74]. The Kampagne für säubere Kleidung, as it is known in Germany, is quite literally a broad church with numerous Christian group affiliations. One priest in particular, Dietrich Weinbrenner who was a member of the German CCC, was so moved by the plight of the Spectrum workers and their families that he used his attendance at the World Council of Churches in Porto Alegré in the same month to bring the demand for the trust fund to the attention of the assembled 582 delegates from seventy-two countries. Organising a petition of all their signatures he called on those German companies sourcing from the company to commit to the fund, and succeeded at the World Council in getting high profile officials in the German Evangelical Church, Bishop Wolfgang Huber and Konrad v. Bonin chair of the Church's Development Arm[75] to sign up. On the 3 April, the Frankfurter Rundschau ran with the story mentioning the petition and the Church's request for a meeting with KarstadtQuelle[76].

Since the breakaway group of companies had expediently declared that their initiative was intended to run parallel to the Inditex scheme, Javier Chercolés and Neil Kearney were still intent on sending the Trust Fund proposal out to all sourcing companies. There had been technicalities with the KPMG scheme leading to a delay and it was not until July that the scheme was ready to be sent out to the buyers. This greatly disappointed NGWF and CCC, who repeatedly asked for, but failed to obtain, progress updates. The matter of advance payments, crucial to the Spectrum workers, also remained unsettled. It is clear that some further company lobbying was going to be necessary and most efforts would continue to focus on the two largest companies: KarstadtQuelle and Carrefour. On 20th September 2006, Dietrich Weinbrenner, and two senior church colleagues met with Professor Merkel, one of the supervisory board members of KarstadtQuelle. The campaign efforts in Germany had finally paid off, for Merkel announced that the company was prepared to make a substantial donation to the Trust Fund[77]. When the company finally pledged €100,000 in December 2006 this was with the proviso that it be paid into a fund account and that it would *not* be involved in the administration of the scheme[78]. In the end KarstadtQuelle, found itself financially supporting both the Inditex and Friendship relief efforts. In the same month, Neil Kearney and Javier Chercolés met with the head of CSR at the Carrefour headquarters in Paris. It was a difficult meeting[79]. The Carrefour assistance to the Friendship Garments Rehabilitation Project Phase 1 had now been exhausted and the company had no intention of contributing to the Trust fund or providing any further assistance. The company's position was that it was the role of the Bangladesh government to provide social insurance[80]. By now, however, the second Friendship initiative– the 'Garments Rehabilitation Project (Phase II)'[81], supported by the other buyers, Cotton Group, Steilmann, Scapino and KarstadtQuelle, was well underway. In less than a year, intensive campaigning and lobbying at international and national level had yielded two quite distinctive voluntary relief schemes for the victims and shaken the employers and the authorities in Bangladesh into action to clean up the industry. The coming years would be a crucial time to see how these responses would in fact deliver on the ground.

CHAPTER 6

The Relief Schemes in Operation

Three distinct initiatives emerged to assist the Spectrum victims: the 'cash assistance' provided by the owners, the immediate relief effort provided by the Bangladeshi NGO 'Friendship' and funded by a number of Spectrum buyers over a period of two years, and the joint relief scheme developed between Inditex and the ITGLWF which had a longer term perspective. As has been seen, for the owner, relief was viewed as 'cash assistance' rather than compensation. The Friendship initiative consisted in fact in two stages of support: the first, a pragmatic response funded by Carrefour, ran between 2005 and 2006 and the second which was funded by KarstadtQuelle and Cotton Group[1] and ran between 2006 and 2007. For the NGO and its associated buyers,their initiative was not viewed as compensation but was based on the principles of immediate relief, income generation and sustainability The Inditex/ITGLWF scheme, whilst focussing on immediate assistance, nevertheless approached the situation from a different intervention perspective seeking to provide *de facto* compensation in the form of payments for loss and a long term pension to cover loss of earnings. By its very nature the Inditex/ITGLWF Voluntary Relief Scheme would be longer term but in fact closed after six years following requests from the local stakeholders in Bangladesh. It is necessary to look at each of these in turn.

Cash assistance provided by the spectrum owners

In the immediate aftermath of the collapse the owners were faced with a huge financial black hole. The factory insurance did not cover the eventuality of collapse. It was only indemnified against a fire.

In addition to the loss of capital assets, and therefore the ability to generate funds to repay the existing loan and interest payments, Spectrum and Shahriyar Fabrics had existing product destroyed in the collapse as well as materials in transit which required payment. A source of funding from which to pay the required statutory WCA compensation payment and the voluntary BGMEA payment had to be found. Through the officers of the BGMEA and directly through the company management, the owners disbursed cash to cover medical expenses of the injured in the first instance. In addition, following concerted efforts to raise funds from a range of their own sources, the owners covered the compensation amounts of BDT 100,000 to each of the families of the dead and on a series of occasions to the injured workers. In this first phase of cash assistance, some ninety Lakh (nine million BDT) was disbursed[2]. In a second phase a further cash payment of BDT 100,000 was made to each family (amounting to six million BDT) in December 2010 by the owners purely 'on humanitarian grounds[3]' and a commitment made to continue financial assistance to the families as and when future funds became available.

The Carrefour/Friendship Scheme 2005

Within days of the collapse, officers from Friendship, an organization well-known for its relief and rehabilitation work, especially in the char[4] areas of Northern Bangladesh during the 2004 floods, had visited the rescue site and drafted an intervention proposal to assist the victims of the disaster[5]. For Runa Khan, Friendship's Executive Director, this was the first disaster relief involving a factory in which Friendship had elected to become involved[6]. On the 17 April, Carrefour responded to the proposal by Friendship by seeking clarification of the type of assistance they might provide to the victims. Friendship submitted its proposal and budget on the 24 April, remarking that:

> ... no policy of rehabilitation or compensation has been discovered by us so far. The owners and the BGMEA may have something in their mind but they really do not have the experience or expertise to handle the compensation system effectively. Nor is it clear at this stage who the beneficiaries of any support would be: the deceased families alone, or the deceased families and the injured, or all the workers who were on site[7].

Friendship was thus the first organisation off the mark with an intervention plan. When they turned up at the disaster site and visited the hospitalised workers, they discovered that the medical expenses had been taken care of and that these immediate matters as well as seeking justice for the workers were the main focus of the trade unions and other NGOs[8]. Friendship decided to devote its attention elsewhere to the families of the dead workers and to issues of rehabilitation for the injured. By the time Carrefour had responded to the letters from the ITGLWF and the CCC in May, Friendship had already been commissioned to undertake this outreach work. The so-called Savar Garments Rehabilitation Project[9] was supported to the tune of €15,000 by the French multinational.

The project was initially conceived in four parts with Part 1 consisting of data collection on the families, Part 2 involving actual outreach to the same while Part 3 focussed on needs analysis and assistance in determining an independent source of income generation. The fourth and final phase was intended to provide financial advice and assistance with the compensation sums provided by the owner through the BGMEA[10]. In line with their proposal, Friendship officers would determine the social category of each family for the purposes of intervention according to the following criteria:

- families with an unemployed spouse and/or parent
- families with dependent children and parents
- families where the husbands had an alcoholic or drug dependency
- families where there was a wage earner but which required a supplementary income.

They set up an office in Savar near the site in order to draw up a comprehensive and 'realistic' list and aided by a number of agencies located a total of 118 potential beneficiaries across thirty-eight districts in the country. Establishing the whereabouts of the families of the deceased and injured consisted of a mail shot in the first instance but, given the fluidity of the domestic circumstances of many of the workers, Friendship soon elected to dedicate some outreach workers to the task of tracing the families[11]. What they found in their household survey and needs assessment was not good but to be expected: the majority of the families were living in conditions of extreme rural hardship and poverty. Since agricultural productivity is very low and does not cover the required amount of food grain for a year, family members depend on selling their labour to local farmers to make ends meet. However, employment is casual and in many cases families can only expect a wage from this work for at best for 6 months in any year. All these uncertainties made it impossible to determine the accurate income of the victims' dependants as would later be discovered by INCIDIN working on behalf of Inditex and the ITGLWF.[12]. Friendship employed three social classification criteria: very poor, poor, and moderate. Very poor was categorised as having a sole breadwinner but owning no land, having a straw hut as a dwelling and not being in a position to afford three meals per day. Poor were those who also had a sole breadwinner, owned or rented a small plot of land for cultivation, and who lived in tin shacks but were in a position to provide for three meals a day for 5 to 6 months in any year. Those persons who were in moderate circumstances were deemed to have sufficient land for subsistence, a stone or tin dwelling, and three meals a day all year and were in a family unit with two or more breadwinners[13].

By the end of July 2005 it was reported that Friendship's outreach efforts had involved some 155[14] interventions for the victims' families. Thirty-two families had received a cycle 'van'[15] and thirty-nine families had received a sewing machine. Forty families of the injured had received cash disbursements of between BDT 2,000 and BDT 3,000 (roughly equivalent to two monthly salaries of a garment worker minus overtime) while a further twenty payments were made to cover the costs of medicines and doctor's fees. Friendship assisted eighteen workers with applications for jobs with a BGMEA member company and six families were assisted with setting to set up a bank account to deposit their BGMEA compensation cheque[16]. In some instances the sum of BDT 100,000 proved disorientating for the recipients, one father using all of the money to erect a proper grave for his son, while another spent the entire compensation amount on food for the whole village[17]. Such a financial sum was of course nowhere near what was necessary to lift these families out of their hardship and coupled with the delay in establishing the Inditex/ITGLWF Trust Fund, Maren Böhm felt compelled to report on the second phase of the Rehabilitation effort that even after a year following the disaster, the victims' families still had received no noticeable relief[18].

Already in June the NGWF had been making representations to the Carrefour sourcing office in Dhaka about the Friendship initiative. Although the union welcomed the efforts, they argued that Carrefour was not doing sufficient and that assisting the victims of the factory collapse had to be seen as a trade union issue, urging the company to support the Inditex/ITGLWF promoted trust fund which was in the process of being set up[19]. However Amin's calls fell on deaf ears. When later that month the Belgian trade unions within the Carrefour works council sought clarification about the relationship between the Friendship initiative and the various appeals for compensation within Bangladesh, they were informed that the company had made a donation to a third party to provide material assistance and that this was not to be seen as compensation[20].

The fasttrack relief/friendship scheme 2006–2007

At the end of 2005, KarstadtQuelle, Scapino, Steilmann and Cotton Group, having lost patience with the protracted roll out of the relief scheme initiated by Inditex/ITGLWF, decided to opt for a more immediate approach which they termed the Fasttrack Relief Scheme. Within weeks the initial proposals including lump sum relief payments were abandoned in favour of a Phase 2 of the Friendship Savar Garments Rehabilitation Project.

In February 2006, KarstadtQuelle acting on behalf of the other buyers, approached Friendship. In a press release to coincide with the first anniversary of the collapse, the German company announced that Scapino, Steilmann and Cotton Group were contributing to Phase 2 of the Friendship Scheme[21], 'focussing on a fair, transparent and reliable concept with trustworthy partners' and reaffirmed that the companies were continuing to support the plans for an international trust fund. Phase 2 was time bound until February 2007, with the possibility of a two month extension. Some eight full-time staff at Friendship were to be funded to provide logistical support to the project and monitoring would continue until after the project period had officially ended[22]. The first part of new phase was a repeat of the exercise undertaken for Carrefour. Out of the 118 families, 108 interviews were conducted but ten families declined to meet with Friendship for their own safety. Such is the depth of rural poverty, word carried quickly that certain individuals were to get pay outs/relief in kind and there was envy[23].

Ten families were classified as very poor, while the majority – some seventy-one families – were categorised as poor, with a further twenty-seven families being termed as having *moderate* living circumstances.

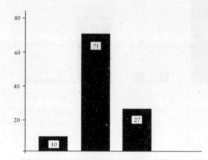

Figure 12 Friendship's economic classification of the families of the victims.

Under the scheme, seed corn funding was to be awarded for Income Generation Activities (IGAs) on the following basis:

1. A dead worker's family (total sixty to sixty-four families) [actual figure sixty-two, Author's note] would receive BDT 23,000 through a bank account.

2. A severely injured worker (total fifteen workers) would be given an award of BDT 27,000 (BDT 17,000 for an IGA and BDT 10,000 for ongoing medical costs).

3. A traumatized worker (total ten workers) would receive BDT 17,000 (BDT 12,000 for IGA and BDT 5000 for medical costs).

4. An injured worker (total fifty-five to sixty workers) would be awarded BDT 10,000 for an IGA[24],

All sums were to be fixed amounts and paid through bank accounts (although withdrawals could only be made with authorisation from Friendship). Those families which did participate in the second needs analysis were requested to indicate their preference for one of four income generation activities (IGAs) on offer: establishing a small shop/business, purchasing or leasing a plot of land, buying a cow, or setting up a fish or poultry farm.

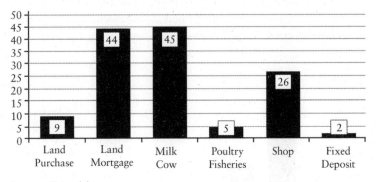

Source: Friendship

Figure 13: Distribution of forms of assistance to Spectrum families under the Friendship Phase 2 initiative. Courtesy: Friendship.

The first cheques were disbursed to the victims' families at the end of July 2006. A total of 131 people received monetary assistance for sustainable income generating activities. This figure included sixty-two victims/families from nineteen districts and fifty-four injured who had received their first instalments and were being put through monitoring and follow up. Of the fifty-four injured, twenty-two had sought medical assistance, sixteen had sought assistance with job hunting while a further twenty had requested training. Up to March 2007, 116 out of 118 victims had received ongoing support from Friendship but were deemed to have reached a point where they were no longer in need of any external livelihood/ income generation support[25].

In some cases a greater number of beneficiaries were assisted than on the official count. Where, for example the widow of the dead victim lived separately from the victims' parents but both parties required support, the money was divided among the claimants according to their need[26]. Friendship had hoped to press on with a third phase involving an education project for the forty-four children of the families, but the buyers ceased funding in 2007[27]. At the end of this initiative there were, according to Friendship, eight families who still had not received compensation either from the owner through the BGMEA or the Labour Court. In two of these cases, there had been a duplication of names and in the others there was a dispute regarding the rightful claimant of the money. In some cases the families had not been in touch[28].

The Inditex/ITGLWF Voluntary Relief Scheme/Aka Trust Fund

The proposal for an actuarially calculated relief scheme had been first mooted in a discussion between Javier Chercolés and Neil Kearney at the offices of the ITGLWF in Brussels in the immediate aftermath of the collapse. Following sustained international pressure, it received the initial backing of the major buyers at Spectrum – Inditex, KarstadtQuelle and Cotton Group. By this time, Carrefour had already contracted with Friendship. Establishing such a fund and scheme was uncharted territory. No existing benchmarks or guidelines for such a scheme appeared to exist anywhere. But the purpose for both Inditex and the ITGLWF at least was clear: it would be a fund designed to take care of the urgent needs – medical and financial – and to support the dead and injured workers and their families, in the aftermath of the collapse of the Spectrum Factory (Inditex/ITGLWF, 2006).

The first task of the relief effort was the expenditure of resources to provide immediate medical attention to the injured. During their repeated visits to Bangladesh in 2005 and early 2006, Kearney and Chercolés went to some length to ensure that the victims, particularly the injured, were properly cared for. One of their first actions at the time of the first buyer mission was to move eighteen severely injured workers who were being treated in different private and public hospitals and clinics to the 'Trauma Center' in Dhaka – a high quality private medical service specializing in orthopaedics and pain treatment. These would be eventually joined by a further four workers bringing the total to twenty-two. Food was also made available for those family members caring for the injured at the Centre (Inditex and ITGLWF, 2006: 10). In total, some seventy workers were eventually examined and treated here, some for prolonged periods of time. All received basic medical treatment. Fifty-four of the more seriously injured, whose injuries ranged from fractures and hearing problems to damaged vital organs and amputated limbs, received more extensive treatment. Some were and still are in constant need of painkillers. S, who was undergoing physiotherapy and occupational therapy at the

Trauma Centre was airlifted to Spain for special rehabilitation at the National Hospital for Paraplegics in Toledo. In another case, a worker whose pelvis had been fractured, underwent surgery to reconstruct his urinary tract. Another worker, whose leg had been amputated, was fitted with a prosthetic limb, as were all who lost limbs as a result of the collapse. In total eight workers received surgical treatment. The injured were invited for regular examinations and periodic assessments by a medical board consisting of the Deputy Director of the Trauma Centre, a specialist from Spain and a local GP[29].

In terms of the mechanics of the actual relief scheme, a major piece of work had to be undertaken. This involved the formulation of definitions, terms of reference, criteria for eligibility, and the determination of formulae for calculating actuarial valuations for the families of the deceased and the injured and their families. With the support (at this time) of KarstadtQuelle and Cotton Group, and the ITGLWF, Inditex commissioned KPMG, the international accountancy and consultancy firm to undertake this work. The first draft of the scheme was delivered in September 2005 (KPMG, 2005). It established two categories of beneficiaries for the deceased (definitively agreed to number sixty-two). For those who were married, the beneficiaries were deemed to be the spouse and children under the age of eighteen. For those who were single, the beneficiaries were deemed to be the father (where both father and mother survived the deceased), the spouse surviving the deceased (parent), and primary family members financially dependent on the deceased.

In the case of the injured, the number of victims was fixed initially at eighty-four but then revised down to fifty-four following diagnosis and successful treatment. Two categories of severity were established, but again without a thorough medical assessment of this group it would not be possible to determine precise payments and therefore the accrual amounts under the scheme (KPMG, 2005:3). Since there were some inconsistencies in the first version of the scheme, there was a delay in the production of the first draft to be presented to the stakeholders. This delay became protracted leading to some tensions between the companies and between Inditex and the ITGLWF and the CCC, which saw itself as acting on acting on behalf of the NGWF. Two additional pieces of work were, moreover, now outstanding – the precise determination of the number and status

Figure 14: Neil Kearney (ITGLWF) and Javier Chercolés (Inditex).
Photo: Courtesy BBC.

of the beneficiaries and a medical assessment of the injured. It was now certainly becoming clear to both Chercolés and Kearney that developing and applying such a scheme was going to be an involved and time consuming business, particularly since this would have to be done remotely in the first instance and, for both these instigators, on top of the considerable workloads which came with their respective global responsibilities. The magnitude of the task in hand certainly provided a group of buyers, which had initially showed support for the initiative, with a pretext for breaking ranks, although within the BSCI and also the BGMEA there were probably concerns that such a Fund would set a precedent. As we have seen, as 2005 drew to a close, the Inditex/ITGLWF Relief Scheme began to lose support amongst the other buyers as they mounted a break away in favour of the Friendship model. They were however at pains to stress that they were not ruling out support for the scheme if and when it should emerge[30]. Inditex and the ITGLWF were nevertheless determined to press on with the next major task – a household and employment status survey of the victims. Although some information was already available via the Friendship initiative, they turned to the Bangladesh NGO INCIDIN to co-ordinate this fact finding mission.

The INCIDIN Fact Finding Mission

The acronym INCIDIN Bangladesh stands for Integrated Community & Industrial Development Initiative. A partner organisation of Oxfam Bangladesh, it was first launched in 1995 as a research organisation, taking on issues it deemed 'unconventional... and politically challenging'[31]. In discussions with Inditex, the BNC and the ITGLWF, the BGMEA and Oxfam, INCIDIN was asked to put together a tripartite fact finding mission to identify the victims and assess their economic situation for the purposes of determining the magnitude of assistance which would be required from the Fund. Four teams of three were formed, each consisting of one member from the BNC unions, the BGMEA and a professional researcher from INCIDIN respectively and allocated a zone covering specific districts and places of origin of the Spectrum victims. Although some of the information was clearly already available and about to be duplicated by a parallel exercise undertaken by Friendship, INCIDIN were keen to develop their own approach[32] and Kearney saw the fact finding mission as a unique training experience and an opportunity for BNC members to develop relations with the BGMEA[33]. The initial meeting to establish the team did not take place until February 2006 (INCIDIN, BNC, and BGMEA, 2006)[34], and Inditex agreed to fund the mission.

The task was not easy. The families of the dead and many of the injured were scattered in villages across Bangladesh (see Map in Chapter 1) and each of these had to be visited in order for profiling to be undertaken, which would include details of dependent relatives and the extent of the disability of those injured. Since written records are not always kept in rural Bangladesh, much of the information gathered would have to be cross-checked with local officials. The Northern Zone for example covers twelve Upazila (districts) and the number of dead workers identified in this zone was seventeen. The family of one of the dead, and identified by a fellow worker as coming from Joypurhat could not be traced. In the South Zone, the team reported taking whole days just to reach one victim's family and finding villages often with the same name. Tracing the victims in the

Central Zone (Dhaka and Manikganj districts) proved to be more straightforward at least as far as the injured were concerned – since some could be interviewed at the offices of the Bangladesh Garment Workers Federation, while others could be approached at the clinic where they had come for ongoing medical treatment.

Additional cultural and legal barriers hampered the initiative. All but two of the sixty-two deceased were male and of these thirty were married. Under Muslim Family Law in Bangladesh there are strict inheritance shares for each member of the family in the case of a death (Asian Development Bank (ADB): 2001; Bangladesh National Women Lawyers' Association (BNWLA): 2002). In some cases it was alleged that the wives of the deceased had been cast out and were now living considerable distances from the victim's former place of abode, and/or without any intervention, were likely to be disenfranchised from receiving any payments by their parents in law[35] (Azam, 2006: 22–27). The general custom in the villages was that the head of household would normally receive any official payments. The Inditex/ITGLWF scheme had established the principle that for those dead workers who were married, the beneficiaries would be the spouse (predominantly the widows in this case) and their children under the age of eighteen. Little thought had been given to this eventuality, although news of disputes over entitlement began to trickle back from some of the villages. This was to have a marked effect on Javier Chercolés who began to realise that some initiative would have to be developed to attempt to address the issue, a point to which we must return.

Overall the report identified the dependants of all sixty-two deceased and fifty-four injured and noted the extent to which they were struggling in dire poverty. It recommended capacity building for income generation, a pension scheme, and education for the children (Azam, 2006). Since two of these three recommendations were already being addressed by the Friendship initiative, the data was going to be essential for assisting in the computation of the funds needed to launch the Project Spectrum Voluntary Relief Scheme, details of which were provided to the buyers in February 2006[36].

In the case of the injured, before any payments could be calculated, however, an official medical assessment had to be conducted in order to determine the magnitude of financial input from the Trust Fund to the Scheme. Inditex enlisted the services of a team of medical practitioners including an occupational injury specialist from Juan Canalejo Hospital (A Coruña, Spain), a specialist from the Trauma Centre and a general medical practitioner to undertake these examinations. Under the terms of the Relief scheme fifty-four of the original eighty-four workers were categorised into four groups:

Group 1: Long-term or permanent injury including loss of limbs (eleven workers).

Group 2: Serious injuries likely to result in prolonged inability to work (twelve workers).

Group 3: Injuries likely to result in shorter term inability to work (eight workers).

Group 4: Minor injuries with no medium or long-term effects (twenty-three workers).

Periodic medical assessments were written into the revised scheme as a mandatory element (Inditex and ITGLWF, 2006: 35). On 11 April 2006, the first anniversary of the Spectrum collapse, KarstadtQuelle publicly announced Phase 2 of the Friendship Scheme, while the ITGLWF issued a press release updating progress on the relief scheme in which the initiative was announced as a national and international effort involving Spectrum Sweater Industries Ltd, the BGMEA, the BNC, NGOs, the Bangladesh Government, multinational clothing buyers led by Inditex of Spain, and the ITGLWF to provide fair and equitable relief to the families of those who died and to workers injured when the Spectrum factory collapsed:

> … temporary humanitarian relief has been given to those injured and to the many who lost their jobs in the collapse. Some of the more seriously injured are still receiving a monthly stipend. Most of the funds for all of this work have been provided by Inditex. The Scheme will provide for lump-sum payments in the case of dead and injured victims, lost wages and a regular payment or pension to the dependents of the dead and to those whose injuries render them incapable of full-time work in the future. The overall governance of the Relief Scheme will rest in the hands of a board of trustees assisted by a committee of contributors and an oversight committee, while its management will

be in the hands of a manager appointed by the trustees (ITGLWF, 2006b).

Those brands and retailers who had business with Spectrum Sweater Industries Limited were invited to attend a round table meeting to finalise the details of the Project Spectrum Voluntary Relief Scheme with local stakeholders and to put in place a Trust to administer the Scheme. The first such Round Table meeting was scheduled for 2 May 2006 in Dhaka, Bangladesh to coincide with the follow up MFA Forum Conference where many of the companies in question would be taking part. The companies were invited to make a public announcement regarding their participation in the scheme and to take part in a meeting to discuss the operational details of the fund once the initial fact finding mission had reported. It was suggested that by assessing the volume and value of production for individual brands and retailers at Spectrum Sweater Industries Ltd during the years prior to the factory collapse, and factoring in the total turnover of the brand or retailer, it should be possible to calculate what might reasonably be expected from each brand or retailer in terms of their contribution.

When the final draft of the scheme was presented later in the month, it included an actuarial determination of lump sums and pensions for the families of the deceased and injured as well as a final accrual amount:

For the families of the deceased:

> ...a voluntary relief payment (lump-sum) payment for pain and suffering of 168,000 BDT per worker, for the surviving spouse or in the absence thereof, for the surviving head of family, and a monthly pension payable in arrears for life, non-reversible and incremental in line with the consumer index in Bangladesh fixed at fifty per cent of the average of the minimum inter-professional salary for the textile sector in Bangladesh (18.77 Euros per month, or 1,500 BDT as at 2005) or the employee's consolidated salary at the date of the accident, which ever was greater[37].

The pension was to be calculated using the average earnings of the deceased worker at the time of the collapse but based on the projected age of the beneficiary from the time of the collapse. Actuarial calculations applied to the starting pension made an allowance for a 4.2 per cent annual inflation rate and a discount rate[38] of eight per cent. The total accrual value of the pension (excluding the lump sum) for the beneficiaries of the deceased was estimated at 252,711.12 Euros.

For the injured:

A lump-sum payment as compensation equal to ten per cent of the total compensation entitlement based on severity of the injury, and

A pension equal to fifty per cent of the average of the consolidated salary (as a minimum 1500 BDT) for life, in the case of Group 1 victims; for ten years for Group II, six months for Group III and nothing if included in Group IV.

The total accrual value of the pension (excluding the lump sum) for the injured was estimated at 137,122.88 Euros. The total accrual value of the relief fund was calculated at €533,323.39 (BDT 42,623,205.17). See Table 5.

	Deceased	Injured	Total
LUMP SUM			
Euros	134,534.53	8,953.87	**143,488.40**
Taka	10,752,000.00	715,593.31	11,467,593.31
PENSION			
Euros	252,712.11	137,122.88	**389,834.98**
Taka	20,196,751.46	10,958,860.40	31,155,611.86
TOTAL			
Euros	387,246.64	146,076.75	**533,323.39**
Taka	30,948,751.46	11,674,453.71	42,623,205.17

Source: Inditex and ITGLWF (2006) Project Spectrum Voluntary Relief Scheme – Final version (Dhaka: Bangladesh).

Table 5: The Spectrum Voluntary Relief Scheme Estimated Value.

The final draft of the scheme was sent out by Inditex to the buyers, Oxfam, INCIDIN and the BNC and, the BGMEA and the Government of Bangladesh at the end of July, inviting prompt comments on the proposal since their aim was have the Trust Fund and Voluntary Relief Scheme up and running by September 2006. The proposal had broad support from the ITG affiliates in the BNC and the CCC and its partner organisations in Bangladesh. Of the buyers, only New Wave Group and Solo Invest had committed to join Inditex by contributing to the Scheme. Despite their public pronouncements to the contrary, the other key buyers KarstadtQuelle and Cotton Group ultimately declined to participate. At the end of November 2007, the ITGLWF drafted a series of next steps for Inditex. This included formally establishing the Spectrum Trust in Spain[39] and seeking nominees and their formal attestation from BNC, INCIDIN, Oxfam Bangladesh, a lawyer/banker, the ITGLWF and Inditex and electing a chairperson for the trust[40]. Funds were to be transferred into the OXFAM account and disbursed by its partner organisation INCIDIN. BNC and the NGWF were to undertake the more challenging task of conducting the outreach to the injured workers and families of the deceased. The fund was however, never consolidated with the result that payments were made in tranches, usually just before the anniversary of the factory collapse, to avoid any adverse publicity from the Clean Clothes Campaign.

Relief payments

Payments to former Spectrum employees

Although only two categories of beneficiaries were nominated under the Scheme, namely the injured, and the families of the deceased, those Spectrum workers who lost their jobs as a result of the disaster, were also seen as part of the relief effort in the immediate aftermath of the collapse. The official Spectrum workforce size as declared to the BGMEA was 1,016[41]. 191 workers were identified in the first instance by the BNC and the NGWF and on 26 June each of the listed unemployed workers received BDT 2,000 as an immediate support payment. Six weeks after the collapse many workers had been compelled to seek employment elsewhere and therefore did not appear in the unions' manifest. When a second list was drawn up a fortnight later, the list had expanded to 487 as more workers (296) came forward. These workers received BDT 2,000 each, and some were provided with alternative job information by the unions. In October, a further 193 workers (including ninety-six women) were given a relief payment. Accounting for the dead and injured, financial outreach was made to approximately two thirds of the workforce. No further relief payments were given to former workers beyond this.

Payments to the injured

For the injured (and the families of the deceased), the administration and calculation of amounts owing under the terms of the scheme were going to be complicated. Firstly, interim emergency relief payments had already been made by Inditex during the first year to the most seriously injured. Secondly, pension amounts were likely to vary according to severity of injury and recalculations were going to be necessary as periodic medical assessments established the extent of recovery of the victims. In the case of the injured, their salary at the time of the accident and the nature of their injuries were all to be taken into consideration. Accordingly, a form of relief was calculated on the basis of four categories of injury sustained where ten per cent of the sum owing would be made as an initial lump sum payment, and the remaining ninety per cent would be applied to establishing a monthly pension the duration of which would be dependent on the level of injury group. Thus for those in Category One, the monthly pension would be made during the full period of disability with recipients subject to periodic medical re-evaluation. For those in Category Two the monthly pension would be paid for a maximum of 5 years which could reduce subject to periodic medical examination indicating the possibility of an earlier return to work. Where an evaluation recommended an extension of the payment beyond five years, the monthly pension would then continue until a full medical discharge. For Category Three injured, a monthly pension was to be paid for a maximum of 6 months. Category Four workers were not entitled to any relief under the terms of the scheme although an *ex gratia* payment of BDT 10,000 was awarded. Following the formulation of the Scheme, all those injured who so desired were medically assessed at the Trauma Centre in Dhaka and relief scheme payments were based on this assessment. In December 2007, a medical board comprising an international medical team from Juan Canalejo

Hospital (A Coruña, Spain) specializing in occupational injuries, a specialist from the Trauma Centre and a general medical practitioner met and re-assessed all of the injured who presented themselves. The medical board confirmed most of the original assessments, but in a handful of cases determined that the injuries sustained merited a higher group rating. For the purposes of the Scheme, this rating was back-dated to April 2005, the date of the accident at Spectrum. Where the assessment indicated a lower group rating, the original group rating was maintained through to 31 December 2007.

The actual payments commenced in August 2005. Two of the most seriously injured received 2 years wages in the first instance as support (based on a monthly average wage of BDT 2,500). These were paid in monthly instalments by banker's draft. The remaining twenty severely injured workers each received BDT 5,000 as a lump sum relief support. A further payment of 2,500 was made in October to eighteen of the injured. Some days before the second anniversary of the collapse on 1 April 2007, the first official payments based on medical assessments and calculated under the terms of the scheme were made at a meeting in Dhaka attended by Inditex, the ITGLWF, BNC members and Oxfam and INCIDIN. On this date €20,757 was distributed to twenty-one of the injured. Over the coming months further payments were made to individual workers based on medical assessments at the Trauma Centre in Dhaka.

From the outset a position had been taken to rehabilitate the Spectrum injured and a skills audit was undertaken. In April 2008 positions were found for fourteen of the most severely injured in the offices and factories of Inditex agents and suppliers. Their employment commenced 1 June[42]. At the end of 2008 after a gap of one year, thirty-six of the injured received all outstanding payments including lump sums and pensions up to 31 December 2008. Because of the changed circumstances of the injured In August 2008, KPMG was instructed to issue an amended actuarial valuation of the scheme to reflect the reductions in entitlements arising from the medical reassessments of the injured.

As at June 2009 there were only six of the injured workers in Category One and a further four in Category Two. These individuals had received their pension payments up until 30 June 2009 but were due further medical reassessment. Since the latter were now in employment, it was deemed unlikely that these workers would be eligible for benefit beyond the end of 2009[43]. However, during July 2010 the NGWF was able to open up dialogue with the owner in pursuit of legal claims for the Category One and Two workers under the terms of the law as at 2005. These workers were paid additional amounts up to a maximum of BDT 30,000 from the company through the labour court.

Payments to the families of the deceased

In addition to the BDT 100,000 lump sum compensation provided by the owner through the BGMEA and the Government, fifty-nine of the sixty-two families of the deceased received an additional payment of BDT 68,000 in December 2008 through to February 2009 from Inditex. Taken together this constituted the lump sum amount owing to the families under the terms of the scheme. Inditex and the ITGLWF had always conceived the funds for the scheme to include the BDT 100,000 lump sum compensation amounts paid by the owner through the Government and BGMEA compensation schemes. In three of the outstanding cases, there was an ongoing dispute over the nominee/beneficiary which, in two cases, had gone to court. The principle of paying compensation to the widow had led in some cases to problems. In one case the dead worker was the only son of his father and the Ward (*Pouroshova*) Chairman determined the next of kin as wife, son, father and mother. However the wife had drawn the total amount of compensation from the BGMEA and moved back into her father's house, leaving the frail parents destitute. In this particular case the widow was planning to remarry[44].

Payment issues

The Spectrum Relief Scheme start-up date was announced as September 2006. At the request of the workers and the families, payments were to be made in the form of a lump sum and a regular pension projected over a working lifetime[45]. There was therefore an expectation that regular payments would be forthcoming from this date. However the families had to wait three and a half years before receiving their first payment which came as a lump sum. This clearly became a source of consternation and frustration for the beneficiaries whose expectation levels had understandably been heightened. Following repeated attempts to get information and, acting on behalf of the NGWF, the CCCs of Belgium, Germany, France, Spain and the Netherlands along with the CCC international secretariat formally wrote to both Inditex and the ITGLWF in November 2006 requesting an update and clarification about the start date of the Fund[46]. At the beginning of 2007, CCC commissioned AMRF to undertake a small survey of the widows and injured in the Dhaka/Savar area. The survey found that many of the Spectrum families had been plunged further into debt and poverty as they struggled to make ends meet. Z, for example, a cleaner at the Spectrum factory and widow of S, one of the workers who perished in the collapse, and living in rented accommodation in Savar with her daughter and two sons, had debts of BDT 19,000. Although her daughter was working in a clothing factory, her monthly wage of 2,600 was the family's only source of regular income and she had grave doubts that her debt would ever be repaid[47]. For N, with a dependent family of six, including his wife and two sons in Savar and his mother and sister who were living in his village home some 100km south of Dhaka life had been tough given school costs for his son, and BDT 1,000 a month on which his mother and sister were dependent. Although his wife had found work in a sweater factory, she had had to give up her job due to pregnancy. All those interviewed were struggling to make ends meet and required money to cover food, rent, medicines and school fees[48]. There was frustration at the lack of communication from the BNC and the NGOs who were supposed to be administering the fund on the ground[49].

Noor Alam and Jahangir Alam, the two workers who went on the speaker tour in Europe during early 2006, and who had been acting as a communication link to the families and other injured as well as collecting bank account details, felt compelled to write on their behalf in the middle of 2007[50]. Their concern, apart from delays in payments, related to a lack of transparency and access on the part of INCIDIN/BNC. Since they were members of NGWF, their concerns were relayed through to the CCC, which in turn began to correspond with the ITGLWF and, through its partner (SETEM) in Spain, also began to exert pressure on Inditex.

How are the delays to be explained? The first critical explanation relates to the long drawn out process of determining the precise status of each family. The second critical explanation relates to complications arising from the proposal to establish a trust fund. Although a decision was taken to register the fund in Spain, the process of consolidating the trust had *de facto* ground to a halt by the end of 2006. Firstly, there was a lack of willingness on the part of the buyers to participate in its administration. Secondly, there was an apparent reluctance on the part of INCIDIN and OXFAM to nominate trustees[51]. Thirdly, although lobbying efforts, which continued through 2006, led to a number of commitments of small amounts of funds from Scapino, New Wave Group and Solo Invest, and a significant pledge of €100,000 from KarstadtQuelle (now Arcandor), the latter declared that it had no desire to participate in the management of the fund or the scheme. The pledged amount would be released on consolidation of the Fund and creation of an account. Fourthly, Inditex management became concerned that the administration of the Fund would require a level of management input in Spain which would be unsustainable[52]. Moreover, despite being invited to make a contribution, and to join the board of Trustees, support from the BGMEA and the government was not forthcoming. Indeed during the unrest in the RMG in the summer of 2006, accusations of an international conspiracy was soon taken to mean anyone critical of the industry and Kearney and Chercolés were nearly always followed by the intelligence services during their periodic visits to the country[53].

Although the original BDT 100,000 compensation sums paid to each family of the deceased by the BGMEA and the Ministry of Labour were to be discounted against the overall actuarial value, these sums were borne by the owner[54]. The owner was thus *de facto* involved in the scheme, and he also made separate payments on several occasions to the injured and ultimately a further cash sum of BDT 100,000 to the each family of the deceased[55]. Since most of the additional funding for the initiative was being footed by Inditex in the end, it would appear that some choices had to be made in prioritisation of funds allocation in favour of up front support for the injured, who despite legal provisions stood to receive nothing in the wake of the disaster, given that support in kind had been made available to the families of the deceased by Friendship. Finally, there was the complexity of initiating bank transfers in Bangladesh. It was reported that payments into bank accounts were preferred in the form of a banker's draft, rather than electronic transfer since inter-bank business was alleged to be complex in the extreme in Bangladesh[56].

Although Inditex and the ITGLWF remained committed to honouring the commitments made under the terms of the Relief Scheme, the absence of a Trust Fund meant that there was no Relief Scheme account either in Spain or in Bangladesh into which neither deposits from third parties nor withdrawals for the beneficiaries could be made. Moreover, Bangladesh law required amounts in excess of €2,000 or the equivalent amount from foreign sources to receive Bangladesh Bank approval before a withdrawal could be made, and ministerial approval from the BNP government was unlikely to be forthcoming in this case. Some payments in the early stages could be made by Inditex through the Oxfam Bangladesh account, but eventually the company fell back on alternative 'creative' means of getting money to the workers[57]. As workers made repeated enquiries about their pension, INCIDIN deferred to the ITGLWF which had no direct access to resources. Calculations of pension entitlements were dependent on accurate assessments of each family's circumstances which either kept changing or were the subject of dispute. This monitoring role fell largely to the member unions of the BNC which did not have the resource to undertake this task, and, moreover, during the 2007 to 2008 state of emergency, were forced, along with the NGWF and other unions, to go to ground (Asia Legal Resource Centre 2008).

This paralysis of administration prompted the CCC (with the support of the NGWF), to propose to Inditex and the ITGLWF the appointment of an in country project manager on a fixed term, first in November 2006 and then in October 2007[58]. The offer was, however, not taken up. Payments to workers thus tended to be made as lump sums on the occasion of Chercolés' and Kearney's periodic visits to Bangladesh. With the appointment by Inditex of an in country CSR director in September 2008, who took over on the ground administrative responsibility for expediting payments, some progress could finally be made. However, in February 2009, when representatives of Inditex, BNC, INCIDIN and the NGWF met to discuss the compensation process, there was a general recognition that the ongoing method of disbursement was simply too problematic as bank transfers were too complex and the delivery of bankers drafts to the hands of the beneficiaries was too burdensome a process to be undertaken repeatedly at regular intervals.

The logical conclusion was now pointing towards a one off lump sum payment to the families to effectively bring the scheme to a close. In June 2009, fifteen of the victims' families who live in Dhaka and the surrounding area attended a meeting convened by Inditex, INCIDIN and the BNC for an update. Whilst not representative of the entire group of beneficiaries, the overwhelming mood was for a lump sum closure payment, a position supported by both the BNC and INCIDIN. In the same month, lawyers acting on behalf of Arcandor AG (formerly KarstadtQuelle), filed a case with the Essen District Court in Germany to open insolvency proceedings. Faced with loan repayments due in the order of €710 million and a failure to secure state loan guarantees[59], the company, which had originally pledged €100,000 to the Spectrum Trust Fund was clearly no longer in a position to fulfil this financial commitment. With the exception of some €10,000 pledged in total by New Wave and Solo Invest, but with no account to hold the money, Inditex was effectively left bearing the major part of financial burden of the entitlements due under the Spectrum scheme. In July, the Spanish Campaña Ropa Limpa (a sister organisation of the Clean Clothes Campaign) wrote to Inditex seeking an update on the situation and clarification of the position. In its response, the company reported that they had opted for a twice yearly settlement having estimated that a monthly pay out would consume in the order of one and half week's fieldwork, and that calculations to bring payments up to date were about to be made in conjunction with the ITGLWF[60]. It was in this communication that mention was first made of a voluntary 'portfolio' proposal to assist the widows in particular with the management of what would be unprecedented large sums of money. The portfolio idea was conceived as a new project to assist with the transition to a final lump sum payment, which Inditex also now appeared to support. As Javier Chercolés, Razaul Karim Buiyan and Neil Kearney met in at the offices of the ITGLWF in Brussels to calculate the outstanding pension payments to date, and to discuss how best to move forward, Neil Kearney was less than enthusiastic about this proposal. More practical issues soon proved to dominate, however, as it became clear to Razaul Karim Buiyan that unfreezing the transferred amount to the new account in Dhaka was going to be a major headache requiring approval from an appropriate Government ministry. Since Inditex was not registered in Bangladesh under company law as a trading company, the company was not authorised to make transfer payments to individuals. Once again efforts to pay the pensions had been thwarted and since this was an important point of principle, action would need to be undertaken by both the company, the ITGLWF and the BNC whose member unions sponsored the new Government party, to lobby for a relaxation or change to the banking rules.

The widows' issue

In November 2009, shortly before the tenth World Congress of the ITGLWF, whilst on a joint visit with Javier Chercolés and journalists from the BBC to look at the progress made on 'cleaning up' another Inditex supplier in Dhaka, and to expedite the payments issue, Neil Kearney suddenly and tragically died of massive heart attack. In an unprecedented demonstration of affection and bereavement, thousands of RMG workers thronged the streets around the Central Minar in Dhaka as his coffin was paraded in line with Muslim tradition and 3 days of mourning were declared in the RMG sector. Pending the election of a new General Secretary at the World Congress of the ITGLWF later that month, one half of the management team of the Inditex/ITGLWF relief scheme was now gone. As Javier Chercolés undertook the necessary arrangements in Dhaka to repatriate Kearney's body, a new dimension to their joint project suddenly began to loom large in the thinking of the CSR director:

> I had to remain in Bangladesh to take care of the repatriation of Neil's body as I had promised to his wife, and I had to wait eighteen hours in the morgue waiting for the autopsy. In those long hours I saw too many dead women on stretchers and... Realised that there was maybe something behind this. The day after, I had to get the mortuary passport for Neil and the final papers had to be approved by the embassy...

> And a consular official invited me to wait while he checked that the papers were correct and in the meantime I was waiting in the lobby and I noticed a book with the title 'Violence Against Women (VAW) in Bangladesh'[61] and then I realised that it was a very dark situation for women in the country[62].

As events unfolded and the prospect of large and unprecedented lump sum pension payments loomed large, Javier Chercolés was keen to consider a new phase of project work which would provide a level of financial advice, where requested, to the Spectrum beneficiaries, particularly the widows. Although Inditex and the ITGLWF had formally committed to the joint resolution of industrial relations issues in the company's supply chain in October 2007 with the signing of the first international framework agreement in the sector (Miller 2011), a joint Inditex/ITGLWF widows' project had been for Neil Kearney one step too far, and he had made this known some months earlier.

Chercolés was nevertheless concerned in particular about the well-being of the widows[63], who stood, under the gender equity terms of the scheme, to receive substantial amounts of money made out in their name as the scheme was wound up:

> ... to pay a cheque to any widow in this kind of situation would be the end of the project and the end of the life of the widow. I realised I had to dramatically change the approach and the calculation. I decided to spend my whole Xmas time at home because I didn't feel so happy after the death of my friend and I began to read everything about Bangladesh... The first book I read was published by the World Health Organisation. This showed Bangladesh as worst country in the world for VAW[64].

The ITGLWF at this time had been cast in turmoil by Kearney's death and Patrick Itschert, the incoming General Secretary, was too preoccupied with the responsibilities of his new position to be able to grasp the complexities of the now unfolding situation concerning the payment of pensions in Bangladesh. (As Regional European Secretary of the ITGLWF, he had however been acutely aware of the Spectrum case since it had been largely European headquartered multinationals which had been sourcing from the company). Consequently Chercolés would be driving this new 'phase' of the project unilaterally until the new General Secretary was in a position to meet his counterpart early in 2010 to discuss the continuation of the global framework agreement and those elements of joint work which fell within its scope.

It is widely accepted that in most disaster situations women and children are among the groups most frequently at risk[65]. From his initial researches on violence against women in Bangladesh, the Inditex director of CSR, felt that a risk assessment needed to be undertaken in relation to the widows and their children. To make this robust, some triangulation of data would be necessary. During the first few months of 2010, he commissioned research from three organisations which had published reports on VAW in Bangladesh – ASK, which had been previously involved in Spectrum related activities, Naripokkho, a women's activist NGO[66] and BJMAS[67], the Bangladesh National Woman Lawyer's Association (aka BNWLA). ASK was commissioned to provide data on VAW at a national level, while Naripokkho was tasked with researching the incidence of police cases at Thana level (local police station) in the communities where the widows lived, and with identifying local social partners who might be in a position to support the widows in future and with interviewing each woman to subjectively determine the extent of the perceived risk. BNWLA was requested to compile data of cases concerning VAW which had come before the courts in those districts where the widows resided. The findings, focusing on data from cases filed under suppression of violence against women and children regarding the matter of dowry from 2008–9 revealed a dark picture as can be seen from Table 6 below:

Location	Torture for Dowry 2008	Torture for Dowry 2009	Total	Murder for Dowry 2008	Murder for Dowry 2009	Total
DHAKA	1316	1888	3204	212	73	285
CHITTAGONG	848	485	1333	61	62	123
RAJSHAHI	1810	1903	3713	231	562	793
KHULNA	1013	889	1902	409	327	736
BORISAL	513	141	654	93	126	219
SYLHET	284	69	353	144	75	219

Source: BNWLA.

Table 6: Cases filed under Suppression of Violence against Women and Children Tribunal (2008–2009) regarding Dowry[68].

Significantly, over fifty per cent of acid attacks on women and children in 2009 were related to dowry and land, property and money[69]. The survey of seventeen of the widows covered by the Spectrum scheme revealed that twelve of their families had handed over dowry during their marriages, while only one had received dower following the wedding[70]. Moreover seventy per cent of the widows had come under pressure from their in laws following the disaster and fifteen of the seventeen had moved back into their parent's home or were living independently at the time of the research interview. Receiving compensation under the Friendship initiatives had already made some widows fearful for their daughter's safety[71] and it was clear that this assistance (both financial and in kind) had not reached all the widows, being diverted instead to the in-laws[72]. Finally, when interviewed, half of the widows responded that they had seen little of the income generation activities provided by the two Friendship relief initiatives[73].

Chercolés had begun to steep himself in a study of Islamic law and the culture of village life in Bangladesh and now understood that three potential obstacles stood in the way of the widows being able to enjoy their entitlements under the scheme: *'patrilineal kinship'* – the expectation (strong in Muslim culture) that the (male) head of the household should be the sole recipient of any benefit, the *'para'*, or local neighbourhoods in which the family remains a tightly knit unit, and *'Purdah'*, the practice of segregating women from men (2011). This brought him to the somewhat paradoxical conclusion that in order to ensure that a widow received (formally at least) her due entitlement, there might have to be a re-apportionment of the entitlements to the beneficiaries in line with the shares as set down in Muslim Family Law in Bangladesh. This would retreat from the principle of gender equality, which had always guided the development of the scheme, since the share would be reduced from full entitlement as a spouse to one quarter if with child, and to 1/8th without child in line with the Koran[74].

Chercolés was of the view that if at the same time the head of household received a 'just' share under the common law, then a degree of risk to the widow, who would now receive her entirely legitimate but significantly reduced entitlement, might be lifted. This of course would by no means be guaranteed within a family unit. The research which he had commissioned now became the so-called 'Purdah Project', and the triangulation could be completed late in

July, when seventeen remaining widows were interviewed in detail for the purposes of assessing the level of subjective risk and the need for voluntary local monitoring and support systems to be put in place. In order to address the differential in their awarded benefit, his plan, still to be approved by Inditex and the ITGLWF/BNC, was for the widows to be offered separate and confidential financial advice with three quarters or seven eighths of their true entitlement made available in a voluntary separate 'Portfolio' project established specifically for their benefit.

In March 2010, Chercolés sent a draft strategy document in March to the newly elected President of the BGMEA. His intention was to persuade the employers of the need for a voluntary protocol which could act as a framework relief scheme for the RMG sector. At the end of April he invited senior officers of the BGMEA to talks at the Inditex company headquarters in la Coruna, where progress might be made towards the adoption of his draft industry wide compensation protocol based on the modified Spectrum relief scheme for workers in the RMG sector[75]. The employers were now in a somewhat different frame of mind. There had been new elections in the BGMEA, and the new Awami League government of Sheik Hasina had created a different environment for dialogue. There was also a new sense of urgency brought about a spate of factory fires in the first few months of the year. The employers appeared ready to countenance a discussion about a protocol for the sector.

Since the ITGLWF had convened a multi-stakeholder meeting on fire prevention in Dhaka for July this proved a favourable moment for Inditex to expedite the payment of outstanding lump sum pensions which were owing to the families up to 2009, the aim being to close the scheme in October that year. Since this would be an opportunity for the unions to continue to press for a compensation fund for the RMG, the BNC was anxious to invite government ministers along to the distribution of the cheques. Chercolés for his part was most keen to hold the meeting at the offices of the BGMEA to keep their commitment to a compensation protocol for the RMG sector alive, something which would have been inconceivable two years previously. His plans, however, were thrown into disarray as the date for the declaration of a new national minimum wage for the sector clashed with the dates which had been set for the July cheque distribution.

Since the BNC had been campaigning for a BDT 5.000 minimum and the employers were unprepared to concede even a 3,000 figure without a package of support measures from the government, it was clearly not politic for the two parties to be sharing a platform at this time.

The RMG sector was in a volatile state during this period, fuelled by the contradictory forces which had been unleashed by the global recession and the lifting of the China safeguards. Business continued to boom[76], with apparel exports amounting to US$12.496bn value worldwide during in 2009–2010 – some seventy-seven per cent of the country's total exports of US$16.204bn. Consumer demand for cheap clothing remained as high as ever, with knitwear continuing to perform well. In order to offset their losses brought on by the recession, many buyers had turned to increasing their sourcing from Bangladesh, but again the workers were bearing the brunt of the boom on the back of a 'price war' (Mirdha, 2009). Amid official reports of delayed wage payments, failure to pay the minimum wage and wage cuts, the RMG sector had begun to unravel once again in 2009 with persistent riots at RMG factories in Ashulia, near Savar. Underlying tensions which had been simmering during much of the first half of 2010 boiled to the surface as the deadline for the declaration of the new minimum wage for the sector approached. July was marked, once again, by serious worker disturbances both inside and outside factories in Dhaka[77].

Having brought a number of the families to Dhaka in anticipation of the BGMEA event Inditex nevertheless arranged cheque distribution events in late July, early August. The group of widows, agreed to assist the company with its research, and a small number of other beneficiaries (nine) were handed cheques covering interim payments at events at Caritas and the Inditex offices on the 27 and 29 July. Once the new Minimum Wage had been declared on the 29 July the remaining families and injured were invited to a high profile event held at the offices of the BGMEA on 3 August. The meeting was attended by Minister for Labour, the Chairman of the Parliamentary Standing Committee for Labour and Employment, and representatives of the BGMEA, the BNC and Inditex. At the event Roy Ramesh of the BNC served notice that the final payments would be made later in the year. In September 2010, however, events took a dramatic turn. Quite suddenly and unexpectedly, Javier Chercolés, the sole remaining

Last Nightshift in Savar

architect and driver of the Spectrum scheme, tendered his resignation. All efforts in respect of the widows and the closure of the scheme now had to be put on hold as the company looked for a successor. When an appointment was made in November, the ITGLWF swiftly moved to secure undertakings from the company that the incoming director of CSR would secure the final transfer of pension payments in line with the principles of the original scheme.

Although there was now no one personally driving the protocol initiative outside of Bangladesh, the issue of a trust fund was still very much on the agenda for the BNC and other unions in the RMG, and their demands were given renewed impetus when, within just days of a follow up multi-stakeholder meeting on fire prevention convened by the ITGLWF in Dhaka on 4 and 5 December[78], a serious fire broke out at the *That's It* sportswear factory belonging to the Hameem group (Daily Star, 2010c). Because *That's It* was supplying numerous US brands and retailers, key North American NGOs[79] were now drawn into the debate. Anxious to ensure that negotiations on a compensation package remained in Bangladesh and involved all stakeholders, the ITGLWF convened a meeting with the key buyers, the owner, the BGMEA, the CCC, the Worker Rights Consortium, the BNC and a number of other Bangladeshi trade union organisations to coincide with the final Spectrum payout scheduled for 16 April 2011.

Figure 15. Distribution of cheques to the families of the deceased at the BGMEA headquarters August 2010. Photo courtesy: Inditex.

As the parties to the meeting gathered to digest a new set of compensation proposals (See Appendix 6) based on the principles of the Spectrum scheme in the offices of the BGMEA, elsewhere in the building a final cheque distribution ceremony was taking place attended by the Minister of Commerce, the President of the BGMEA and BNC, a representative from the Spanish Embassy, the new General Secretary of the ITGLWF and the new global director of CSR at Inditex. Representatives of all the families of the victims were in attendance, as were some eighteen unaccounted for injured Spectrum workers who had come forward to request a medical assessment from Inditex. At the back of the hall sat the owner who had, some three months earlier, paid a further 100,000 Taka to each of the families. Significantly, Javier Chercolés' concerns for the widows' safety had been heeded as the announcement was made that any widow requiring support and assistance in managing her benefits would be provided support on a voluntary basis from Naripokkho and the BNLWA.

CHAPTER 7

Plus ça change,
plus c'est la même chose.
Assessing the Outcomes

The Spectrum factory collapse was a wake-up call for the authorities in Bangladesh, rendered all the more urgent by the need for the RMG sector to maintain its competitiveness in the light of the expiry of the Agreement on Textiles and Clothing at the end of 2004. The Bangladesh Government and the exporters' associations knew that some major changes were going to be necessary both in the civil service and in the RMG sector, specifically in the area of building safety, worker compensation and risk and disaster management to meet the social compliance requirements of their international buyers. However, the responses demanded by the national and international unions and labour rights organisations were far reaching and, significantly, involved the buyers too. In assessing the impact of the Spectrum disaster it is necessary to examine the original sets of demands in relation to each party and attempt to explain the reasons for the particular outcomes in relation to those demands.

As we saw in Chapter Four, a number of trade union and labour rights organizations in Bangladesh articulated a series of demands made at demonstrations and rallies into a Charter which they submitted to the BGMEA and then formalized into the PIL writ submitted to the High Court of Bangladesh. The first set of demands focussed on the arrest of the owner, a prompt enquiry to determine the actual reason for the collapse, a determination of the ownership of the land, the legality of the construction and the liability of the owners for compensation of the victims. Pending the outcome of such an enquiry, appropriate action was called for in respect of the owners continued membership of the

BGMEA. Although the owners did finally surrender themselves to a Dhaka court almost a month after the collapse, and were later sent to jail, they were released on bail after a two week period of custody but had to make numerous court appearances between 2005 and 2007. There was probably never any intention on the part of the BGMEA to expel the Spectrum owners and, any future court case notwithstanding, the current evidence, as contained in the most authoritative unofficial study to date of the structural causes of the collapse tends to suggest that it was caused by systemic collective failure rather than any negligence on the part of the owners. (IEB report Part 2) This of course did not stop civil society organisations in Bangladesh from demanding changes in labour law to apply the principle of corporate criminal responsibility as a means of enabling companies to take compliance systems much more seriously (Islam 2006:2).

Demands also focussed on very specific material redress for the victims of the disaster – namely a determination of the precise workforce size for the purposes of establishing a pool of beneficiaries, and compensation for the families of the dead varying from an unspecified amount in excess of BDT 100,000 to BDT 700,000 (approx €8,471 as at April 2005), short and long term medical care and hospitalisation costs for those injured (including replacement of limbs) and arrangements for rehabilitation, and re-employment of the Spectrum workers. Local trade unions and NGOs had called for compensation to always take into account expected lifetime earnings of the deceased or injured worker and the number of dependants. Although legal action commenced in Bangladesh for the case to be tried under the Fatal Accidents Act of 1955, which would, according to some lawyers, have seen pay outs in excess of BDT one million (€12,677), the combined pay outs under both the Friendship and Inditex/ITGLWF schemes far exceeded this figure in a number of cases. Moreover there was the issue of payment of outstanding wages and overtime and redundancy entitlements, since under Bangladesh labour law workers were entitled to four months wages in the event of factory closure.

Although the compensation amounts to each of the families of the deceased were nominally split between an amount determined under the WCA (BDT 21,000) and awarded through the Labour Court[1] and a further BDT 79,000 which the BGMEA had specified as an appropriate additional amount to round the total compensation figure to BDT 100,000, the whole amount was bankrolled by the owner as were some of the initial medical costs. The additional amount of BDT 79,000 was deposited by the owner in the BGMEA account for distribution by the employer's association to the families in a separate event. Further 'cash assistance' was provided by the owner on numerous occasions principally to the injured although a further cash payment of BDT 100,000 was made to each of the victims' families in March 2011[2]. No financial assistance was forthcoming, either from the Government or the BGMEA. The long term rehabilitation costs of the injured and those of the families of the deceased were met by the efforts of the buyers in the form of sporadic lump sum payments under the medium- to long-term voluntary relief scheme initiated by Inditex and the ITGLWF and the short term rehabilitation efforts initiated by Carrefour and continued by KarstadtQuelle, Cotton Group, Scapino and Steilmann.

Figure 16: Shafiqul Islam in his new job at the reception of the Inditex sourcing office in Dhaka.

All of the fifty workers cited in the NGWF claim to the Labour Inspection Department were finally paid their outstanding wages by the owner and it was estimated that by September 2005 some sixty per cent of the workers had found new jobs. One year after the collapse, the NGWF approached Carrefour to accommodate some fifty-seven workers in their suppliers who had still not found employment. To date no severance payments have been forthcoming for the displaced Spectrum workers. In the matter of employment for former workers, it has to be assumed that most workers were able to find employment in the industry, while a number of the injured have now been rehabilitated in some cases and employed by agents and suppliers of Inditex[3]. In Shafiqul Islam's case, he now has a position as a receptionist in the new wheelchair accessible Inditex sourcing office in Dhaka and is learning Spanish and English.[4] A promise of employment was also made by the owner to those eligible family members of the deceased expressing a wish to work in his new factory[5].

The national sectoral demands

In addition to the set of more immediate demands, the Spectrum disaster provoked an offensive by organised labour to bring about more systemic change in the management of health and safety in the RMG sector. Calls came from the Workers Safety Forum, and the Bangladesh unions supported by ITGLWF, and CCC, for some far reaching yet still quite short term measures. These included the establishment of a tripartite committee to undertake an urgent structural review of all multi-storey buildings currently in use as garment production units and an inspection of safety precautions and working conditions in every RMG factory – specifically access and exit routes and evacuation procedures.[6] For the CCC, such an oversight committee had to have international expertise (in the form of ILO technical assistance). Furthermore, should any unauthorized buildings be found without adequate safety measures, the authorities were called upon to take firm action against the owners particularly in the RMG production centres of greater Dhaka, Narayanganj and Chittagong.

Whilst the BGMEA and the BKMEA did not disclose their respective rules of association to the trade unions and NGOs, an additional demand made by Civil Society, the government and the employers were nevertheless spurred into action in relation to the issue of factory compliance. After the Spectrum incident, it became a pre-condition for any new factory to obtain membership with BGMEA to submit the structural design, an engineer approved certificate and the approval from the relevant authority e.g. whether RAJUK, Local Government Regional Development Board, or Paurashava. Already prior to the Spectrum disaster, Group Insurance had become mandatory for member companies covering accidents both inside and outside the factory premises and as at 2011 indemnifying an employer to an amount of BDT 200,000 per worker[7]. Several days after the first buyers' mission (on 11 June 2005), the Government, clearly concerned about the impact of compliance failure on the ability of the RMG to compete effectively in a post quota world, responded to these demands at a roundtable organised by the German GTZ with a decision to establish a so-called 'Social Compliance Forum' (SCF) for the RMG which would be chaired by the Minister of Commerce. The Forum's inaugural meeting was held on 1 August 2005 and one of its first decisions was to set up two proposed taskforces for health and safety and welfare respectively. In addition, a Compliance Monitoring Cell (CMC) was established in the Export Promotion Bureau, the purpose of which was to function as a secretariat for the SCF and collate national data on the compliance status of the RMG factories. The work plan of the CMC involved establishing an overview of garment units and buying houses, and an instruction to member firms to participate in the respective BGMEA and BKMEA group insurance schemes and to submit the structural design and layout plans for approval within 3 months. The submission of approved plans would be critical for registration with the Export Promotion Bureau, without which export licences would not be granted.

One of the first tasks undertaken by the BGMEA was to commission structural surveys of a number of member companies' units. Out of an initial total of 169 inspected factories, three were identified as highly risky structures that might collapse without warning, and served with a notice to either move to different premises or renovate the buildings[8]. This could be interpreted as a somewhat conservative figure when compared with the ninety per cent figure of vulnerable RMG units claimed by a SKOP study following the factory collapse (Daily Star, 2005s). Although the trade unions had called for a tripartite approach to factory inspections, this had not materialised although there was tripartite representation within the SCF. Because of the spate of garment factory disasters early in 2006, BGMEA surveillance teams inspected 2,435 garments factories in Dhaka and 575 factories in Chittagong between April and June to monitor fire safety measures. Fire drills had been undertaken in 1,865 units/factories, during which forty factories had been discovered with locked exits and a further twenty one units with exit routes blocked with merchandise awaiting despatch.[9] The CIFE had already lodged cases against ninety-two garment units in Dhaka city alone for lacking adequate emergency escape facilities, but due to understaffing had been unable to follow this up (Daily Star 2006c). As far as building safety was concerned, an announcement was made at the third meeting of the SCF in April 2006 that the period for submission of structural plans was to be relaxed to one year, and that building inspections would henceforth be the responsibility of the RAJUK and not the task force on Occupational Health and Safety[10]. Furthermore, the Forum dropped its plans to identify and demolish unfit buildings[11]. (Uddin K. 2006)

Demands for changes in the national legislation

Calls for legislative change came in four key areas: the law on occupational health and safety; building regulations; worker compensation and the establishment of a Workers' Welfare Trust Fund. Under the terms of the Bangladesh Labour Act, which was rushed through by the Government in 2006, new offences were introduced for violations of the law leading to death or injury which can result in a fine of BDT 100,000 or imprisonment of up to four years – a small sum but significant in contrast to the BDT 1,000 under the old law. Whereas in the past, criminal offences under the Factories Act were prosecuted in the Magistrate's court, all prosecutions for offences now had to take place in the Labour Court. Under Section 313, the right of prosecution has been given to a wider category of people, in particular an 'aggrieved person or trade union'. The Labour Act also increased the level of compensation for death to BDT 100,000 which can be increased to BDT 125,000 in the event of permanent disability[12]. After the money has been deposited by the owner, the labour court summons the dependents to court to determine how the money is to be distributed, in contrast to the principles of the

Spectrum Relief Scheme which had nominated the spouse/widow in the first instance in the case of a married victim[13].

For injury, the Law established four categories: permanent total disability; temporary total disability; permanent partial disability; and temporary partial disability. Payments in relation to each specific category are made based on a percentage laid down in a schedule under the terms of the Act. Significantly – unlike the parameters of the Spectrum Relief Scheme – such payments are time bound. For the permanently disabled, the victim receives a one off lump sum payment of BDT 125,000 and in the other categories of disability, employers would be expected to continue to pay wages for up to a year but these would reduce after each two months in the case of Category Three and Four victims[14]. The Act does, however, enable individual agreements to be reached between the injured party and the employer in relation to amounts and duration of payment[15].

Whilst this is certainly a move in the right direction, and appears to parallel elements of the Inditex/ITGLWF Relief Scheme, commentators have suggested that this would place a new strain on the Factory Inspectorate, since filing criminal complaints against employers will inevitably be resisted because convictions can lead to imprisonment. This will almost certainly require an increase in legal staff on the part of the CIFE to the potential detriment of further investment in field staff[16]. Given that the old provisions in relation to compensation for accident related incapacity were scarcely heeded by the employers, it remains to be seen whether these changes will impact on employer behaviour in any future cases.

In November 2006 the Government passed a National Building Code to establish minimum standards for the design, construction, quality of materials, use and occupancy, location, and maintenance of all buildings within Bangladesh in order to safeguard within achievable limits, life, limb, health, property and public welfare. Under the organisational enforcement sections of the Code, the Government was to establish an 'authority' for the purpose of administering and enforcing the code provisions including necessary inspectors (section 2.1.3), building notice and orders (section 2.2.5), and construction approval (section 2.2.7). In January 2008, the Bangladesh Legal Aid and Services Trust (BLAST) and the Bangladesh Occupational Safety, Health and Environment Foundation (OSHE) jointly filed a writ petition in the High Court Division to redress the failure of the government to establish an agency to enforce the Code in particular the provisions relating to worker safety issues. Six years into the enactment of this Code, no such authority has been established. However, in October 2010 the High Court Division of the Bangladesh Supreme Court directed the government of Bangladesh to set up an enforcement authority in Bangladesh within a year of the judgement[17].

The fourth legislative enactment which entered the statute books with little fanfare, yet can be viewed as an outcome of the efforts of those involved in the Spectrum campaign, is the creation of a Workers Welfare Foundation. In her May Day speech 2006, Prime Minister Khaleda Zia announced the creation of a Foundation for the Welfare of Labour, clearly in an effort to appease the electorate, and a volatile mass of RMG workers in particular. The Bangladesh Labour Welfare Foundation Act[18], 2006 (Act XXV of 2006) came into force on the 1 October 2006, its main objective being to support victims of industrial accidents and their family members and dependants through grants and projects, to extend financial assistance to any disabled workers, including meeting medical expenses, providing financial assistance to family dependants and crucially, obliging employers to participate in a group insurance scheme. The Foundation Board is tripartite in structure (See Appendix Five) and its finances were to be established through individual grant, and government and industrial donations. However, one year into its life, the Foundation was still rudderless under the interim government which had still not allocated a budget nor made it mandatory for employers to pay into this Fund (Daily Star, 2007) In 2007, the Manusher Jonno Foundation (MJF), the Bangladesh Institute of Labour Studies (BILS), Bangladesh Legal Aid and Services Trust (Blast), INCIDIN Bangladesh, the NGWF, and Karmojibi Nari jointly organised a press conference to publicise the content of the law but also the lack of progress in its implementation. This prompted the Government to formally constitute the Foundation although an injection of funds had still not been forthcoming even after the election of the new Government in 2008. The Foundation has convened on thirty-two occasions since its inception, principally to focus on establishing rules for the governing body and to collate available funds[18]. Understandably, deficiency of funds has been a major issue with the Government expecting companies to allocate five per cent of their profits under section 243(2) of the Bangladesh Labour Act, 2006. In this matter the Government contracted MJF to undertake a study in 2008 on sources and prospects for voluntary funding of the Foundation by business. The study focussed on two major issues – the identification of eligible companies and a review of allocation of profit under the terms of the Act. Having considered the eligibility of fifty major companies in Bangladesh, the authors projected that in 2006 some BDT 32 million would have been available from forty-six of those companies (including twenty per cent from the textile, garment and footwear sector). The figure for 2007 was calculated at 34 million. The Foundation thus could have, year on year, a significant funding base particularly for the Welfare Fund. However, the Act as yet, has no jurisdiction to render such transfers of profit legally enforceable (Sharif, 2008). Significantly, recommendations from a study published in 2007 by Adam Smith International and the Asia Development Bank for a social protection system for women in the RMG not only called for a significant level of subsidisation, but a sector based approach rather than an individual enterprise based scheme (Adam Smith International/ADB, 2007).

The international demands to the buyers

In the demands made to the buyers by the ITGLWF and CCC, four main areas were addressed: ensuring exemplary compensation as well as the payment of any outstanding wages or benefits and, if necessary, taking joint responsibility for this along with the owner; examining the failure to detect the hazards at the factory, including disclosure of any relevant audit reports; taking urgent measures to ensure code compliance throughout the buyer's supply chain and disclosing full details of the same to trade unions and civil society. We have noted the different responses of the buyers, with respect to the issue of compensation and outstanding wages. In the end, only Inditex appeared to acknowledge this through its actions, although this was never formally stated by the company[19]. None of the buyers published any of their audit reports. Apart from an absence of any reports for Spectrum Sweaters, most continue to consider these documents to be confidential and a matter for disclosure only to the supplier. For a number of buyers implicated in the collapse, work was undertaken to tighten up their compliance systems, particularly in Bangladesh.

In its first full year (2005) the BSCI, undoubtedly affected by the Spectrum disaster, had established an auditing guideline that member companies should audit two thirds of their suppliers in the case of soft goods (textiles) in defined risk countries (which included Bangladesh) within three years (BSCI, 2005: 6). In the case of Carrefour, FIDH had already decided to stop its systematic monitoring of audits in 2004 in order to focus on specific initiatives to advance human rights in the company's supply chain (Crabbé, Leroy and Caudron *op.cit.*). Cotton Group, mindful of orders still being processed at Shahriyar Fabrics, commissioned Intertek only two months after the collapse, to undertake an audit of the facility at the behest of the BSCI[20]. Inditex, as part of a broader strategy of moving towards direct sourcing, took the decision to establish an in country sourcing office with a dedicated CSR function. There was little response to the fourth demand for disclosure of locations. Inditex did, however, disclose its Bangladesh supplier base to the ITGLWF affiliates given the concern about factory safety,[21] but no other buyer obliged.

The continuing health and safety crisis in the RMG

Despite the huge concern generated by the Spectrum disaster for safety in the factories, much of the attention had been focussed on cure rather than prevention. Despite new prohibition powers assigned to labour inspectors in the country, permitting them to close down premises deemed unsafe[22], the number of medical/engineering inspectors for the economy as a whole was now down to seventeen (from twenty-one in 1984) (Centre for Corporate Accountability, 2009:5). Every sign pointed towards the need for renewed efforts to deal with preventative OHS, and the employers were once again on the back foot in February 2010, when a fire broke out at Garib and Garib (CCC, 2010c) leading to the deaths of twenty-one workers and the hospitalisation of a further six workers. The following month, there was a stampede at Matrix Sweaters in Gazipur, after a striplight exploded resulting in the death a worker and thirty injured (Daily Star, 2010a). Then, in April, a further twenty workers were injured following a fire at Tung Hi Knit and Sweater (Daily Star, 2010b). Garib and Garib had been the most serious incident of the three, particularly since there had been a fire there six months previously and the familiar pattern – overloaded capacity, poor electrical installation, blocked exits and no ventilation for smoke – was an indication that little appeared to have been learned in terms of occupational health and safety since the establishment of the Compliance Cell in 2005.

The principal buyer in the Garib & Garib case was H&M, but despite efforts by the ITGLWF and Inditex to offer guidance to the Swedish company and calls by the Clean Clothes Campaign to consider the key features of the Spectrum scheme, H&M sought to approach the issue of victim relief differently and unilaterally[23]. Their voluntary programme included a lump sum payment for the children as well as the elderly dependants; monthly payments for children up until the age of eighteen; counselling for the injured workers; and jobs offered to family members of the deceased or injured workers who were over eighteen years old. H&M did not regard this programme as a compensation scheme which they insisted was the responsibility of the Government and employers in Bangladesh. Although they accepted that they had a responsibility to ensure that existing compensation, as laid down in national law and custom and practice, was duly paid in line with their responsibility for ensuring compliance with other standards on worker rights, they were not in favour of launching their own pension scheme for the families of the victims[24].

Although there had been some movement in the lump sum compensation to BDT 250,000 in the Garib & Garib case (100,000 under the Labour Act of 2006 plus a further BDT 150,000 voluntary sum provided by the BGMEA/owner's insurance), across all industries, employers were continuing to flaunt the law, paying the families of the victims of industrial accidents directly instead of through the Labour Court and in three quarters of all cases (102*) less than half of the new statutory entitlement (Centre for Corporate Accountability, 2007:15). An exemplary relief and compensation scheme for the sector was thus still very much the order of the day. Notwithstanding the readiness or otherwise of the parties to resort to existing institutions, the architecture was now available in the form of the Labour Welfare Foundation but the vexed question of resourcing such a fund had still to be addressed.

The fires of early 2010 and the disasters of 2005 (notably KTS and Phoenix) had provided further evidence of the continued absence of a sustainable preventative compliance framework in the RMG sector, an issue which the ITGLWF was acutely aware of and which was in the process of being addressed through a series of meetings with key buyers and BGMEA members. The extent of the problem was revealed, when within just days of a follow up multi-stakeholder meeting on fire prevention convened by the ITGLWF in Dhaka on 4 and 5 December[25], a serious fire engulfed the ninth floor of the ten storey Ha-Meem Group's sportswear factory in the Ashulia industrial area. The incident occurred at lunchtime while most of the 6000 workers were fortunately outside, but 150 workers remained trapped inside and twenty-eight perished, while several dozen suffered severe burns (Daily Star, 2010d). Because *That's It* was supplying numerous US brands and retailers, key North American NGOs[26] were now drawn into the debate and a period of intensive consultations between Washington, Brussels and Dhaka resulted in two meetings being arranged in Dhaka on the 16–18 April to discuss a workable fire prevention programme for the RMG as well as a benchmark compensation package for the victims of the Hameem fire. The Hameem compensation proposals projected some BDT 1.7 million for each worker and drew heavily on the principles of the Inditex/ITGLWF Relief Scheme [27], and the union and NGO side made a strong case for buyer involvement in any package. As the (predominantly) US buyers adjourned to consider the proposals, it was clear to all that this new set of demands was going to push against the existing limits of corporate social responsibility. It is to these issues we must now turn.

CHAPTER 8

Conclusion – Spectrum and the limits of corporate social responsibility

Given the voluntary and privatised nature of buyer interventions in social compliance in their supply chains, multinationals currently have great discretion both in terms of the decision to intervene in any given situation and the magnitude of their intervention. Responses can of course range from zero reaction through varieties of engagement to a 'transformative' action on the part of a buyer (Mirvis and Googins, 2006). The buyer responses to the Spectrum disaster which can be located all along this continuum displayed an acute lack of solidarity. This absence of consensus hinged on different corporate viewpoints on three fundamental and interrelated questions in CSR. Firstly, for what is business responsible? Secondly, how proportionate should a CSR response be? Thirdly, to what extent can individual buyer actions constitute replicable models for intervention across a sector and perhaps beyond?

The privatization of social compliance has entailed a fragmentation of initiatives and duplication of effort in particular as an ever complex ethical trading agenda has opened up across the global apparel sector. At some point, multinational buyers with any commitment to CSR, have to confront the decision whether to go it alone or join with competitors in rationalizing their social compliance efforts, or engage in a mix of both. For a number of European retailers, various options have presented themselves involving essentially national programmes in the countries where they are headquartered such as the Ethical Trading Initiatives of the UK[1] and Norway[2], the Dutch Fair Wear Foundation[3] and the German Round Table on Codes of Conduct[4].

Some of these initiatives have member companies headquartered in other parts of the world and operating in different sectors, and all (to varying degrees) are built on multi-stakeholder principles with trade union and NGO participation in both governance structures and project activities. However, by the middle of the decade new initiatives had emerged as some companies, tired of 'inefficient and unproductive cross-sectoral partnerships', looked to industry initiatives which eschew the stakeholder principle (Egels-Zanden and Wahlqvist, 2007). The Business Social Compliance Initiative, established in 2002, was launched as just such an initiative by the European Foreign Trade Association in Brussels, providing a common platform for European retail companies with the aim of creating convergence in social auditing in particular[5]. A number of the buyers at Spectrum: Inditex, KarstadtQuelle, Multiline[6] and Cotton Group were members of the BSCI at the time of the collapse. As we have seen in Chapter 5, it was indeed the BSCI which posed the first critical CSR question, by taking the position that buyers could not be held responsible for failures to ensure the structural safety of factory buildings in a supplier country. Whilst the BSCI could not prevent its members from engaging individually, it was concerned about any precedents which the Inditex/ITGLWF initiative might set. This was certainly KarstadtQuelle's apprehension of the scheme expressed in their mission report late in 2005, and their questions went to the heart of the matter. Originally conceived as a voluntary indemnity scheme with the immediate purpose of providing relief to the victims of the disaster and their families in the form of a pension, it nevertheless had strategic intent as a replicable intervention model for similar countries where worker compensation schemes are non-existent or underdeveloped. Was the Inditex/ITGLWF scheme in this respect an intervention too far? Was this, moreover, a response which was misguided? In seeking to be a global citizen, and to develop a replicable instrument for poverty alleviation, was Inditex, in partnership with the ITGLWF, and other buyers who were prepared to come on board, not running the risk of becoming 'maverick' (Blowfield, 2008:1) in the process? Critical questions were thus posed regarding the appropriateness of the scheme for Bangladesh. It was this which brought about the ultimate switch by a number of fellow buyers which had been sourcing from Spectrum from the Inditex/

ITGLWF Relief Scheme to the Friendship Rehabilitation initiatives in 2006. However, at the other end, criticisms of the suitability of the Friendship Rehabilitation initiative came from Civil Society, and these same NGOs then turned their critical gaze on to the implementation of the Inditex/ITGLWF relief scheme. Hence it is necessary to look critically at each of these charges in turn.

A response too far?

Spectrum attracted widespread international publicity and as soon as brand names became associated with the case, irrespective of the degree of their corporate social culpability, the task for the respective CSR managers was first and foremost 'reputation management', given that an array of international civil society organisations were hovering above. As we have seen, there was wide variation in buyer response. Some were, and to this day still are, oblivious to the fact that their product was being sourced from the factory. Others chose to bury their heads in the sand. Most of the bigger retailers which were implicated, began in denial, either out of ignorance that they were sourcing there, or because their orders had not been current. As events unfolded, and more information came to light, they felt compelled to respond as the campaigning activities of the Clean Clothes Campaign in particular began to impact at home. Initially, with the exception of Carrefour, they proceeded under the umbrella of the Inditex scheme proposal but disengaged after 8 months because of a desire not to become too committed to an intervention which clearly was now going to be quite a long term effort, where the establishment of a trust fund began to look increasingly unlikely, and also because any buyer involvement in such a fund could be seen as tantamount to an admission of partial if not joint responsibility for the factory collapse. Most certainly, the ITGLWF and CCC took the view that the retailers were 'jointly responsible' for failing to uncover ongoing violations at the factory of their own codes of conduct and national labour law, and urged them to disclose the relevant audit reports for Spectrum. The legal notion of 'joint responsibility' is a concept which nationally has some validity in labour law in the USA where it was developed initially in the wake of the US 1938 Fair Labour Standards Act, and deployed to address the problem of interstate undercutting of wages and conditions by clients and their contractors. More recently this concept has been applied in cases in the USA where the buyer has been 'joined' with the vendor concerning failure to pay due wages (see Greenwald Doherty, 2009). Given falling FOB prices (cf. Miller, 2010), an argument could be construed in a global context that buyers were not accounting for compliance costs in the prices they paid for their garments. As we have seen, at one stage CCC were keen to examine the possibility of mounting an international legal case. However, the absence of existing case law, the testing question of jurisdiction in this area, and crucially, the absence of an International Labour Court were all factors ultimately militating against this course of action.

Had such a case been pursued internationally, the 'responsibility' test might have hinged on the extent to which due diligence was exercised by the buyers, the factory management and those auditing companies acting on behalf of the buyers in respect of health and safety at Spectrum. Whilst there had been some serious lapses in factory safety, the critical question relates to the extent to which such a collapse might have been foreseen by both parties, and here the issue of cracks or gaps opening up and the detection of the same might arguably have been pivotal. However, whilst Spectrum was linked to the Shahriyar building, the two were in fact separate constructions. An official but unpublished document concerning the cause of the collapse found no evidence of cracks or widening gaps[7] and other sources relating to this issue were contradictory[8].

It would have required a fully functioning well trained health and safety committee and managers with the technical competence to have identified the need for a structural survey and possible evacuation of the building. However, at this time Bangladesh labour law made no provision for a workplace health and safety committee. Since at this time, few, if any factory audit schedules in the world included either a structural survey or evidence of the same, and no audits had been undertaken at the factory, it is perhaps unreasonable to have expected anyone other than a qualified structural engineer to have predicted such a structural weakness, which as evidence seems to suggest, had been occurring several feet under the ground over a period of 5 years.

Does this vindicate the position of the BSCI? Whilst the argument is a strong one, that structural defects in factory units are the responsibility of the owner and the relevant national oversight authorities, one has to view the bigger picture of uncontrolled free for all expansion in Bangladesh, as buyers and suppliers went in search of quick profits at the expense of the available resources in the country, and the lack of buyer overview of their own supply chains, where subcontracting appeared to be rife. Ironically in their Annual Report in 2006, the BSCI did establish a link between the actions of buyers and compliance issues including structural safety concerns:

> Due to the low cost of labour, Bangladesh is becoming an increasingly important producer of readymade garments. Strong growth in textile exports and severe competition has proven a challenge to many companies' production capacities, often resulting in extreme overtime work, piece-rate work, salaries below the legal minimum wage and child labour. The expansion of production has led to wild extensions of buildings, especially the construction of new storeys. This is problematic for the buildings' foundations, especially as Bangladesh is prone to flooding and has led to several accidents (BSCI, 2006: 21).

The need for speed in this expansion meant circumvention of any bureaucratic hurdles by whatever means possible, a state of affairs which still prevails today[9]. After Spectrum social audit methodology was nevertheless revised to include structural survey reports.

As the member companies of the BSCI and Carrefour declined on the grounds of non responsibility to be involved in the Trust Fund, this impacted on the ability of the Scheme to deliver payments to the victims/families, and left Inditex isolated within the BSCI. The company ended its association with the Initiative in 2007. Significantly, although Inditex at no point had conceded joint responsibility for the collapse, the company nevertheless sanctioned the continuation of financial support for the victims/families[10]. The Relief Scheme became a dedicated CSR project which focussed not just on what might be termed 'venture philanthropy', otherwise termed 'the adventurous funding of unpopular causes' (Edwards 2008: 21), but sought a higher aim beyond a humanitarian gesture, to 'transform' the system of worker compensation and relief, not just in Bangladesh but also in other countries, where worker welfare systems are particularly underdeveloped.

A disproportionate response?

Was the Inditex intervention disproportionate? Given that an order of only 3,000 Zara Boy units had been placed through Spectrum for the Inditex South American retail network by an Indian trader, and the company projected in excess of €500,000 to cover costs related to the scheme[11], the CSR intervention certainly appeared disproportionate when compared to other companies buying from the factory. However, Spectrum was deemed an 'emergency' item in the Annual Sustainability Reports and Accounts 2006–2009 and the average annual amount spent over the first 4 years was €61,112[12]. Compared with other financial commitments made by the company in respect of other 'emergencies' elsewhere in the world, these were modest annual expenditures.

In August 2006, however, Inditex received a communication from the Far East Asia Sourcing office of KarstadtQuelle raising a number of probing questions in relation to the appropriateness of the planned relief scheme which had been circulated to the buyers. Since KarstadtQuelle was now fully engaged with the Friendship Initiative, they were keen to know about measures in the Relief Scheme which would provide the means of sustainable income generation for the beneficiaries. There were questions about monitoring and the composition of the Board of Trustees, as well as the financial entity which was going to manage and oversee the funds and make transfers and payments in Bangladesh. KQ also had questions about the extent to which the social background and poverty level of the victims were going to be taken into account and the risk management procedures in the Scheme. There was particular concern that the payment of such high sums (by Bangladesh standards) might lead to social unrest and that such a scheme might discriminate against the victims of other accidents[13].

Income generation was a core principle underlying the approach of Friendship and as such was geared towards fast track, pragmatic and sustainable assistance. Until the second phase commenced in 2006, income generation had been provided in the form of a sewing machine to the widows and a rickshaw van to other beneficiaries in the victims' families, but this had done nothing to alleviate the poverty of the families in question[14]. As we have seen in Chapter 6, more substantial

IGAs were introduced to the families during 2006–2007 in place of compensation/pension. Beneficiaries had to choose a specific asset and received a cheque specifically for that purpose. Friendship's approach constituted a mix of paternalism, poverty alleviation and disaster relief. Whilst they were at pains to stress that their goal was long term and sustainable income generation, they stated in their proposal to Carrefour:

> It is easy to give money to the victims without caring for what or how they will manage it[15].

This of course runs counter to the notion of compensation which is a financial entitlement/reparation without preconditions for expenditure. For Runa Khan, Director of Friendship, the goals of their initiative were quite modest:

> What we wanted to do was put them up to a level of where they were before the disaster... You cannot make beggars out of people. You have to give them their dignity otherwise they cannot proceed[16].

Since the second phase of the Friendship initiative closed in the middle of 2007, there had been no follow up survey on the impact of the IGAs on the families of the Spectrum victims. Following discussions between the ITGLWF and Inditex about the possibility of financial advisory work with the families of the deceased, given the substantial lump sums likely to be forthcoming, Inditex undertook a telephone survey during July 2009 of a sample of the victims (ten injured workers and twenty-seven of the families of the deceased) to establish the true impact of the income generation activities provided by Friendship[17]. Amongst the injured, a majority (six) had sold their asset (land) while the majority of the families of the deceased (twenty-four) had kept their asset (land mortgage). Overall, although the beneficiaries expressed their gratitude for the assistance provided by Friendship, a small minority had been able to make a living from their income generation activity. Generally, the families had been struggling. Given the harsh realities of rural poverty in Bangladesh, for many of the dependants, the alternative concept of a *pension* – an arrangement to provide people with an income in the form of periodical benefits in the absence of a means of income – was as unknown as the concept of a 'welfare state' in Bangladesh. Yet if a regular, modest monthly pension could have been administered by the Inditex/ITGLWF Relief Scheme, then this in fact would have been entirely consistent with the sentiment expressed by Runa Khan as the Friendship approach.

The question of replicability

At their first face-to-face meeting in Brussels, Kearney and Chercolés committed to an initiative which had strategic intent. By proposing a scheme to support the victims of a specific industrial disaster both knew that that they would be challenging not only the existing limits of corporate social responsibility but that if such a fund garnered international buyer support, it would bring pressure to bear both on the Bangladesh government and the BGMEA to drastically improve existing safety net provision for workers in the RMG. For Chercolés, who had an actuarial background, there was a bigger goal – to develop a scheme which would have the potential for international replicability in a number of LDCs. This, however, would be dependent first and foremost on elements of the Spectrum Relief Scheme being adopted by the RMG sector in Bangladesh.

Two critical components of any compensation scheme relate to its funding and the institutional framework responsible for its implementation. On the issue of funding the Inditex/ITGLWF scheme sought at the outset to establish a trust fund with multi-stakeholder contributions, in contrast to the existing BGMEA group insurance scheme which indemnified its members against their total compensation commitment of BDT 100,000. As we have seen in Chapter 6, the fund could not be established and there were also critical questions raised concerning its constitution and management. Since clearly the majority of the buyers, the BGMEA and the Bangladesh government were not going to participate, this left Inditex and the ITGLWF with a very difficult administrative task of trying to maintain relief payments from an unconsolidated fund compounded by the problem of remote liaison with Oxfam, INCIDIN and the BNC/NGWF on the ground and during a particularly difficult political period in the country. Although CCC had suggested the appointment of an in country agent to administer the scheme given the apparent paralysis on the part of the BNC and INCIDIN, they themselves declined a request by Inditex and the ITGLWF to become participants in the scheme. Whilst the CCC's proposal was not taken up, Inditex did appoint an in country CSR specialist in 2008, as they began to roll out their policy of direct sourcing in an effort to cut out intermediaries in their supply chain.

It is fair to conclude that the proposal to establish a Trust Fund was an element of the overall Inditex/ITGLWF scheme which failed. As Masud Ali of INCIDIN commented:

> The whole concept of the trust fund... gave an idea that reaction based responsibility should not be event based. If it is not event based then you have to have a knowledge base before you create an institutional setup and... the knowledge base has to be collectively owned and credible. Then a consultative inclusive process has to accompany the entire process of planning, otherwise... whatever institution comes out won't be sustained. No matter how effective the idea sounds, the contextual reality needs to own an ethical idea to really be materialised[18].

The failure to establish the Fund meant that initial pension payments to the victims/families were not only delayed but came as periodic lump sums. Moreover, a consensus appeared to be forming between all parties in Bangladesh throughout 2009 to close the initiative with a final one off lump sum pension payment. Although this was entirely consistent with the spirit of Article 20 of Convention 121, up to his untimely death, Neil Kearney was still holding out for the idea of periodic payments from an account in Bangladesh, a mode which could have diminished the perceived vulnerability of the widows at a stroke[19]. For Runa Khan, the payment of such large sums was seen, however, as a step too far:

> When you give too much to them, that is where they will start to be noticed by others and when you give too much... what is going to happen – every 3 months there is going to be a fire outbreak and somebody else will die or another factory will collapse and you have to sustain this and it becomes difficult for the donors... For me it was not in harmony with the country[20].

There is little question that Friendship provided prompt and necessary relief to the victims:

> We are working with relief work in Bangladesh – as an

> NGO – one of my main concerns and main beliefs is that an
> NGO is a body which actually should not exist in a country
> which can help itself. So we should working always... to
> make the people come up to a certain level of the country
> –not make them anything more but to fit in wherever the
> help is needed.

As Downey has commented however, 'The issue here is not the
effectiveness of the NGOs. In many cases the NGOs are able to
deliver greater expertise and efficiency to the problems at hand' but
by stepping in to plug gaps in service delivery, they have in effect
relieved the Bangladesh government of responsibility to the populace
(2007: 45-6). Responsibility to the victims of industrial disasters had
to come in the form of rights not voluntary relief as Ineke Zeldenrust
of the Clean Clothes Campaign has argued:

> The Inditex/ITGLWF Relief Scheme was a solution that
> would bring in the responsibility issue... (approaching)
> people as employees. These were people working for an
> international supply chain – nobody would ever think about
> giving them a bike (van) to become a bike messenger!'

This 'rights-based' approach was the higher 'transformative' aim
of the CSR intervention by Inditex and the ITGLWF. It was a
genuine humanitarian effort, with the intention of being exemplary
and political at one and the same time and of echoing a sentiment
contained in progressive thinking within the international community,
namely that:

> ... the necessary solutions... point in the same direction:
> Governments adopting policies that induce greater
> corporate responsibility, and companies adopting strategies
> reflecting the now inescapable fact that their own long-
> term prospects are tightly coupled with the well-being of
> society as a whole (Ruggie, 2009: 11).

Finally, the concept of a welfare fund was a demand which RMG
workers not only supported, but one which they considered buyers
should sustain[21]. For Masud Ali of INCIDIN:

> In future I think a trust fund leads us to a situation where
> we claim on the government to create an institution where
> there will be roles and space for trade union, business

and civil society, which wouldn't just monitor but which would also hold resources to react, and this body may not have global actors present but should have a coordinating mechanism with the global actors so that they are not merely informed but held accountable through some kind of MOU or joint declaration and this body should also ventilate information to consumer groups around the world on the role of companies both national and international in ethical production[22].

Figure 17: The new facility on the old site of Spectrum[23].

The establishment of a trust fund has remained a core demand of the BNC since Spectrum, given added impetus by the passage of the Labour Welfare Foundation Act in 2006 outlined in Chapter 7, and rehearsed once again in the campaign for improved compensation arrangements for the victims of the Garib and Garib and Hameem fires of 2010. The critical and contradictory question for CSR focuses once again on the issue of responsibility raising the question whether buyers should, if at all, contribute to such an in-country fund and whether these contributions should be standing or ad hoc. Trade unions in Bangladesh and the international NGOs are unequivocal about buyer involvement in such a fund, viewing this as a compliance cost and citing Spectrum as a model, but targeting the buyers does run the risk of shifting the burden of responsibility away from the employers and the government for the welfare of workers and their families in the country.

There is little doubt that the initiative taken by Inditex, together with the global union, had been unprecedented and in some cases had set an (uncomfortable) precedent for fellow buyers in the RMG. Moreover, it was an exercise – particularly in terms of outreach – which the prime movers were unlikely ever to be in a position to repeat, should such a disaster befall the RMG in the future. Although they had made a major contribution to the overall relief of the Spectrum victims, for both social partners all signs pointed and still point to local solutions to these issues in the future, with or without future buyer involvement. In this respect in attempting to implement the standards laid down in ILO Convention 121 in respect of worker compensation, Inditex and the ITGLWF had shown the powers that be in Bangladesh the way.

APPENDIX 1

List of sixty-two dead workers at Spectrum

Full Name	Age	Sex	District	Job Title
Safiqul Islam Alim	32	M	Madaripur	Distributor
Soikat Hossen	24	M	Madaripur	Operator
Babu Mia	25	M	Faridpur	Quality Controller
Safiqul Islam	23	M	Rajbari	Knitting Operator
Rakibul Islam Rahim	26	M	Rajbari	Supervisor
Akidul Islam	20	M	Faridpur	
Monirul Islam	34	M	Kustia	Assistant Mechanic
Md. Ramzan Ali	35	M	Jahanidoho	Security Guard (Ansar)
Alomgir Hossen Milon	24	M	Joshor	
Belal Hossen	22	M	ShaTakahira	Knitting Operator
Rafiqul Islam	24	M	Barisal	Knitting Operator
Md. Abdul Gani	18	M	Sharitpur	Knitting Operator
Momtaz Begum	25	F	Khulna	Folder
Md. Abdur Rajjak	45	M	Gaibandha	Quality Controller

Full Name	Age	Sex	District	Job Title
Md. Samsul Alam	31	M	Gaibandha	Security Guard (Ansar)
Md. Rashedul Islam	17	M	Dinajpur	
Abdus Salam	17	M	Nilphamary	Clerk
Md. Raqfiqul Islam	19	M	Lalmonirhut	Production Worker
Milon Sarkar	20	M	Kurigram	Knitting Operator
Rajjak	36	M	Bogra	Knitting Operator
Md. Shahidul Islam	20	M	Bogra	Knitting Operator
Abu Bakar Siddique	21	M	Natore	Knitting Operator
Md. Shah Alom	22	M	Natore	Knitting Operator
Md. Afjal Hossain	22	M	Nababgonj	Knitting Operator
Mahbub shiekh	25	M	Naogaon	Knitting Operator
Abdul Barek	17	M	Pabna	Knitting Operator
Abu jafar	18	M	Pabna	Knitting Operator
Md. Abdul Alim	22	M	Pabna	Knitting Operator
Aleya	21	F	Pabna	Folder
Md. Rafiqul Islam	35	M	Shirajgonj	Boiler Operator
Mozammel Hoque (Bulbul)	28	M	Shirajgonj	Quality Controller

Full Name	Age	Sex	District	Job Title
Md. Nazrul Islam	30	M	Jamalpur	Supervisor
Md. Samret Alam	35	M	Jamalpur	Security Guard (Ansar)
Md. Abdul Aziz	18	M	Jamalpur	Knitting Operator
MizaNoor	26	M	Jamalpur	Knitting Operator
Md. Ratan Miah	20	M	Mymensingh	Knitting Operator
Abu Taleb Kayes	30	M	Mymensingh	Knitting Operator
Hafez Abdul Hashem	23	M	Maymenshing	Knitting Operator
Md. Ashadul Islam	21	M	Maymenshing	Knitting Operator
Md. Anwar Hossain	25	M	Sherpoor	Knitting Operator
Md. Sanaullah	25	M	Gazipoor	Knitting Operator
Md. Humayun Kabir	21	M	Netrokona	Knitting Operator
Rubel	21	M	Netrokona	Knitting Operator
Md. Shah alam	21	M	Brahmanbaria	Knitting Operator
Md. Badsha	22	M	Norshingdi	Knitting Operator
Masud	22	M	Jamalpur	Knitting Operator
Soleman Shikdar	45	M	Tangail	Cleaner
Jamal	29	M	Tangail	Knitting Operator

Full Name	Age	Sex	District	Job Title
Shahin	23	M	Tangail	Knitting Machine Operator
Zohirul	30	M	Tangail	Knitting Operator
Mintu	24	M	Tangail	Quality Controller
Anwar	27	M	Tangail	Security Guard (Ansar)
Zahangir	26	M	Tangail	Knitting Supervisor
Abdul Gafur Ahmed	20	M	Dhaka	Knitting Operator
Noorul Amin Palan	24	M	Dhaka	Supervisor (Mechanical) Batch Assistant
Md. Nazrul Islam	32	M	Dhaka	Knitting Operator
Siddikur Rahman	25	M	Manikgonj	Knitting Operator
Hridoy Ahmed	20	M	Manikgonj	Knitting Operator
Robin Hossain	20	M	Manikgonj	Knitting Operator
Elias Khan Kamar	21	M	Manikgonj	Knitting Operator
Abul Kalam Azad	34	M	Manikgonj	Circular Knitting Machine Operator
Md. Jahangir Alam	37	M	Dhaka	Fitter (Mechanical)
Mohammad Ali			Not found any relatives	

APPENDIX 2

List of fifty-four injured workers of Spectrum Sweater Ltd who sought and received medical attention and were assessed for compensation

Name	Age	Job
Md. Shafiqul Islam	20	Knitting Operator
Md. Jinnah Matbar	28	Knitting Operator
Md. Milon Howladar	26	Knitting Operator
Md. Sumon Hawladar	23	Knitting Operator
Md. Mobarak Hossain	22	Knitting Operator
Md. Delwar Hossain Boati	24	Knitting Operator
Md. Abdul Halim	23	Knitting Operator
Md. Lablu Miah	32	Knitting Operator
Sheikh Md. kalim uddin	27	Knitting Operator
Md. Saiful Islam Mridha	21	Knitting Operator
Habibur Rahaman	25	Knitting Operator

Name	Age	Job
Abdul Motin Mollah	36	Knitting Operator
Md. Shipon Miah Bishwas	26	Knitting Operator
Md. Ainul Haque Promanik	30	Knitting Operator
Md. Jahid Hossain Bepari	23	Knitting Operator
Md. Alauddin Promanik	20	Knitting Operator
Sheikh Jahangir Alom	25	Knitting Operator
Md. Manjurul Islam Bepari	23	Knitting Operator
Md. Mojaffar Mandal	25	Knitting Operator
Md. Hafijur Rahaman	37	Knitting Operator
Abdur Sobhan	28	Knitting Operator
Sheikh Monammad Mohidul Islam	21	Knitting Operator
Sheikh Abdul Mannan	40	Cleaner
Gaen Md. Motaleb Miah	25	Knitting Operator
Md. kamal Hossain	22	Knitting Operator
Md. Khalilur Rahaman	22	Knitting Operator
Md. Noor-E-Alom Choukidar	30	Knitting Operator
Md. Jahirul Islam Mollah	30	Knitting Operator

Name	Age	Job
Md. Kamal Hossain Bhuiyan	30	Dyeing Operator
Md. Shahidul Islam	26	Dyeing Operator
Sheikh Rafiqual Islam (Masud)	18	Dyeing Room Helper
Md. Sadek Hossain	27	Knitting Operator
Md. Kamrul	28	Knitting Operator
Md. Nesar Uddin	22	Knitting Operator
Md. Abdul Majid Sheik	61	Cleaner
Md. Jakir Hossain Miah	26	Knitting Operator
Rezaul Karim	25	Knitting Operator
Md. Rashedul Islam Sarkar	24	Knitting Operator
Hasan Mahmud Mridha	21	Knitting Operator
Md. Helal Uddin Fakir	26	Knitting Operator
Sheikh Md. Shakhawat Hossain	22	Knitting Operator
Md. Barek Miah	27	Operator
Golam Robbani Sarker	23	Knitting Operator
Abdul Talukder	27	Knitting Operator
Md. Shamim Ahmed Baperi	24	Knitting Operator

Name	Age	Job
Md. Ruhul Amin Dewan	21	Knitting Operator
Md. Monayem Fakir	28	Knitting Supervisor
Md. Rezaul Karim Pramanik	19	Clerk
Md. Akhter Hossain Khondoker	22	Knitting Operator
Md. Sagor Ahmed Mollah	21	Knitting Operator
Md. Nasir Uddin Shikder	24	Knitting Operator
Abdul Kader Mollah	25	Knitting Operator
Md. Roni Mollah	20	Helper
Sheikh Abdur Rouf	30	Knitting Operator

APPENDIX 3

Bangladesh Garment Workers Unions' 10 Point Charter of Demands 2006

- Workers should be paid Taka 3,000 as minimum basic wage, 35 per cent of the basic as house rent, Taka 300 as medical allowance, Taka 400 as conveyances, Taka 200 as festival allowance, Taka 100 as dress washing allowance and other allowances.

- It also calls for a review of the wages of the RMG workers every four years with additions to wages every two years in conformity with the price hike of essentials and the appreciation of foreign currencies that foreign buyers pay to the factory owners.

- It says workers should work at most 48 hours a week and no way be compelled to work more than 60 hours overtime. In case of overtime, they should be paid double the amount they get for scheduled work.

- Factory owners will pay on-contract operators, during no-production period, a minimum wage, which will be the average of three months' wage earned by the worker, it says.

- Every factory should go by strict safety regulations and in case of an accident factory owners should pay the nominated heir of a dead worker Taka 500,000 and a disabled worker Taka 700,000.

- The government should relocate multi-storey factories to safe three-storey buildings and not allow any new multi-storey factories.

- The employers and the government should also arrange construction of residential facilities for workers in the industrial areas.

- The charter also calls for ensuring the workers' rights to form trade union at every factory in line with the ILO conventions and 'participation committee' in line with the industry relation ordinance.

- It seeks mandatory jobs appointment letters for every worker and 16-week maternity leave for every female worker. It says a woman worker should not be terminated during her pregnancy.

- The charter also calls for provident funds and gratuity facilities for workers, five per cent profit sharing with workers, mandatory day-care centre at every factory for children of workers.

APPENDIX 4

Owner's Statement concerning the collapse

1. Construction of Spectrum was started in the beginning of 2000 and this construction was carried on phase by phase till April, 2005. During the span of 5 years and a half the construction of the 8 storied building was nearing completion.

2. Before taking up the construction work the soil test was carried out by a reputed soil testing firm. On the basis of the soil test report and design made by Bangladesh university of engineering and technology (buet) engineers, another reputed piling company carried out rcc cast in situ piling up to nearly 60 feet deep inside the ground.

3. Thereafter the construction of an eight storey building was carried out with proper structure and due foundation of an eight storey building under the supervision and structural design provided by the BUET engineers.

4. On the late night of 10th April 2005 the entire eight storey building collapsed.

5. Initially the collapse of the building was considered to be caused by foundation failure. Subsequent practical investigation into the cause of collapse by expert engineers revealed that the foundation and the pilings were found intact.

6. After further investigation it was found that during the time of collapse the building tilted towards the north east corner. The two side by side north east corner columns were completely broken down at first. Towards the north east corner there were 05 feet cantilever roofs. As a result of the collapse of the two north east corner columns

a (20 + 20 + 05) = 45 feet cantilever roof was created. Such suddenly created 08 number of forty five feet cantilever roofs pulled the entire building towards the north east corner. Consequently the building lost its equilibrium and completely collapsed.

7. Further investigation revealed that the bottom 02 – 2½ feet of those two columns had no concert mixture with cement. Instead it was only filled with sand and stone. The rest bulk part of those two columns were built with proper cement concrete mixture as all the other columns of the building. Subsequently the iron rods of the bottom parts of those two corner columns started crumbling with the increasing load of the building. At one point the crumbled iron rods of those columns could not bear the load of the building, completely broken down and caused the collapse of the building.

8. The building was constructed with flat slab design. So every individual floor was a single unit roof by itself. Such collapse or disturbance of any part of the building totally disturbed and collapsed the rest part of the building.

9. The basic principle of any RCC structure is that it shows different types of structural cracks in various parts of the building. As time passes these cracks keep on expanding. But in our case no such structural cracks in any part of the building were seen.

10. During the normal working period almost two thousand workers used to be present and most of the machines running. But at the time of accident in mid night ninety percent machines were not in function and ninety percent of the workers had already left the factory. So the possibility of machine vibration and human load on the floors of the building as one of the causes of the collapse as alleged is totally irrelevant.

11. Quality and strength of construction materials like iron rods and concrete chips were tested in the BUET laboratory several times after the accident. The test results furnished by the testing and consultation department of the BUET bureau of research showed that the quality and strength of those construction materials were within satisfactory level even though the materials submitted for test were "disturbed samples" because of the accident.

12. The insurance coverage was made only for fire hazard, natural disasters etc. but not for building breakage. As a result we did not

receive a single taka from the insurance company after the accident.

13. The total financial assistance provided to the dead and injured workers was given by the management of the company under Bangladesh law and in line with BGMEA custom and practice. This was disbursed after thirty days and completed within 6 months of the accident. Subsequent payments to the injured were made on numerous occasions and payments were made to the families of the deceased on two further occasions.

Shahriyar Hossain

Dhaka, 7 July 2011

APPENDIX 5

Bangladesh Labour Welfare Foundation Act 2006

(Act No. XXV of 2006; enforced since October 1st 2006)

*[An unofficial English summary prepared by
Jafrul Hasan Sharif, Advocate)*

Aims to ensure welfare of the workers'...

Applicable to all workers' in Bangladesh in both formal and informal sector...

[Section 1 (3)].

Informal sector refers to that non-governmental sector where a worker's work or job conditions etc. are not covered within ambit of the Labour Act (of 2006) and related rules and where workers' have limited opportunity to be organized [Section 2 (a)].

Formal sector refers to that governmental and non-governmental sector where a worker's work or job conditions etc. covered within ambit of the Labour Act (of 2006) and related rules... Section 2 (e)].

Worker is that person who is employed in any formal and informal sector – in any institution or industry or by any contractor – in exchange of money – involved in any skilled, unskilled, physical or technical, business developmental or clerical work

[Section 2 (k)].

No sooner the act is enforced a foundation named Bangladesh Labour Welfare Foundation will be established as a codified organisation with its head office in Dhaka[Section 3, 4]

Activities of the foundation will be [Section 5];

a. to ensure welfare of the worker and her family;

b. to initiate and implement different projects for the welfare of the worker and her family;

c. to provide financial assistance to worker especially who is incapable or disabled;

d. to ensure treatment or provide financial assistance to ill worker;

e. to provide financial assistance to her family when a worker dies in accident;

f. to grant scholarship or stipend to the meritorious family member of worker for education;

g. to introduce group insurance for the life insurance of worker and for that pay premiums to the insurance company from the fund;

h. to take necessary actions – managing the funds and administration; and

i. To take all necessary action to meet the objectives of the act and fulfill the above mentioned activities.

A **Management Board** will be entrusted with the management and administration of the foundation [Section 6] formed with [Section 7];

a. Honourable Minister, Ministry of Labour and Employment as the Chairperson;

b. Secretary, Ministry of Labour and Employment as the Vice-chairperson;

c. the Director General, who will be the Member-Secretary;

And as Members

d. Labour Director, Labour Department, Ministry of Labour and Employment;

e. Officer of the status of a Joint-Secretary (or someone upwards) nominated from the Finance Division;

f. Officer of the status of a Joint-Secretary (or someone upwards) nominated from the Ministry of Textile and Jute;

g. Officer of the status of a Joint-Secretary (or someone upwards) nominated from the Ministry of Industry;

h. Officer of the status of a Joint-Secretary (or someone upwards) nominated from the Ministry of Welfare of the Repatriated and Overseas Employment;

i. Officer of the status of a Joint-Secretary (or someone upwards) nominated from the Ministry of Law, Justice and Parliamentary Affairs;

j. Officer of the status of a Joint-Secretary (or someone upwards) nominated from the Ministry of Commerce;

k. Five nominated representatives (at least 1 female) from the Employers' side; and

l. Five nominated representatives (at least 1 female) from the Workers' side in consultation with the National Level Employers'/ Owners' and Workers' Federation.

They will be nominated for three years from the date of their nominations. [Section 8 (1)]

Director General appointed by the Government; is the Executive Head of the Foundation [Section 11]. He will mainly be responsible to implement the decisions taken by the board. He will be assisted by officers as per the structure appointed by the Government [Section 12]. The board will meet quarterly [Section 13].

To meet the objectives of this act – the foundation will have a **Fund** [Section 14] gathered from;

a. Government grants, b. Owners' grants, c. Loans (pre-approved by the Government) with no/ low interest, d. Earnings from different institutions of the foundation, e. Institutional and/ or Individual donation, f. Profit from the investments made from the foundation's funds, and f. Any other source approved by the Government. 50% of the consolidated funds of the "Labour Welfare Funds" under the Companies Profits (Workers Participation) Act 1968 would have to be transferred in this fund within 45 days – after the fund is collected – every year [Section 14 (3)].

The board will as per the procedure maintain, manage and record the accounts to be audited by the Auditor General of Bangladesh [Section 16]. It will also prepare and submit a report with financial statement to the Government [Section 17]. The Government will by notification draft Rules to implement the set objectives of the Act [Section 18].

APPENDIX 6

Charter of demands from BNC and other Trade Union Groupings to the Brands Delegation representing the buyers of Hameem Group

In light of the unfortunate incident of fire at the Hameem group's That's it Sportswear Unit, which cost the lives of so many innocent workers, BNC and other Trade Unions of Bangladesh have taken a unified stand on presenting this 'CHARTER OF DEMANDS' to the visiting delegation of Brands... and all other buyers from the Hameem group).

In the name of the workers of Hameem, the Trade Unions of Bangladesh demand the following:

1. The total compensation paid to the worker's family by the Brands to be based on the loss of earning of the dead or injured workers. (So far, Hameem group has given 1,050,000 taka to the next of kin and family members of the deceased workers on 31/1/2011).

2. The Brands along with the industry to put together a comprehensive plan using national and international technical experts in fire safety to support the Bangladeshi RMG industry in becoming fire proof, so that such incidents are prevented in the future and the safety of each worker is ensured.

3. An urgent appeal is made that the Brands should use their influence to ensure that Freedom of Association and the Right to Collective Bargaining is respected in their supply chain in line with the International Labor standards for Decent work. A stronger, more

unified workforce will be more empowered and vigilant when it comes to matters of their Health and Safety as well as other Human rights.

4. The Hameem incident follows a series of other fire safety related incidents over the years that have negatively affected the lives of workers in the Bangladeshi RMG sector. So far the issues of compensation and related themes have followed an ad hoc approach. BNC and the other trade unions have been one of the first unified groupings to ask for the setting up of a 'Bangladeshi Garment Workers Trust Fund' (BGWTF), which is a fund set up by the various stakeholders active in the RMG sector. These include all the Brands, retailers and Agents sourcing from Bangladesh; all the manufacturers who supply garments to the international labels; and the Government of Bangladesh. This 'Trust Fund' would be a fair way of ensuring that the current and future needs of the worker and their families would be taken care of.

5. The BNC and other trade unions of Bangladesh recommend that the BGWTF be set up in the following way:

– All Brands, Retailers and Agents sourcing from Bangladesh to contribute 10 cents per garment into the BGWTF.

– All Suppliers to contribute 5 taka per month per worker into the Trust fund, which will be matched by the worker's own contribution of 5 taka per month into this fund.

– The Government of Bangladesh contributes 5 taka per worker per month into this fund.

– This fund will have a multi stakeholder oversight committee, constituting the industry, government, brand and trade union representatives who will frame the rules and mechanisms for compensation, disbursement etc. to workers in the event of any unfortunate tragedy or even as a pension fund.

6. BNC and other trade unions of Bangladesh would like to convene a high level multi stakeholder meeting related to all the above issues in early March in Dhaka, in order to move the process of compensation and the Trust Fund forward.

Chronology

1995
Shahriyar Fabrics commences build.

1997
Shahriyar Fabrics commences production in Palashbari.

2000
Construction commences on the four-storey Spectrum factory.

2002–2005
Extension work is carried out to build up a further four storeys.

2004
Agreement on Textiles and Clothing expires but US and EU impose so-called China safeguards which displaces demand to countries like Bangladesh on certain garment categories, including sweaters.

2005
April 11 Shortly before 1 a.m. the Factory collapses. Rumours circulate it was a boiler explosion.
April 12 Police file a case implicating the owners of the company and 'others unknown' in death due to negligence'. The Planning Authority RAJUK establishes a five-man investigation committee.
April 13 An assistant to the boiler operator is rescued thirty-two hours after the collapse. He confirms that there was no explosion.
April 19 Having conducted an eight-day round-the-clock operation involving 1,500 rescuers, the officers in charge call off the rescue effort. In total sixty-two bodies have been recovered and eighty-four injured workers rescued. The company claims that the workforce register which was kept on the fifth floor has been destroyed in the collapse.
April 24 Friendship, a Bangladeshi NGO, submits a proposal to Carrefour for funding to assess the victims and provide immediate income generation relief. Carrefour approves.
April 30 2,000 garment workers of the Jatiya Garments Sramik Federation participate in a protest rally in front of the Home Ministry, demanding the arrest of the owners of Spectrum Sweaters.
May 3 The owners of Spectrum pay compensation to the families of the deceased workers at the offices of the BGMEA.

May 4 The Director of the Department of Labour and the Chief of the Department for Inspection of Factories and Establishments meet representatives of Sramik Nirapotta Forum (Workers Safety Forum) to discuss ways of improving OHS in the RMG industry.

May 6 A symbolic one-hour hunger strike is organised by garment workers demanding that the government meet its responsibilities to the Spectrum victims.

May 8 The owners surrender themselves before a Dhaka court on May 8 with a plea for bail.

May 12 Court refuses application for bail. The owners are sent to jail.

May 24 The owners are freed on bail. A writ petition is filed by four injured workers and nine rights based organizations seeking judicial redress of their grievances and directions to prevent further disasters in future. The National Garment Workers' Federation sends a memorandum to the Bangladesh Labour Inspectorate regarding the outstanding wages owing to some fifty workers.

June 3–9 Under pressure from the ITGLWF and campaign groups, a mission of the main buyers at Spectrum is organised to travel to Bangladesh to assess the situation and determine what needs to be done in the aftermath of the collapse. The delegation accompanied by the General Secretaries of the ITGLWF and one of its Spanish affiliates Fiteqa and an official from the BSCI visits the site of the factory, the residential areas where most of the workers lived, and the homes of a number of workers and different hospitals. The Inditex and ITGLWF representatives make arrangements for the injured workers to be admitted to hospital for treatment and for others to be medically examined.

A public consultation is held on the aftermath of the disaster. The delegation begins the process to put in place a plan for a compensation scheme for families of those who had died and for the injured.

June 19 An inter-ministerial meeting decides to establish National Forum on Social Compliance in the textile and garment industry, two task forces on occupational safety and labour welfare in RMG sector and a compliance monitoring cell in the Export Promotion Bureau.

June 22 BNC calls a press conference to call for the establishment of a trust fund and a national investigation body.

June 24–29 A follow-up visit to Bangladesh takes place to deal with the aftermath of the y collapse, led by Neil Kearney, Javier Chercolés and Lakshmi Bhatia. The delegation meets with the BGMEA, BKMEA, officials at the Ministry of Labour and Ministry of Commerce and with the UNDP.

June 28 The NGWF and the BGMEA agree upon an official and definitive list of 62 dead Spectrum workers.

June 30 A follow-up meeting is held to oversee progress on the establishment of a compensation fund for the Spectrum Sweater factory victims and to ensure that the injured are adequately treated. Arrangements are made for further medical treatment for a number of injured workers.

Neil Kearney and Javier Chercolés travel to Savar to see some of the injured workers and travel to the hospitals where other workers were still detained. Meetings are held with the German Technical Cooperation Bureau (GTZ) and with officers of the United Nations Development Programme.

June 26 First payments are made to the injured and unemployed Spectrum workers.

Sep 6–14 A delegation returns to Bangladesh for a series of meetings with the Garment Manufacturers and Exporters' Association regarding the relief fund for Spectrum workers.

The ITGLWF, Inditex and KPMG work together and agree on the relief fund formulae for compensation. The delegation visits the homes of injured workers and hospitals where workers were detained. Further meetings are held with the Minister of Commerce, the Secretary of Commerce, the Secretary of Labour, the Executive Chair of the Bangladesh Export Processing Zones Authority, and with other Government officials regarding the aftermath of Spectrum, trade in textiles and clothing and worker rights' abuses.

Nov 16 KarstadtQuelle signals its withdrawal from the Trust Fund.

Nov 26 Report from IEB confirms that there was no concrete support in the Spectrum factory building's north east corner underground columns.

Nov 26–27 A protest demonstration and condolences rally is organised by garment worker federations.

Dec 5 KarstadtQuelle and Cotton Group representatives on behalf of Scapino and Steilmann meet at the offices of INCIDIN and agree with Oxfam Bangladesh to set up their own fast track relief fund.

Dec 10 Unions and NGOs demonstrate in front of the Office of Chief Inspector of Factories.

Dec 18–24 Neil Kearney and Javier Chercolés visit Bangladesh to follow up on the issue of the treatment of the victims of the Spectrum factory collapse and on developing a compensation scheme for the families of the dead and those injured. They meet with the Bangladesh Garment Manufacturers' Association on a number of occasions, and with the Ministries of Labour and of Commerce.

2006

Feb 8 Inditex and the ITGLWF agree to establish a fact-finding mission.

Feb 10–18 Neil Kearney and Javier Chercolés visit Dhaka to meet with the BGMEA regarding developments on the compensation package for the victims of the Spectrum factory collapse. The procedure for building profiles on the families of the dead and on the injured is agreed. Neil Kearney briefs representatives of the BGMEA, the BNC and specialist information gatherers who will conduct the profiling.

Mar 22 Demonstration is organised by the National Garment Workers Federation, Bangladesh demanding follow-up on health and safety problems in garment factories.

April 11 First anniversary of the Spectrum collapse. Roy Ramesh Chandra, President of the United Federation of Garment Workers, demands a series of measures to ensure the safety of workers in an industrial sector in which 425 workers have been killed and 2,399 have been injured in twenty-four accidents since 1990.

May 1–6 Round table meeting on compensation for the victims of the Spectrum collapse is held in Dhaka.

May–Jun Riots in Bangladesh's garment industry.

May 29 RMG workers agree on a Charter of demands.

Jun 4–6 ETI mission to establish the causes of workers uprising in Bangladesh.

Jul 6 Inditex officially invites brands to participate in a Voluntary Relief Scheme for Spectrum victims.

Jul 31 – Aug 5 Neil Kearney,and Javier Chercolés meet with Grameen Bank, with the Bangladesh Garment Manufacturers' and Exporters' Association, with INCIDIN and Oxfam, the Ministry of Commerce and the former Governor of the Central Bank with a view to his joining the Board of Trustees.

Oct 1 Passage of the Worker Welfare Foundation Act.

Dec 18 KarstadtQuelle pledges €100,000 to the Trust Fund. A General Election is scheduled for the end of 2006, however it does not take place. The caretaker government is accused of BNP bias by the Awami League and there are nationwide protests and shutdowns.

2007

Jan 11 State of emergency is declared as President Iajuddin Ahmed and other members of the interim government resign.

Jan 25 The caretaker government uses the provisions stated in section 3 of the Emergency Powers Act to issue a set of Emergency Power Rules (EPR).During the next sixteen months these laws are used to suppress opposition to the government and the freedoms of association, assembly and expression for a wide variety of groups including trade unions and other labour rights activists.

Mar 28 – Apr 2 Neil Kearney and Javier Chercolés visit Bangladesh to meet with injured workers from the Spectrum factory and progress work on the development of the Spectrum Trust with Oxfam, INCIDIN and officers of the BNC.

Apr 1 Inditex distributes about US$ 3,000 total, divided over twenty-two of the victims, and pledges that the rest of an announced $60,000 advance would reach the remaining families in due course.

Jul 19–23 Various meetings aimed at progressing the Spectrum Trust are held in Dhaka.

Oct 5–12 Publication in the national press of parts 1 and 2 of a report by the Bangladesh Institute of Engineers' (IEB) of their own independent and unofficial investigation into the causes of the collapse.

Oct 5 Inditex and the ITGLWF formally sign an international framework agreement.

Nov 6–10 Arrangements are made for all of the injured to have further medical attention and to have their injuries classified before a board of three physicians, the Deputy Director of the Trauma Centre in Dhaka, a trauma specialist from Spain and a general medical practitioner.

2008

Mar 22 Neil Kearney and Javier Chercolés hold meetings with the different agencies working to establish the modalities for the trust fund for Spectrum victims.

Jul 22–26 Neil Kearney travels to Bangladesh, together with representatives of Inditex. Meetings are initiated with suppliers to secure employment opportunities for all of the Spectrum injured.

Sep 20 Inditex appoints an in country CSR director for the Bangladesh cluster.

Nov 11–13 Medical board treats and reassesses all injured workers.

Nov 12–16 Neil Kearney and Javier Chercolés visit Bangladesh to get updates on the families of the dead where investigations are ongoing. Discussions take place about arrangements for payments.

Dec 17–18 Neil Kearney and Javier Chercolés travel to Bangladesh to work with the bank, the union and INCIDIN on the preparation of documents on payments.

Dec 29 Awami League wins general election by a landslide.

By the end of 2008 payments for all injured workers are ready to be collected. In all but three cases, where the beneficiaries are contested, the lump sum part of the pension has been paid to the families of the dead. All injured workers, with the exception of Shafiqul and two others, are in new employment. Opportunity is taken to discuss employment opportunities with these workers.

2009

Jan 1 Lifting of 'China safeguards' by EU and USA means all quantitative restrictions on Chinese garment imports into these markets have now disappeared.

Feb 14 Joint meeting of Bangladesh partners involved in the Spectrum Compensation Process decide to recommend a lump sum final payment to a meeting of the nominees.

Jun 9 Arcandor (formerly KarstadtQuelle) files for bankruptcy. Pledge of €100,000 for Spectrum Fund is lost.

Jul Calculations undertaken to bring pension payments for families up to date.

Sep Pension payments are frozen in an Inditex bank account in Dhaka pending authorisation by the Government.

Oct–Nov New factory on the former site of Spectrum Sweaters begins production.

Nov 19 Neil Kearney dies of a heart attack in the Pan Pacific Sonargoan Hotel in Dhaka.

Dec 2–4 Tenth ITGLWF World Congress Frankfurt elects Patrick Itschert as new General Secretary.

2010

Feb 25 Fire at Garib and Garib resulting in twenty-one deaths and six injured.

Mar 1 Javier Chercoles opens up negotiations with the BGMEA on a protocol for a sector wide disaster relief scheme.

Mar 20 Worker dies at Matrix Sweaters. Inditex compensate the family in line with the Spectrum scheme.

Mar 31 The owners of Shahriyar Fabrics Ltd. begin discussions with Gildan Activewear about the future of the factory.

Apr 23 Twenty workers are injured in a factory fire at Tung Hi Knit and Sweater.

Apr 29 Meeting between Inditex and a delegation of officers from the BGMEA discuss the issue of an MOU on disaster relief for the sector in la Coruña.

Jul 27 Meeting to distribute cheques to the Spectrum widows.

Jul 28 Government announces the new minimum wage for the RMG.

Aug 3 Meeting in Dhaka hosted by the BNC at the BGMEA headquarters and attended by Inditex, to oversee the disbursement of interim lump sum cheques to families and the injured. This brings families' payments up to June 2009.

Sep 7 Javier Chercolés tenders his resignation as Global CSR Director of Inditex. The Company accepts his resignation.

Nov 2 Inditex appoints Felix Poza Pena as Director of Corporate Social Responsibility.

Dec 5–6 ITGLWF convenes a joint multi-stakeholder meeting on fire safety and prevention in Dhaka.

Dec 14 Fire at the *That's It* factory in Ashulia belonging to the Hameem Group. Twenty-nine workers die and fifty-seven are injured.

Dec 22 The owners distribute a further 100,000 BDT to each of the families of the deceased.

2011

Apr 16 Meeting to disburse final payments to the victims of the Spectrum factory disaster.

Apr 17 Joint BGMEA/BNC convening on Fire Prevention in the RMG.

Apr 18 Roundtable meeting to agree a compensation protocol for the victims of the fire at the *That's It* factory.

Bibliography

Chapter 1

Abernathy, F. H., Dunlop, J. T., Hammond, J. H., and Weil, D. (1999) *A Stitch in Time: Lean Retailing and the Transformation of Manufacturing – Lessons from the Apparel and Textile Industries*, Oxford: Oxford University Press.

Afsar, R. (2003) 'Internal migration and the development nexus: the case of Bangladesh', Bangladesh Institute of Development Studies, Dhaka, Bangladesh.

Alam, K. (2005) 'Workplace Profile Spectrum Sweater Industries', Unpublished Report, Dhaka: Alternative Movement for Resources and Freedom.

Bair, J. L. (2009) 'Embattled Labor, Embedded Ties: Industrial relations and inter firm networks in New York's garment district', Paper presented at the 2009 American Sociological Association Conference, San Francisco, California, 8–11 August 2009.

Bakhta, Z., Salimullaha, Md., Yamagatab, T. and Yunusa, M. (2008) 'Competitiveness of the Knitwear Industry in Bangladesh: A Study of Industrial Development amid Global Competition', Discussion Paper No. 169, Chiba: Institute of Development Studies.

Barrientos, S., Kabeer, N. and Hossain N. (2003) 'The Gender Dimension of Globalization of Production', ILO Working Paper No. 17, Geneva, International Labour Organization.

Berik, G. and van der Meulen Rodgers, Y. (2008) 'The Debate on Labor Standards and International Trade: Lessons from Cambodia and Bangladesh, Department of Economics Working Paper Series No. 2007–03, Rutgers University, USA.

Blackburn, S. C. (2002) 'Princesses and Sweated-Wage Slaves Go Well Together: Images of British Sweated Workers, 1843–1914', Journal of *International Labor and Working-Class History*, vol. 61: 24–44.

Blackburn, S. C. (2007) A *Fair Day's Wage for a Fair Day's Work*, (London: Ashgate).

Brandon, R. (1977) *Singer and the Sewing Machine: A Capitalist Romance* (New York: Kodansha International).

Bruce, M. and Daly, L. (2006) 'Buyer behaviour for fast fashion', *Journal of Fashion Marketing and Management*, vol. 10: 329–344.

Bythell, D. (1978) *The Sweated Trades: Outwork in Nineteenth Century Britain*, (New York: St. Martin's Press).

CCC (2005c) 'List of companies reportedly sourcing at the Spectrum–Shahriyar factory in Bangladesh', 1 July 2005. Available at: http://cleanclothes.org/news/list-of-companies-reportedly-sourcing-at-the-spectrum-shahriyar-factory-in-bangladesh (Last accessed 13 May 2011).

Chowdhury, R. A. R. and Ahmed M.S . (2005) 'Social Economic Costs of Post-MFA: Workers' Perspectives', Working Paper, Bangladesh Institute of Labour Studies, and International Labour Organization.

Fairwear Foundation (2006) Background *Study Bangladesh* (Amsterdam: FWF).

Ferenschild, S. and Wick, I. (2004) The Global Game for Cuffs and Collars, Siegburg/Neuwied Suedwind Texte 14.

Gereffi, G. (1994) 'The organization of buyer-driven commodity chains: how United States retailers shape overseas production networks' in G. Gereffi and M. Korzeniewicz (eds.) *Commodity Chains and Global Capitalism* (Westport: Praeger): 95–122.

Hausen K. (1978) Zur Sozialgeschichte der Nähmaschine *Geschichte und Gesellschaft* 4 pp. 148–169.

Hübner, K. (ed.) (2005) *The New Economy in Transatlantic Perspective. Spaces of Innovation* (London: Routledge).

Hurley, J. and Faiz N. (2005) 'Assessing the impact of on code compliance. A case study of the Bangladesh garment industry', MFA Forum and Gesellschaft fur technische Zusammenarbeit. Available at: http://www.mfa-forum.net/downloads/ mfaforum_Assessing%20the%20Impact%20of%20Purchasing%20Practices%20 on%20Code%20Compliance.pdf (Last accessed 22 February 2009).

Joshi, G. (ed.) (2002) *Garment Industry in South Asia Rags or Riches? Competitiveness, productivity and job quality in the post-MFA environment* (New Delhi: International Labour Organisation).

Kahn, S. (2004) 'Bangladesh Braces for Trade Law Changes', Verite. Available at: www.verite.org/news/Bangladesh%20Braces%20for%20Trade%20Law%20 Changes.htm (Last accessed 13 May 2011).

Kee, H. L. (2005) Foreign Ownership and Firm Productivity in Bangladesh Garment Sector (Washington D.C.: World Bank Development Research Group, Trade).

Kingsley, C. (1850) 'Cheap clothes and nasty', *Tracts by Christian Socialist II*, in preface to Charles Kingsley, *Alton Locke* (London).

Mason, P. (2007) *Live Working or Die Fighting. How the Working Class Went Global,* London: Harvill Secker.

Miller, D. and Williams P. 2008 What Price a Living Wage? Implementation issues in the quest for decent wages in the global apparel sector, *Global Social Policy*, Vol. 9 No. 1.pp. 99–125.

Miller, D. (2010) Towards sustainable labour costing in the Global Apparel Industry: some evidence from UK Fashion Retail. *Proceedings of the Textiles Institute Centenary Conference,* 3–4 November 2010.

Muqtada, M., Singh, A. and Rashid M. A. (2002) *Bangladesh: Economic and Social Challenges of Globalization* (Dhaka: University Press Limited).

Nordås, H. K. (2004) 'Labour implications of the textiles and clothing quota phase-out', Study commissioned by the International Labour Organization, Geneva, ILO.

Olberg, O. (1894) Das Elend in der Hausindustrie der Konfektion Leipzig.

Paratian, R. and Torres R. (2001) 'Bangladesh', Studies on the Social Dimensions of Globalization, Geneva, ILO.

Pfeifer, M. O. (2007) 'Fast and Furious', *Latin Trade*, 15 September 2007.

Pratima, P. M. (1998) 'Health Status of the Garment Workers in Bangladesh: Findings from a Survey of Employers and. Employees', Mimeo, Bangladesh Institute of Development Studies (BIDS), Dhaka, Bangladesh.

Rahman, M., Bhattacharya, D. and Moazzem K. G. (2007) *Bangladesh's Apparel Sector in Post-MFA Period A Benchmarking Study on the Ongoing Restructuring Process* (Dhaka: Centre for Policy Dialogue).

Rashid, M. A. (2006) 'Rise Of Readymade Garments Industry In Bangladesh: Entrepreneurial Ingenuity Or Public Policy', Paper presented at the Workshop on Governance and Development organized by the World Bank and BIDS, Dhaka, 11–12 November 2006.

Ross, R. (2004) *Slaves to Fashion: Poverty and Abuse in the Sweatshops* (Michigan: University of Michigan Press).

Siddiqi, H. G. (2004) *The Ready Made Garment Industry of Bangladesh* (Dhaka: The University Press Limited)

Stein, L. (ed.) (1977) *Out of the Sweatshop*, (New York: Quadrangle).

Stiglitz, J. E. (2003) *The Roaring Nineties – A new history of the world's most prosperous decade* (New York: W.W. Norton).

Uddin, Md. A. (2006) *Readymade Garment Industry of Bangladesh: How the industry is affected in post MFA period?* (Perth: Curtin University of Technology, Unpublished MA Thesis).

United Nations Conference on Trade and Development (UNCTAD) (2005) *TNCs and the removal of textiles and clothing quotas* (New York and Geneva: United Nations).

Wells, D. (2009) Local Worker Struggles in the Global South: reconsidering Northern impacts on international labour standards, *Third World Quarterly*, Vol. 30, No. 3, : 567–579.

Wolensky, K. C., Wolensky, N. H.,Wolensky, R. P., (2002) *Fighting the Union Label*, Pennsylvania: Pennsylvania State University Press.

Zohir, S. C. (2001) 'Social Impact of the Growth of Garment Industry in Bangladesh', *The Bangladesh Development Studies,* vol. 27 (4): 41–80.

Zohir, S. C. (2003) 'Emerging Issues in the RMG Sector of Bangladesh: Insights from an enterprise survey', Paper presented at the Seminar on A Value Chain Analysis of the RMG Sector in Bangladesh: Beyond MFA, Bangladesh Institute of Development Studies and OXFAM GB Bangladesh Programme.

Chapter 2

Arens, J. (2005) *Preliminary Report of CCC visit to Bangladesh in connection with collapsed Shahriyar Spectrum Sweater factory* (Amsterdam: Clean Clothes Campaign).

Bangladesh National Council of ITGLWF affiliated Unions (BNC), BGMEA, Incidin (2006) *Fact Finding Report on Spectrum Disaster Victims* (Dhaka: Incidin).

CCC (2005a) 'Interviews with workers, survivors and relatives of workers who died in the Spectrum-Shahriyar disaster', 1 June 2005. Available at: http://www.cleanclothes.org/component/content/article/1-news/189-interviews-with-workers-survivors-and-relatives-of-workers-who-died-in-the-spectrum-shahriyar-disaster (Last accessed 13 May 2011).

Daily Star (2005a) 'Cover Story – Death at Work', Daily Star Weekend Magazine, 22 April 2005. Available at: http://www.thedailystar.net/magazine/2005/04/04/cover.htm (Last accessed 13 May 2011).

Daily Star (2005b) 'Agonising Wait', 12 April 2005. Available at: http://www.thedailystar.net/2005/04/12/d5041201022.htm (Last accessed 13 May 20011).

Daily Star (2005c) 'Rescue goes slow on lack of equipment', 12 April 2005. Available at: http://www.thedailystar.net/2005/04/12/d5041201033.htm (Last accessed 13th May 2011)

Daily Star (2005d) 'Relatives hope only to identify their dear ones', 16 April 2005. Available at: http://www.thedailystar.net/2005/04/16/d5041601066.htm (Last accessed 27 May 2009).

Daily Star (2005e) 'No compensation yet for relatives of the Savar victims', *The Daily Star*, 26 April 2005. Available at: http://www.thedailystar.net/2005/04/26/d50426012521.htm (Last Accessed 13 May 2011).

Disaster Database (2005) 'Miscellaneous', *Disaster Prevention and Management*, vol. 15 (3).

Farazi, A. N. (2005a) 'Future Decimated', *New Age*, 25 April 2005. Available at: http://www.newagebd.com/2005/apr/25/front.html (Last accessed 27 May 2009).

INCIDIN (2006) *A brief report on the Spectrum Disaster response Program*, Unpublished Report, Dhaka: INCIDIN.

Sramik Nirapotta Forum (2005) The injured workers of Spectrum Sweaters Industries need our help, Dhaka: SNF.

Chapter 3

Ahmad, M. (2005) '*Governance, Structural Adjustment and the State of Corruption in Bangladesh*', Transparency International Bangladesh. Available at: http://www.ti-bangladesh.org/index.php?page_id=332 (Last accessed 11th May 2011).

Alam, H. (2005) 'National building code on hold for 11 years', *New Age*, 20 April 2005. Available at: http://www.newagebd.com/2005/apr/20/front.html#e3 (Last accessed 5 March 2009).

Ascoly, N. and Zeldenrust, I. (2003) *Monitoring and Verification Terminology Guide for the Garments and Sportswear Industries* (Amsterdam: SOMO).

Azad, A. K. (2005) 'Building collapse toll now 26, 100 missing', *New Age*, 13 April 2005. Available at: http://www.newagebd.com/2005/apr/13/front.html#2 (Last accessed 20 February 2009).

BOSHE and Centre for Corporate Accountability (2006) 'Report to the ILO Committee of Experts on the Bangladesh Government's Compliance with the Labour Inspection Convention – ILO Convention 81'. Available at: http://www.corporateaccountability.org/dl/International/bang/ilo/cca_iloreport2006.pdf (Last accessed 13th May 2011).

BSCI (2007) BSCI System: Rules and Functioning (Brussels: BSCI)

CCC (2006) 'What is the BSCI and how does it measure up? 1 May 2006. Available at: http://www.cleanclothes.org/news/newsletter21-05.htm (Last accessed 13 May 2011).

Choudhury, S. R. and Hussain, M. (2005) Post MFA Issues and Challenges: Social Dimension, Geneva:ILO.

Daily Star 2005a *op.cit.*

Daily Star 2005b *op.cit.*

Daily Star (2005f) 'Bangladesh: Workers' warnings of cracks overlooked', the Daily Star 25 April 2005 Available at: http://www.thedailystar.net/2005/04/25/d5042501044.htm (Last accessed 13 May 2011)

Daily Star (2005g) 'We had approval for four-storey building', The Daily Star, 14 April 2005. Available at: http://www.thedailystar.net/2005/04/14/ d5041401022.htm (Last accessed 13 May 2011).

Daily Star (2005h) 'JS body blames owners, Rjauk; suggests action', The Daily Star, 25 April 2005. Available at: http://www.thedailystar.net/2005/04/25/ d50425011210.htm (Last accessed 13 May 2011).

Daily Star (2005i) 'Owners Blamed for Knitting Factory Fire', The Daily Star, 9 January 2005. Available at: http://www.thedailystar.net/2005/01/09/ d5010901022.htm (Last accessed 13 May 2011).

Daily Star (2005j) 'Most garment units lack safety measures', The Daily Star, 12 April 2005. http://www.thedailystar.net/2005/04/12/d5041201077.htm (Last accessed 13 May 2011).

Farazi, A. N. and Islam K. A. (2006) 'A year on, Spectrum collapse probes still on', New Age, 11 April 2006. Available at: http://www.newagebd.com/2006/ apr/11/front.html#2

Fairwear Foundation (2006) Background Study Bangladesh (Amsterdam: FWF).

Harney, A. (2008) The China Price: The True Cost of Chinese Competitive Advantage, London: Penguin Press.

Institute of Bangladesh Engineers (IEB) (2007a) 'Savar Spectrum sweater factory failure – Investigation Report: Part I' The Daily Star, 10 May 2007. Available at: http://www.thedailystar.net/story.php?nid=6625 (Last accessed 13 May 2011).

IEB (2007b) 'Savar Spectrum sweater factory failure – Investigation report: Part II', The Daily Star, 12 October 2007. Available at: http://www.thedailystar.net/ story.php?nid=7568 (Last accessed 13 May 2011).

International Labour Organisation (ILO) (2006) General Survey of the reports concerning the LabourInspection Convention, 1947 (No. 81), and the Protocol of 1995 to the Labour Inspection Convention, 1947, and the Labour Inspection Recommendation, 1947 (No. 81),the Labour Inspection (Mining and Transport) Recommendation, 1947 (No. 82), the Labour Inspection (Agriculture) Convention, 1969 (No. 129), and the Labour Inspection (Agriculture) Recommendation, 1969 (No.133) Report III Part1b http://www.ilo.org/public/ english/standards/relm/ilc/ilc95/pdf/rep-iii-1b.pdf (Last accessed 9 May 2011).

Islam, K. A. (2005) 'BGMEA probe echoes Rajuk findings', New Age, 3 may 2005. Available at: http://www.newagebd.com/2005/may/03/front.html (Last accessed 12 February 2009).

Islam, S. (2005) 'Spectrum Sweater bldg caved in for faulty foundation', The Daily Star, 26 November 2005. Available at: http://thedailystar.net/2005/11/26/ d5112601108.htm (Last accessed 13 May 2011).

Islam, S. and Ashraf, S. (2005) '23 killed, 350 trapped', The Daily Star, 12 April 2005. Available at: http://www.thedailystar.net/2005/04/12/d5041201011.htm (Last accessed 13 May 2011).

Juberee, A. and Farazi, A. N. (2005) 'No compensation yet for Savar building collapse victims', New Age, 25 April 2005. Available at: http://www.newagebd. com/2005/apr/25/front.html (Last accessed 12 February 2009).

Islam, S. (2005) 'Spectrum Sweater building caved in for faulty foundation', The Daily Star, 26 November 2005. Available at: http://thedailystar.net/2005/11/26/ d5112601108.htm (Last accessed 13 May 2011).

Kabeer, N. and Mahmud, S. (2006) Compliance versus accountability: Struggles for dignity and daily bread in the Bangladesh garment industry in Newell P. And Wheeler J. *Rights, Resources and the Politics of Accountability*: London: Zed Books.

Khan, M. A. (2005) 'Foundation failure led to collapse', The Daily Star, 14 April 2005, http://www.thedailystar.net/2005/04/14/d5041401076.htm (Last accessed 13 May 2011).

Locke, R., Qin, F., Brause, A. (2007) "Does Monitoring Improve Labor Standards?: Lessons from Nike", *Industrial and Labor Relations Review* Vol. 61 No.1, 3–31.

Morshed, M. M. (2007) *A study of labour rights implementation in the ready made garment sector in Bangladesh: Bridging the gap between theory and practice*, University of Wollongong Master Thesis, Centre Asia Pacific Social Transformation Studies.

Murshid, K. A. S., Zohir, S. C., Milford A., and Wiig A. (2003) *Experience from Bangladesh with ethical trading initiatives,* Bergen: Michelsen Institute.

New Age (2005a) 'Rajuk forms probe body', *New Age*, 12 April 2005. Available at: http://www.newagebd.com/2005/apr/12/front.html (Last accessed 12 February 2009).

New Age (2005b) 'Taka 6,796cr paid in bribes every year, says TIB', *New Age*, 21 April 2005. Available at: http://www.newagebd.com/2005/apr/21/front.html#1 (Last accessed 12 February 2009).

O'Rourke, D. (2002) 'Monitoring the Monitors: A Critique of Corporate Third Party Labor Monitoring', in R. Jenkins, R. Pearson and G. Seyfang (eds) *Corporate Responsibility and Labour Rights: Codes of Conduct in the Global Economy* (pp. 196–208). London: Earthscan.

Pruett, D. (2007) *Looking for a Quick Fix* (Amsterdam: Clean Clothes Campaign).

Sedex Members Ethical Trade Audit (SMETA) Best Practice Guidance, SMETA 2009 Version 2.2. as at January 2009, http://www.sedex.org.uk/sedex/_WebSite/PDF/SMETA_Best_Practice_Guidance.pdf (last accessed 13 May 2011).

SAI – Social Accountability International (2004) *Guidance Document for Social Accountability 8000* (New York: SAI).

Tombs, S. and Whyte, D. (2010) *A deadly consensus: Worker safety and regulatory degradation under New Labour, British Journal of Criminology*, volume 50, number 1, pp. 46–65.

Transparency International Bangladesh (2005) 'Corruption in Bangladesh: A Household Survey', 20 April 2005. Available at: http://www.ti-bangladesh.org/HH%20Survey/Household%20Survey%20-%202005.pdf (Last accessed 13 May 2011).

Chapter 4

Daily Star (2005k) 'SKOP demands punishment to those responsible', *The Daily Star*, 14 April 2005. Available at: http://www.thedailystar.net/2005/04/14/d50414060252.htm (Last accessed 13 May 2011).

Daily Star (2005l) 'Negligence led to tragedy', *The Daily Star*, 18 April 2005. Available at: http://www.thedailystar.net/2005/04/18/d50418060153.htm (Last accessed 13 May 2011).

Daily Star (2005m) 'Impartial investigation demanded', *The Daily Star*, 22 April 2005. Available at: http://www.thedailystar.net/2005/04/22/d50422060865.htm (Last accessed 13 May 2011).

Daily Star (2005n) 'Collapse of Spectrum sweater industries and non-compliance of laws – A review', 4 June 2005. Available at: http://www.thedailystar.net/law/2005/06/02/monitor.htm (Last accessed 13 May 2011).

Daily Star (2005o) 'Factory owner surrenders, sent to jail', The Daily Star, 9 May 2005. Available at: http://www.thedailystar.net/2005/05/09/d5050901033.htm (Last accessed 13 May 2011).

Daily Star (2005p) 'Garment workers lay siege to court', *The Daily Star*, 13 May 2005. Available at: http://www.thedailystar.net/2005/05/13/d50513060475.htm (Last accessed 13 May 2011).

Daily Star (2005q) 'Mirpur garment worker lynched for a T-shirt', *The Daily Star*, 31 December 2005. Available at: http://www.thedailystar.net/2005/12/31/d5123101033.htm (Last accessed 13 May 2011).

Daily Star (2006a) 'Ensure safe workplace for garment workers', *The Daily Star*, 11 March 2006. Available at: http://www.thedailystar.net/2006/03/11/d60311060370.htm (Last accessed 13 May 2011).

Daily Star (2006b) 'Spectrum Tragedy – 1st Anniversary Today', *The Daily Star*, 11 April 2006. Available at: http://www.thedailystar.net/2006/04/11/d60411061066.htm (Last accessed 13 May 2011).

Downey, K. (2007) 'Sequenced reforms as a response to Governance challenges in Bangladesh', Asian Affairs, vol. 29 (2): 40–59.

Hasan, Md. (2006) 'Accords with workers hardly implemented', *The Daily Star*, 31 May 2006. Available at: http://www.thedailystar.net/2006/05/31/d6053101085.htm (Last accessed 13 May 2011).

Islam, K.A. (2006) 'RMG workers agree on 10 common demands', *New Age*, 30 May 2006. Available at: http://www.newagebd.com/2006/may/30/front.html#4 (Last accessed 12 February 2009).

Islam, S. (2006a) 'Workers' Rights', Ain O Salish Kendra. Available at: http://www.askbd.org/web/?page_id=511 (Last accessed 13 May 2011).

ITUC (2006), 'International Labour Standards in Bangladesh', Report for the WTO General Council Review of Trade Policies of Bangladesh, Geneva, 13 –15 September. Available at: http://www.icftu.org/www/pdf/corelabourstandardsbangladesh2006.pdf (Last accessed 13 May 2011).

Khan, S. I. (2002) 'Trade Unions, Gender Issues and the Ready-Made-Garment Industry of Bangladesh', in Vivian J. and Miller C. (eds.) *Women's Employment in the Textiles Manufacturing Sectors of Bangladesh and Morocco* (Geneva and New York: UNRISD and UNDP).

Kumar, A. (2006) 'Bangladesh: Industrial Chaos Worsens Political Instability', South Asia Analysis Group, Paper N. 1852, 17 June 2006. Available at: http://www.southasiaanalysis.org/%5Cpapers19%5Cpaper1852.html (Last accessed 13 May 2011).

National Labour Committee (2006) 'Ask US companies for justice for the killed and injured workers'. Available at: http://www.nlcnet.org/article.php?id=112#Contact (Last accessed 20 March 2009).

Rahman, M., Bhattacharya, D. and Moazzem, K. G. (2007) *Bangladesh's Apparel Sector in Post-MFA Period A Benchmarking Study on the Ongoing Restructuring Process* (Dhaka: Centre for Policy Dialogue).

Rahman, W. (2007) 'Is Bangladesh heading towards disaster', BBC News, 8 January 2007. Available at: http://news.bbc.co.uk/1/hi/world/south_asia/6241263.stm (Last accessed 13 May 2011).

Saha, B. C. and Farazi, A. N. (2006) '16 Killed as building collapses in city', *New Age*, 26 February 2006. Available at: http://www.newagebd.com/2006/feb/26/front.html#8 (Last accessed 20 March 2009).

Chapter 5

Appelbaum, R. P. (2005) 'TNCs and the Removal of Textiles and Clothing Quotas' (*Center for Global Studies,* Paper 3. Available at: http://repositories.cdlib.org/isber/cgs/3 (Last accessed 13 May 2011).

Arens, J. (2005) *Preliminary Report of CCC visit to Bangladesh in connection with collapsed Shahriar Spectrum Sweater factory* (Amsterdam: Clean Clothes Campaign).

BSCI (2006) *Annual Report 2006* (Brussels: BSCI).

Burckhardt, G. (2006) *Tchibo – Jede Woche eine neue Welt? Dokumentation der Tchibo-Kampagne* (Tübingen:Terre des Femmes).

Campagne Vetements Propres (2005) 'Interpellation et réponses des entreprises clientes en Belgique,' 5 July 2005. Available at: http://www.vetementspropres.be/index.php?p=g&search=oui&id=131 (Last accessed 13 May 2011).

CCC (2005b) 'Major European Buyers Sourcing at Collapsed Factory in Bangladesh', Amsterdam, 15 April 2005. Available at: http://www.cleanclothes.org/news/major-european-companies-sourcing-at-collapsed-bangladesh-factory (Last accessed 13 May 2011).

Crabbé, C., Leroy, N. and Caudron J-M. (2008) Profil Carrefour (Louvain-La-Nueve, Belgium: Campagne Vêtements Propres).

Croucher, R. and Cotton, E. (2009) *Global Unions, Global Business* (Middlesex: Middlesex University Press).

Daily Star (2005r) 'RMG order to shift unless work condition improves', *The Daily Star*, 9 June 2005. Available at: http://www.thedailystar.net/2005/06/09/d5060901085.htm (Last accessed 13 May 2011).

Doorey, D. (2005) 'Who Made That?: Influencing Foreign Labour Practices Through Reflexive Domestic Disclosure Regulation', *Osgoode Hall Law Journal*, Vol. 43: 353–405.

Hearson, M. (2009) *Cashing In: Giant Retailers, Purchasing Practices, and Working Conditions in the Garment Industry* (Amsterdam: Clean Clothes Campaign). Available at: http://www.cleanclothes.org/resources/ccc/working-conditions/cashing-in (Last accessed 13 May 2011).

ITGLWF (2005a) 'Bangladesh Factory Collapse Tantamount to Murder, Says Global Union Federation', Press Release, 11 April 2005. Available at: http://www.itglwf.org/lang/en/documents/ITGLWFPressReleases2005_000.pdf (Last accessed 13 May 2011).

ITGLWF (2005b) 'Bangladesh: 72-Hour Work Weeks and Inattention to Industrial Safety Makes Accidents Inevitable', Press Release, 13 April 2005. Available at: http://www.itglwf.org/lang/en/documents/ ITGLWFPressReleases2005_000.pdf (Last accessed 13 May 2011).

ITGLWF (2006) 'Organising in a Global Economy', Regional Asian Workshop Executive Summary, Bangkok, 4–5 December 2006.

Klawitter, N. (2005) 'Blood in the Supply Chain', Der Spiegel Online International, 13 December 2005. Available at: http://www.spiegel.de/ international/spiegel/0,1518,390198,00.html (Last accessed 13 May 2011).

Meeran, R. (2001) 'Victory for Cape Asbestos Miners and Residents', LabourNet UK, 21 December 2001. Available at: http://www.labournet.net/world/0112/ cape3.html (Last accessed 13 May 2011).

Merk, J. (2004) 'The Business Social Compliance Initiative: An initial assessment', Internal discussion document, Amsterdam, Clean Clothes Campaign.

MFA Forum and UNDP (2005), 'Action Report', Forum on the Future Conference on an Internationally Competitive Textile and Garment Industry in Bangladesh, Dhaka, Bangladesh, 27–28 June 2005. Available at: http://www.mfa-forum.net/ groups/Bangladesh/ConferenceJune2005.aspx (last accessed 13 May 2011).

Miller, D. (2004) 'Preparing for the long haul: Negotiating International Framework Agreements in the Global Textile, Garment and Footwear Sector', *Global Social Policy*, vol. 4 (2): 215–239.

Miller, D. (2008) 'The ITGLWF's policy on crossborder dialogue in the textiles, clothing and footwear sector: Emerging strategies in a sector ruled by codes of conduct and resistant companies,' in K. Papadakis (Ed.) Cross-*Border Social Dialogues and Agreements – An emerging global industrial relations framework?* (Geneva: ILO Publications): 161–189.

New Age (2005c) 'Buyer's help sought to make RMG factories compliant', *New Age*, 29 June 2005. Available at: http://www.newagebd.com/2005/jun/29/busi. html (last accessed 20 May 2009).

NGWF (2005) *Report of Belgian Delegation to the Shariyar Fabrics facility December 4th 2005* (Dhaka: National Garment Workers Federation).

Tokatli, N. (2008) Global sourcing: insights from the global clothing industry— the case of Zara, a fast fashion retailer, *Journal of Economic Geography*, 8 (2008) pp. 21–38.

Webb, T. (2003) 'Human rights litigation risk on the increase for multinational companies', *the Ethical Corporation*, 24 November 2003. Available at: http://www. ethicalcorp.com/content.asp?ContentID=1366 (last accessed 13 May 2011).

Chapter 6

Asian Development Bank (2001) *Country Briefing Paper Women in Bangladesh* (ADB Programs Department West: ADB Publication Unit). Available at: http://www.adb.org/Documents/Books/Country_Briefing_Papers/Women_in_ Bangladesh/women_ban.pdf (last accessed 13 May 2011).

Asia Legal Resource Centre (2008) 'BANGLADESH: Prolonged State of Emergency threatening the judiciary and human rights defenders' ability to work', Written submission to the 9th Session of the UN Human Rights Council, 21 August 2008. Available at: http://www.alrc.net/doc/mainfile.php/hrc9/519/ (Last accessed 13 May 2011).

Azam, S. (2006) *Fact Finding Report on the Spectrum Disaster Victims* (Dhaka: INCIDIN).

Bangladesh National Women Lawyers Association (2002) *Widows' Plight in Bangladesh: Rethinking Policies*, Dhaka: BNWLA.

Chercoles Blasquez J. (2011) Navigating the Spider's Web. Multinational interventions in an industrial disaster scenario: the Spectrum case. Unpublished PhD thesis.

Daily Star (2010c) '26 killed in factory fire', 15th December 2010. Available at: http://www.thedailystar.net/newDesign/news-details.php?nid=166145 (Last accessed 13 May 2011).

INCIDIN, BNC, and BGMEA (2006) *Fact Finding Report on Spectrum Disaster Victims* (Dhaka: INCIDIN).

Inditex and ITGLWF (2006) *Project Spectrum Voluntary Relief Scheme – May Draft* (Dhaka: Bangladesh).

ITGLWF (2006b) 'One Year on Groundwork on Spectrum relief nears completion', Press Release 11 April 2006. Available at: http://www.itglwf.org/DisplayDocument.aspx?idarticle=1535&langue=2.

KPMG (2005) *Spectrum Garments Accident Definitions, Criteria, Terms of Reference and Actuarial Valuations –First Draft September* (Dhaka: Bangladesh).

Mannan, M.A., Choudhury Zohir S. (2009) An Inventory and Statistics on Violence Against Women in Bangladesh, Dhaka: Bangladesh Institute of Development Studies.

Miller, (2011) Global social relations and the limits and possibilities of transformative CSR in outsourced apparel supply chains: The case of the Inditex GFA in Papadakis (ed) In Kostas Papadikis (ed.) *Practices and Outcomes of an Emerging Global Industrial Relations Framework*, London: ILO/Palgrave.

Mirdha R.U. (2009) 'Falling Prices pare down apparel profits, *The Daily Star*, August 06.09. Available at http://www.thedailystar.net/newDesign/news-details.php?nid=100340 (last accessed 13 May 2011)

Chapter 7

Adam Smith International/Asian Development Bank (2007) *Social Protection for Poor Female Garment Workers in the Context of Changing Trade Environment, Final Report*. Available at: http://www.adb.org/Documents/PRF/BAN/Final-Report-Bangladesh-SP.pdf (Last accessed 4 May 2011).

Basak, B. K. (2006) 'Loopholes in the Labour Act, 2006', *The Daily Star*, 11 October 2008. Available at: http://www.thedailystar.net/law/2008/10/01/info.htm (Last accessed 13 May 2011).

CCC (2010) 'Compensation Deceased Garib Workers still Inadequate' Clean Clothes Campaign, Amsterdam 21 June 2010. Available at: http://www.cleanclothes.org/urgent-actions/compensation-deceased-garib-workers-still-inadequate (Last accessed 13 May 2011).

Centre for Corporate Accountability (20079) *Obtaining Compensation for Workplace Death and Injury in Bangladesh*, Dhaka: Centre for Corporate Accountability and Bangladesh Occupational Health, Safety and Environmental Foundation. Available at: http://www.corporateaccountability.org/dl/International/bang/reports/compreportenglish.pdf (last accessed 13 May 2011).

Daily Star (2005s) '90pc garment factory buildings vulnerable to collapse', 15 June 2005. Available at: http://www.thedailystar.net/2005/06/15/d50615060362.htm (Last accessed 13 May 2011).

Daily Star (2006c) Booming RMG cares little for workers' life, The Daily Star, 13 March 2006. Available at: http://www.thedailystar.net/2006/03/13/d6031301022.htm last accessed 20 May 2011.

Daily Star (2007) 'Labour Welfare Foundation – Government urged to allocate budget', The Daily Star, 29 May 2007. Available at: http://www.thedailystar.net/2007/05/29/d70529060276.htm.

Daily Star (2010a) 'Stampede at RMG factory', The Daily Star 21 March 2010. Available at: http://www.thedailystar.net/newDesign/news-details.php?nid=130919 (Last accessed 13 May 2011).

Daily Star (2010b) '20 injured in fire at an RMG factory', the Daily Star April 24, 2010. Available at: http://www.thedailystar.net/newDesign/news-details.php?nid=135683 (Last accessed 13 May 2011).

Daily Star (2010c) op.cit.

IEB (2007b) 'Savar Spectrum sweater factory failure – Investigation report: Part II', The Daily Star, 12 October 2007. Available at: http://www.thedailystar.net/story.php?nid=7568 (Last accessed 13 May 2011).

Islam, S. (2006) 'Workers' Rights', Ain o Salish Kendra – A Legal Aid and Human Rights Organization. Available at: http://www.askbd.org/web/?page_id=511 (Last accessed 13 May 2011).

Just-Style.com (2006) 'Bangladesh: 3 factories at risk of collapsing,' 20 March 2006. Available at: http://www.just-style.com/article.aspx?id=74014 (Last accessed 13 May 2011).

Sharif, J.H. (2008) Profit Status of Company: Action Towards and Opportunities of Raising Funds for Bangladesh Workers' Welfare Foundation, Research Report, Dhaka: Manusher Jonno Foundation.

Uddin, K. M. (2006) 'Demolition of unfit buildings – Compliance Forum for RMG deviates from its decision', New Age, 26 February 2006. Available at: http://www.newagebd.com/2006/feb/26/front.html#e (Last accessed 20 May 2009).

Chapter 8

Blowfield, M. (2008) Business Corporate Responsibility and Poverty, Background Paper Geneva:United Nations Research Institute fo Social Development.

BSCI (2006) Annual Report 2006 (Brussels: BSCI).

CCC (2010) 21 Workers Die at Bangladeshi Factory Fire. Amsterdam: Clean Clothes Campaign, 2nd March, available at: http://www.cleanclothes.org/urgent-actions/21-workers-die-at-bangladeshi-factory-fire (Last accessed 13 May 2011).

Downey, K. op.cit.

Edwards, M. (2008) Small Change: Why Business won't save the World, San Francisco: Berrett-Koehler.

Egels-Zanden, N. and Wahlqvist, E. (2007) Post-Partnership Strategies for Defining Corporate Responsibility: The Business Social Compliance Initiative Journal of Business Ethics (2007) 70:175–189.

Greenwald Doherty (2009) "Joint Employers" May Be Liable in Wage & Hour Cases http://www.overtimeadvisor.com/articles/joint-employer-liability/ (Last accessed March 3 2011).

Klawitter, *op.cit.*

Miller, D. (2010) *op.cit.*

Mirvis, P.H. and Googins, B.K. (2006) *Stages of Corporate Citizenship: A Developmental Framework,* Chestnut Hill: MA Center for Corporate Citizenship at Boston College.

Ruggie, J. (2009) '*Business and human rights: Towards operationalising the "Protect, Respect and Remedy" framework*' Report of the Special Representative of the Secretary-General on the issue of human rights and transnational corporations and other business enterprises, United Nations General Assembly A/hrc/11/13, 22 April 2009.

Notes

Preface

1   Richard Greenwald (2005) The Triangle Fire, the Protocols of Peace, and Industrial Democracy in Progressive Era New York. Philadelphia: Temple University pp.14–15

2   Jennifer Bair (2009) Embattled Labor, Embedded Ties: Industrial relations and inter-firm networks in New York's garment district, Paper presented at the American Sociological Association Conference.

3   http://abcnews.go.com/Blotter/workers-die-factories-tommy-hilfiger/story?id=15966305

Chapter 1

1   The 'new economy' mantra called for a refocussing of business functions away from manufacturing and customer service to brand and product development cf. Hübner (2005) and Stiglitz (2003).

2   Justice, 5 May 1906 quoted in Blackburn, S.C. (2002) p.44.

3   Interview with Inditex CSR manager, Bangladesh, 07.06.09.

4   Before its replacement in 2008 with GSP PLUS, this was a formal system of exemption from World Trade Organisation rules which permits member countries to discriminate in favour of LDCs in terms of import duties and quotas.

5   BGMEA figures available at: http://www.bgmea.com.bd/home/pages/TradeInformation (Last accessed 13 May 2011).

6   Interview with Inditex CSR manager, Bangladesh, *op.cit.*

7   BGMEA figures for 1995–6 *op.cit.*

8   http://www.bkmea.com/history_of_development.php (Last accessed 13 May 2011).

9   A Cantonment denotes a military station in South East Asia. A Cantonment Board is an administrative office within such a military district.

10 Interview with the owner, 08.06.2009.

11 Bangladesh Garments and Textiles Directory (2002) Local agents of foreign buyers, Dhaka: Peoples Publication pp. 329–380. See also http://www.just-style.com/analysis/new-eur4m-initiative-aims-to-boost-bangladesh_id111148.aspx (Last accessed May 23 2011).

12 Figure supplied by the owner.

13 See: BGMEA, 'List of the BGMEA members'. Available at: http://www.bangladeshgarmentsmanufacturer.label.com.bd/p70.html (Last accessed 13 May 2011).

14 An initiative of the European Union which entered into force in March 2001 and established quota and duty free status under on all imports from LDCs into the EU with the exception of armaments.

15   Interview with Fazrul Hoque, then President of the BKMEA in Fibre2Fashion. Available at: http://www.fibre2fashion.com/face2face/bkmea/bkmea.asp (Last accessed 13 May 2011).

16   Maxine Frith 2008 Revealed: How Bra Wars devastate world's poor, *The Independent* 27 August 2005 Available at: http://www.independent.co.uk/news/world/politics/revealed-how-bra-wars-devastate-worlds-poor-504425.html (Last accessed 13 May 2011).

17   Interview with Fazrul Hoque, *op.cit.*

18   Information provided by the owner.

19   Interview with Inditex CSR manager, Bangladesh, *op.cit.*

20   Interview with the owner, *op.cit.*

21   Interview with Javier Chercolés, then Inditex Director of Corporate Social Responsibility, 10.06.2009.

22   Quoted in Flanagan M. (2009) Sourcing: Is fast fashion starting to fade? In: www. just-style.com, 8. September (Last accessed Sept 12 2009).

23   Information provided by the owner.

24   US DOL 2000 quoted in Fairwear Foundation, 2006: 44.

25   Some of the data here is contained in the transcripts and testimonies of Spectrum workers taken by the CCC in May 2005 (2005b) 'Interviews with workers, survivors and relatives of workers who died in the Spectrum disaster', 1 June 2005. These are available at: http://www.cleanclothes.org/component/content/article/1-news/189-interviews-with-workers-survivors-and-relatives-of-workers-who-died-in-the-spectrum-shahriyar-disaster (Last accessed 13 May 2011). However these have not been independently verified. Similarly the AMRF (cf Alam, 2005) compiled a factory profile of Spectrum on behalf of the NGWF. The data contained in this report has not been verified.

26   The worker in question claimed to have worked until nine or twelve p.m. and often until three o'clock in the morning. This was disputed by the owner.

27   Eighteen hours overtime for the nightshift and six hours for the dayshift was paid as an overtime premium on Fridays. CCC (2005b) Testimony 6: Helper working on ground floor – dyeing section.

28   ILO Conventions 87 (Freedom of Association and Protection of the Right to Organise Convention), adopted 17 June 1948 and ILO Convention 98 (Right to Organise and Collective Bargaining Convention), adopted 8 June 1949).

Chapter 2

1   This is a reconstruction based on a set of interviews given anonymously by survivors, injured workers and family members to Jenneke Arens of the Clean Clothes Campaign (CCC). See: CCC (2005a) 'Interviews with workers, survivors and relatives of workers who died in the Spectrum disaster', 1 June 2005. All the transcripts and testimonies are available at: http://www.cleanclothes.org/component/content/article/1-news/189-interviews-with-workers-survivors-and-relatives-of-workers-who-died-in-the-spectrum-shahriyar-disaster (Last accessed 13 May 2011). Additional information provided by the owner.

2   There are conflicting accounts as to the numbers of workers in the factory that night. The record book on the fifth floor was allegedly destroyed in the collapse. Adding up testimonies of the workers on different floors in the factory arrives at a figure of around 400. We know for certain that 148 (sixty-

two dead and eighty-four injured) were present but a further unspecified number were hauled free or escaped as the factory went down. Figures provided by the Bangladesh Garment Manufacturers and Exporters Association (BGMEA) and mentioned in the Friendship report put the total at 230. See: Friendship (2005) Brief proposal "Friendship Survey Report on possible intervention for the victims of the disaster of the Spectrum Sweater Collapse on 11 April 2005"; unpublished document Friendship dated 14.4.05.

3   It has been claimed that there had been a dispute concerning overtime/ nightshift pay. This has been denied by the employer which suggests that the dispute may have been between some workers who were directly employed by line managers rather than by the company which could account for such a dispute. This was said to be one of the reasons for the difficulty in establishing precise number of workers in the factory that night (Reported by Neil Kearney).

4   Workers refer to this floor as the seventh floor in their testimonies which includes the ground floor.

5   CCC (2005a) 'Testimony No. 10: of knitting machine operator on the 7th (6th floor Author's note) floor', and 'Testimony No. 4: of a knitting machine operator who was not working the night of the collapse but who had left at 9 p.m.'. The former estimated 130, the latter put the figure at between eighty and eighty-five and 110–120 on the fourth floor.

6   CCC (2005b) 'Testimony No. 10: Machine operator on 7th Floor left arm amputated'.

7   INCIDIN 2006 Fact Finding Report on the Spectrum Disaster Victims, Dhaka: BNC, BGMEA, INCIDIN, p.12.

8   '...the workers (are) in a very poor state, not only physically, but also in a state of shock. Some have lost their limbs and... running a temperature due to post surgery infection. Their families who... attend upon them [are] equally distressed, because they had no other means of survival except the monthly wages their son, brother or husband earned' (Sramik Nirapotta Forum, 2005: 2).

9   As at 25.5.2005.

10 Elita Karim After the disaster, Daily Star Magazine, available at: http://www. thedailystar.net/magazine/2007/04/04/education.htm (Last accessed 13 May 2011).

11 Interview with Neil Kearney, Brussels, 31.3.2009.

12 Interview with the owner conducted 8. 6.2009.

13 Figures as at 11.4.2005.

14 Section 4 Workmen's Compensation Act 1923

Chapter 3

1   Interview with the owner, *op.cit.*

2   A statutory body entrusted with the responsibility of initiating and implementing urban development through planning.

3   Interview with the owner, *op.cit.*

4   Institute of Bangladesh Engineers (IEB) Report, Part 1.

5   *Ibid.*

6   Evidence submitted by the owner based on BUET test reports.

7   IEB Report Part 2.

8   *Ibid.*

9   Legislation which was in force at the time of the factory collapse.

10 For a discussion of lack of health and safety enforcement of factories in the UK, for example, see Tombs and Whyte (2010). Cf. also ILO *op.cit.*

11 For a discussion of the bigger picture see Ahmad (2005).

12 The combined turnover of brands involved in multi-stakeholder code monitoring constitutes only ten per cent of total sales revenue of the apparel and footwear industries, R. Casey 2006 *Meaningful Change*, Working Paper 29, Cambridge MA: Kennedy School of Government, Harvard University, p.31 quote in Wells (2009).

13 An exception is Convention 138 on Minimum Age.

14 Providing a common auditing platform means aligning the company code with a commonly agreed code and following a single auditing procedure with its auditors accredited in line with a specific auditing standard. The BSCI opted for auditor accreditation under the Social Accountability International scheme. The SA 8000 standard is a robust code and the guidance document for auditors very thorough, but even this included no reference to structural surveys in the rubric on health and safety at the time (SAI, 2008: 37–55).

15 'An eight storey building in four and half years is the slowest construction – we were adding one new floor every six months as finances permitted – we didn't need the sweater business immediately', Interview with the owner, *op.cit.*

16 BSCI Code of Conduct March 2004 version 7.6.

17 Three months prior to the collapse a woman worker had been injured by an electric shock after her shawl became tangled in a live 11 KV line adjacent to exit door, and earlier a worker from the dyeing section had been scalded to death when he opened a tap on the machine. Reported in Alam, K. (2005) *Worker Profile Spectrum Sweaters*, Dhaka: Alternative Movement for Resources and Freedom Society.

18 Unpublished official report in Bangla shown to the author and translated and witnessed by an interpreter, which refutes the appearance of cracks. However, see also CCC (2005a) and Klawitter (2005).

Chapter 4

1   See: www.drishtipat.org.

2   See: www.uttorshuri.org.

3   See: Drishtipat Writers' Collective (Blog). Available at: http://dpwriters. wordpress.com (Last accessed 13 May 2011).

4   See: Drishtipat, 'Palashbari Tragedy Justice Wanted'. Available at: http://www. drishtipat.org/images/Garments_disaster/index2.htm; See also: A Drishtipat Initiative, 'Death and Destruction'. Available at: http://www.drishtipat.org/ images/Garments_disaster/Death%20and%20Destruction/index.html (Last accessed 13 May 2011).

5   See: Drishtipat, 'Drishtipat Rehabilitation Programme Spectrum Victims'. Available at: http://www.drishtipat.org/images/Garments_disaster/ beneficiaries.html (Last accessed 13 May 2011).

6   SKOP was established in a joint meeting of the top leaders of 12 national trade unions in Dhaka on 13 April 1983.

7   See: Bangladesh National Workers Federation. Available at: http://www.nadir.org/nadir/initiativ/agp/s26/banglad/index.htm (Last accessed 13 May 2011).
8   Email from Amin NGWF to CCC 23.4.2005.
9   Email to CCC 22.4.2009.
10 Email to CCC 22.4.2009.
11 Eighteen unions were politically aligned at the time according to information provided by AMRF.
12 Article 18 ILO Convention 121.
13 The Fatal Accidents Act, 1855 (ACT NO. XIII OF 1855) [27 March, 1855.]
14 One Lakh is a unit in the Indian numbering system equal to one hundred thousand.
15 A director of the association is reported to have said that the BGMEA fixed the amount equal to life insurance claims, and that the association compelled those owners of garment factories without employee liability insurance to pay the same amount to the victims that they would otherwise receive as life insurance.
16 Interview with the owner, *op.cit.*
17 The New Nation, http//www,nation.ittefaq.com 29 May 2005, p.8 (Last accessed 2 July 2009).
18 Letter from Neil Kearney ITGLWF to the Bangladesh Government 28 April 2005.
19 Clean Clothes International Secretariat 2006. Three tragedies hit Bangladesh factories in one week leaving scores dead and wounded. http://www.cleanclothes.org/news/three-tragedies-hit-bangladesh-factories-in-one-week-leaving-scores-dead-wounded (Last accessed 13 May 2011).

Chapter 5

1   In June 2012 the ITGLWF will formally cease to exist and merge with two other global unions: the International Chemical, Energy and Mineworkers' Union (ICEM) and the International Metalworkers' Federation (IMF). The new Global Union is to be called IndustriALL.
2   In 2005 there were 8 ITGLWF affiliates in Bangladesh with a further 6 with applications for affiliation pending. The ITGLWF had suggested the formation of the BNC to deal with the problem of multi unionism in the sector.
3   Email from the Bangladesh National Garments Workers and Employees League (BNGWEL) dated 12.4.05. Email from the Bangladesh Textile & Garments Workers League dated 13. 4. 2005. Email from the Bangladesh Garments Workers Unity Council (BGWUC) representing ten National Federations in the RMG 13.4.2005. Email from the Shadhin Bangla Garments Sramik Kormochari Federation (SBGSKF) 22.4.2005.
4   *Ibid.*
5   Clean Clothes Campaign 2005 'Bangladeshi Garment Workers buried alive', cf. http://www.cleanclothes.org/newslist/363-bangladesh-workers-buried-alive (Last accessed 13 May 2011).
6   On 19 September, 2004 the Bangladesh Government passed a temporary derogation to the existing law on working time permitting a seventy-two

hour week in the RMG sector. The derogation which was to become permanent expired on 18 March 2005 under pressure from the unions and the opposition.

7   Telephone interview with Amirul Haque Amin, 21.06.2009.

8   Interview with Javier Chercolés 11 June 2009.

9   Inditex (2004) Tested to Wear Audit methodology for external manufacturers and suppliers, 2004 la Coruna: Inditex.

10 Federación Estatal de Industrias Textil-Piel, Quimicas y Afines de Comisiones Obreras.

11 Unión General de Trabajadores.

12 For a comprehensive bibliography,cf. http://www.alyssaalappen. org/2002/12/04/bibliography-on-bhopal-disaster/ (Last accessed 13 May 2011).

13 The NUTGW merged with the General and Municipal, Boilermakers and Allied Trades Union in 1991.

14 Cf. http://www.fidh.org/spip.php?rubrique919 (Last accessed 13 May 2011).

15 See also: Labour Behind the Label (2009) 'Cashing In: Giant retailers, purchasing practices, and working conditions in the garment industry', 9 February 2009. Available at: http://www.labourbehindthelabel.org/ component/content/article/269-giant-retailers-cashing-in-on-poverty-ws- (Last accessed 13 May 2011).

16 http://www.vetementspropres.be/.

17 http://www.schonekleren.be/.

18 The German Textile Workers Union merged with the IG Metall in 1998.

19 http://www.steilmann.de/en/04_00_presse_artikel.php?show=00013 (Last accessed 26.07.2009).

20 Cfr. 'Carrefour-UNI Union International'. Available at: http://www.ewcdb.eu/ show_pdf_first_page.php?document=9934.pdf (Last accessed 13 May 2011).

21 ITGLWF 2005 Decisions of the 9th World Congress, Brussels: ITGLWF.

22 Interview with Neil Kearney 19.2.2009.

23 Email from Ineke Zeldenrust to partner organisations and the ITGLWF 22 April 2005.

24 Communication from Carrefour management to the BBBDT-ABVV branch 18.4.2005.

25 Carrefour statement and response to questions relating to the Spectrum Sweater disaster in Bangladesh as raised by CNE (Centrale Nationale des Employés) and Setca / BBBDT (Syndicat des Employés, Techniciens et Cadres de Belgique). The International Textile, Garment and Leather Workers' Federation (ITGLWF) reported previously on the disaster in ITGLWF (2005c) 'Irresponsible European Retailers Put Lives of Garment Workers at Risk'. Available at: http://www.reports-and-materials.org/Carrefour-responses-re-Spectrum-Sweater-Bangladesh-15-June-2005.doc (Last accessed 13 May 2011).

26 See: 'Carrefour Statement on Social Responsibility Relations with suppliers and subcontractors'. Available at: http://www.carrefour.com/ docroot/groupe/C4com/Commerce%20responsable/Espace%20ISR/ Responsabilit%C3%A9%20sociale/SOCIAL%20RESPONSIBILITY-%20 SUPPLIERS.pdf (Last accessed 13 May 2011).

27 Interview with Manjur Morshed, Social compliance advisor and former Intertek auditor who conducted an audit on behalf of Cotton Group/BSCI at the Shahriyar Fabrics factory 11.06.2009.

28 ITGLWF Letter sent by email to CEOs 28 April 2005.

29 This figure was later revised down significantly to 3,000 units. Interview with Javier Chercoles *op.cit.*

30 Letter from the CEO of Inditex to ITGLWF dated 2 May 2005.

31 Letter from Carrefour to ITGLWF dated 11 May 2005.

32 Inditex/ITGLWF (2005) Project Spectrum – Voluntary Indemnity Payments Scheme, A Coruna/Brussels:Inditex/ITGLWF. First Draft.

33 Arcandor finally went into receivership in June 2009

34 Letter from the Head of Social Affairs, Karstadt–Quelle (now Arcandor) to Neil Kearney, General Secretary of the ITGLWF, 5.5.2005

35 It is of course possible that these were old labels which were found but given the level of subcontracting in the RMG it is also reasonable to come to a conclusion that such work was being undertaken without the knowledge of KarstadtQuelle.

36 Source: CCC.

37 The Richard Howitt speech is available for download at:http://www.ethicaltrade.org/Z/lib/2005/05/eticonf/plen-richard-howitt.shtml#resources (Last accessed Feb 14 2009).

38 http://www.cleanclothes.org/spectrum-disaster-bangladesh/188 (Last accessed Feb 14 2009).

39 Carrefour statement and response to questions relating to the Spectrum Sweater disaster in Bangladesh as raised by CNE (Centrale Nationale des Employés) and Setca / BBBDT (Syndicat des Employés, Techniciens et Cadres de Belgique).

40 Email from CCC Netherlands to the CCC International Secretariat dated 13 April 2005.

41 *Ibid.*

42 BSCI 2005 Press Release Spectrum Factory in Savar, Bangladesh, Brussels 2 June 2005.

43 Email from Neil Kearney to Baddrudoza Nizam, 22 May 2005.

44 Email from Neil Kearney to the author 15.08.2009.

45 Interview with Lakshmi Bhatia 22.07.2009.

46 *Ibid.*

47 Interview with Neil Kearney Feb 19 2009.

48 BSCI 2005 *'After the Collapse of the Spectrum Factory in Savar, Bangladesh,' Report of the delegation visit of BSCI from 6–9 June* released Brussels 23rd June 2005, pp. 2–4.

49 Interview with Lakshmi Bhatia 22.07.2009.

50 Interview with Razaul Karim Buiyan 9.06.2009.

51 See: MFA Forum, 'In Country Working Group'. Available at: http://www.mfa-forum.net/groups/Bangladesh/Introduction.aspx (Last accessed 13 May 2011).

52 Email from Neil Kearney 15.08.2009.

53 *Ibid.*

54 Inditex/ITGLWF, *op.cit.*p.1.

55 Cf. Rosen H. 2005 Labor Market Adjustment to the Multi-Fiber
    Arrangement Removal http://www.mfa-forum.net/LinkClick.aspx?fileticket=
    ylduW5WAPZo%3D&tabid=57 (Last accessed 13 May 2011).
    There is no available comprehensive overview of worker compensation
    schemes worldwide. However Rosen lists 88 countries which have no
    unemployment insurance scheme in place and it can be reasonably assumed
    that in such societies provision in this area is likely to be underdeveloped if
    non-existent.

56 Email from International Commission of Labor Rights to Clean Clothes
    campaign 1.10.05.

57 See: HCCH 'Convention of 1 July 1985 on the Law Applicable to Trusts and
    on their Recognition', Entry into force 1 January 2002. Full text available at:
    http://www.hcch.net/index_en.php?act=conventions.text&cid=59

58 KPMG 2005 Spectrum Garments Accident: Definitions, Criteria, Terms of
    Reference and Actuarial Valuations, Dhaka, September 2005, FIRST DRAFT.

59 Report of Third BSCI mission 17.09.2005 Courtesy: Clean Clothes
    Campaign.

60 *Ibid.*

61 *Ibid.*

62 A technique in economics used to determine the relative value of two
    currencies by taking some international measure and determining the cost for
    that measure in each of the two currencies and comparing the amount.

63 Email to Clean Clothes dated 13.09.2005.

64 *Ibid.*

65 *Ibid.*

66 Email from CCC to unions in Bangladesh dated 29 September 2005.

67 Further legal advice received by CCC suggested that it might be possible
    to threaten litigation *vis-á-vis* those brands which were not contributing
    sufficiently into the trust fund once the proposal was on the table but this
    would have depended very much on the specific wording of the fund.
    Source CCC.

68 Council Directive 94/45/EC of 22 September 1994 on the establishment of a
    European Works Council or a procedure in Community-scale undertakings and
    Community-scale groups of undertakings for the purposes of informing and
    consulting employees.

69 Email to Javier Chercoles dated 19.10.2005.

70 BSCI 2006 Press Release: European Commerce pushes for improvement of
    social standards in Bangladesh Press Release available at http://www.bsci-eu.
    com/index.php?id=2041&PHPSESSID=r710ponhei8g9svq83sn89end3
    (Last accessed 13 May 2011).

71 Minutes of a meeting held at the Offices of INCIDIN to discuss Immediate
    Relief Support for Spectrum Workers, Dhaka, Bangladesh 05.12.2005.

72 Email from Oxfam Bangladesh to KarstadtQuelle 12.12.2005.

73 www.cleanclothes.org/urgent/05.12.15 (Last accessed March 21 2009).

74 Cf Klawitter *op.cit.* and Dietrich Weinbrenner *Eine Welt ohne Armut ist moeglich* (A world without poverty is possible) 03.04.2006 See: http://www. ik-armut.de/inhalt/Eine%20Welt%20ohne%20Armut%20ist%20moeglich. htm (Last accessed 13 May 2011).

75 Email exchange with Dietrich Weinbrenner.

76 See: http://www.ik-armut.de/inhalt/Eine%20Welt%20ohne%20Armut%20 ist%20moeglich.htm (Last accessed March 24 2009).

77 Tagung der Solidarische Kirche Westfalen / Lippe am 1.11.2006 in Bochum Referat zum Thema „Weltweite Gerechtigkeit im Zeichen der Globalisierung" von Dietrich Weinbrenner (Amt für MÖWE in der EKvW) www.123people. de/s/dietrich+weinbrenner (Last accessed Sept 7 2009).

78 Letter from Professor Merkel, KarstadtQuelle to Javier Chercoles and Neil Kearney dated 18.12.2006.

79 Interview with Neil Kearney, *op.cit.*

80 Crabbé, C. & N. Leroy. 2007. *op.cit.* p.14.

81 Mail from Arcandor (KQ) to the author 2.05.2009.

Chapter 6

1 Steilmann was taken over by the Italian Group Miro Radici during 2006.

2 Interview with the owner 14.1.2012.

3 The Daily Janakantha 23.12.2010.

4 Char areas are small islands which emerge from silt deposits in some of the larger rivers in Bangladesh.

5 Friendship 2005 Brief proposal "Friendship Survey Report on possible intervention for the victims of the disaster of the Spectrum Sweater Collapse on 11th April 2005 dated 14.4.05.

6 Interview with Runa Khan 10.6.09.

7 Friendship 2005, *op.cit.*, p.2.

8 Interview with Runa Khan, *op.cit.*

9 http://friendship-bd.org/site_pages/donors.aspx?id=43 (Last accessed Feb 23 2009).

10 Friendship 2005 *op.cit.*

11 See: Friendship website, 'Savar Garments Rehabilitation Project'. Available at: http://friendship-bd.org/site_pages/relief.aspx?pid_sub=109 (Last accessed 23 February 2009).

12 INCIDIN, BNC, and BGMEA (2006) Fact Finding Report on Spectrum Disaster Victims (Dhaka: INCIDIN). p.6

13 Karstadt Quelle – Friendship Projekt zur Rehabilitation für die Opfer des Spectrum-Unglückes. Status Report on the Friendship Project to rehabilitate the Spectrum victims by Maren Böhm 14.09.06 Author's translation from the German.

14 Friendship intervened more than once in the case of certain families.

15 A cycle van is a pedal-powered three-wheeler which can be used for carrying people or goods.

16 Friendship Rehabilitation project of Savar Garments Final List of beneficiaries as at July 31st 2005. Internal document.

17 Interview with Runa Khan, *op.cit.*

18 KarstadtQuelle Status Report, *op.cit.* p.2.

19 Report of a telephone conversation between Jenneke Arens and Amin (NGWF), 22.6.2005.

20 Written responses from Carrefour management to the union questions posed by CNE and le Setca/ BBBDT on the Belgian works council received by CCC on June 21st.

21 KarstadtQuelle Press release dated 10 April 2006.

22 Khorshed Alam 2006 Friendship Rehabilitation Fund for Spectrum victims (2nd Phase) Research Report submitted to CCC 26.9.06.

23 Status Report by Maren Böhm on the Karstadt Quelle Rehabilitation Project 14.09.06 Sept 2006 Author's translation from the German.

24 This totals BDT 2,647,000 (€28,931 as at March 2007).

25 Cf. 'Savar Garments Rehabilitation Project'. *op.cit.*

26 Friendship 2006 Current Status Report on Garment Rehabilitation Project (Phase 2) supported by Cotton Group and KarstadtQuelle. Friendship: Dhaka p.12.

27 *Ibid.* p.16.

28 Friendship Status Report 2007.

29 Spectrum Relief Fund Medical Report to Year end 2007.

30 Minutes of a meeting held at the Offices of INCIDIN to discuss Immediate Relief Support for Spectrum Workers, 5 December 2005, Dhaka.

31 See: INCIDIN website, 'Background of the organisation'. Available at: http://www.incidinb.org/org_back.html (Last accessed 7 May 2009).

32 Interview with Masud Ali, INCIDIN 09.06.09.

33 Interview with Neil Kearney, 6.2.2009.

34 Minutes of a meeting held at La Vinci Hotel Auditorium, Dhaka, to establish a data collection process attended by ITGLWF, BNC, Oxfam, Inditex, GAP, BGMEA and INCIDIN 17.02.06 (Annex 5 in INCIDIN 2006 Fact Finding Report on Spectrum Disaster Victims, Dhaka: INCIDIN.

35 Interview with Neil Kearney, *op.cit.* The veracity of Kearney's comment is corroborated by research conducted by the Bangladesh National Women Lawyers Association, (BNWLA, 2002)

36 Letter from Inditex SA to the Spectrum buyers dated 11.2.2006.

37 Also calculated as the last consolidated wages of the deceased worker upon occurrence of the collapse.

38 The discount rate in pension calculations refers to the rate of investment return on the overall amount of pension owed if paid now.

39 Bylaws of the Spectrum Victims Trust, Internal Document Inditex SA.

40 Email from Neil Kearney, ITGLWF to Inditex dated 22.11.07.

41 Interview with the owner, *op.cit.*

42 Information provided by Razaul Karim Buiyan Inditex Bangladesh 21.6.09.

43 Interview with Neil Kearney and Javier Chercolés 29.6.09.

44 INCIDIN *op.cit.* Annex 3 Family Circumstances of the dead workers.

45 Text of letter sent to buyers 28.7.2006.

46 Letter from CCC to Javier Chercolés, Inditex and Neil Kearney ITGLWF 29.11.2006.

47 Unpublished Report to Clean Clothes Campaign by Khorshed Alam AMRF dated March 2007.

48 *Ibid.*

49 *Ibid.*

50 Letter from Noor Alam and Jahangir Alam on behalf of the family members of the victims and injured workers of Spectrum to Javier Chercolés and Neil Kearney 22.7.2007.

51 Email from Neil Kearney to CCC 14.11.2007.

52 Interview with Javier Chercolés, 11.06.09.

53 Interview with Neil Kearney, 11.2.09.

54 Interview with the owner, 08.06.09.

55 Notes from a meeting with the owner 14.06.09.

56 There is no centralised clearing and settlement system for the electronic transfer of funds in Bangladesh, although there are arrangements available for the telegraphic transfer of funds between cities. The primary payment mechanism in Bangladesh is by cheque. The use of pay orders and demand drafts is very common with the former used for payments within the same city or clearing zone. Domestic wire transfers are possible but primarily intra-bank, rather than inter-bank. Kamal Ahsan, *Cash management in Bangladesh* originally published in HSBC Guide to Treasury and Cash Management in Asia Pacific 2007.

57 Interview with Javier Chercolés 11.6.2009.

58 Letter from Clean Clothes International Secretariat to Neil Kearney, 26.10.07.

59 Arcandor Press Release dated 9.06.09 http://www.arcandor.com/en/presse/6579.asp (Last accessed September 7 2009).

60 Email from Javier Chercolés to Campana Rope Limpa 25.6.2009.

61 Mannan and Chaudhuri Z.S. (2009).

62 Interview with Javier Chercolés 21.7.2010.

63 There were originally 19 but 2 had remarried. Fact Finding Report 28.

64 Interview with Javier Chercolés *op.cit.*

65 The Sphere Project 2011 Humanitarian Charter and Minimum Standards on Disaster Response http://www.sphereproject.org/dmdocuments/handbook/hdbkpdf/hdbk_c1.pdf (Last accessed December 3 2010).

66 Naripokkho and Bangladesh Mahila Parishad 2005 *Baseline Report: Violence Against Women in Bangladesh* International Women's Rights Action Watch Asia Pacific (IWRAW Asia Pacific) Kuala Lumpur, Malaysia.

67 Bangladesh Jatiyo Mohila Ainjibi Samity 2001.

68 J. Chercolés Blasquez (2011) *Navigating the Spiders Web. Developing A Rights Based Approach To Industrial Disaster Management— The Case of The Spectrum Sweaters.* Unpublished paper.

69 Acid Survivors Foundation Bangladesh 11.2010. http://www.acidsurvivors.org/statistics.html (Last accessed October 27 2010).

70 Unpublished survey of widows undertaken by Inditex CSR team Bangladesh August 2009.

71 It was reported that widows received 100% compensation if they had a son but mothers of only daughters had to share the amount with their in-laws.

72 *Ibid.*

73 *Ibid.*

74 Q'uran 4:12.

75 Just-Style.com: BGMEA in MOU talks with Inditex, 29.4.2010. Interview with Javier Chercolés 21.7.2010. Draft Inditex/ITGLWF Relief Scheme for Industrial Accidents.

76 Refayet Ullah Mirdha: More apparel buyers look to Bangladesh http://www.thedailystar.net/story.php?nid=96490 08.09.09 cf also Just-Style.com Bangladesh in brief, apparel trade overview. August 2. 2010.

77 Shafiq Alam: Bangladesh textiles unravelled by price war, protests. Agence France Presse 1.7.2009. http://www.textiletodaybd.com/News/news_detail.php?news=NEWS000394. Daily Star 2010 Ashulia erupts into violence 29.7.2010 the Daily Star available at: http://www.thedailystar.net/newDesign/news-details.php?nid=94665.

78 ITGLWF 2011 Report of Multi-Stakeholder Meeting on Fire Safety in Bangladesh, 4th–5th of December, Dhaka, unpublished report. Brussels: International Textile Garment and Leather Workers' Federation.

79 International Labour Rights Forum, United Students Against Sweatshops, Maquila Solidarity Network, Worker Rights Consortium were the authors of the joint communiqué issued December 21 along with the Clean Clothes Campaign.

Chapter 7

1   As updated in Chapter 2, Clause 26, Bangladesh Labour Act 2006.

2   Payments were made on nineteen separate occasions according to the owners.

3   Some nine workers were accommodated at Moreen Apparels, an Inditex supplier.

4   In order for Shafiqul to withdraw his salary from his local bank, the company was able to persuade the bank to install a ramp to the ATM machine and entrance to the premises.

5   Interview with the owner, 08.06.09.

6   Letter from Neil Kearney ITGLWF to the Bangladesh Government 28.4.2005.

7   Following the 2006 Labour Act statutory compensation has been increased from 21,000 to 100,000 and this amount is now enhanced to 200,000 by the BGMEA. Email from Jenefa Jabbar former counsel to the BGMEA dated 7.7.09.

8   Just-Style.com 2006 Bangladesh: three factories at risk of collapsing – BGMEA 20 March 2006 | Source: just-style.com (Last accessed June 26 2009).

9   Bangladesh Export Promotion Bureau (EPB) http://www.epb.gov.bd/index.php?NoParameter&Theme=default&Script=cmc (Last accessed March 23 2012).

10 *Ibid.*

11 *Ibid.*

12 Section 169 ((1) & (2)).Bangladesh Labour Act 2006 Available at: http://complytex.com/bangladesh_labor/Bangladesh_Labor_Law.pdf

13 *Ibid.* Section 155 (6).

14 *Ibid.* Section 151(1)(d) and Schedule V.

15 *Ibid.* Section 168.

16 Bikash Kumar Basak, Loopholes in the Labour Act, 2006. http://www.thedailystar.net/law/2008/10/01/info.htm (Last accessed May 20 2011).

17 M. Rahman Construction Sites go unwatched http://www.thedailystar.net/newDesign/news-details.php?nid=180240 (Last accessed May 20 2011).

18 Not to be confused with Bangladesh Labour-Welfare Foundation which is an NGO established in 1997 and registered with the Department of Social Welfare.

19 Email from Jafrul Hasan Sharif, Manusher Jonno Foundation, 01.09.09.

20 New Wave Group, Solo-Invest made pledges of €5000 to the Trust Fund while KarstadtQuelle pledged €100,000, however none of these buyers played any role in ensuring any payments reached the victims.

21 Interview with a former social auditor at Intertek, Dhaka 11.06.09.

22 N. Kearney 2005 Annex to the ITGLWF urgent appeal for the victims of the Savar disaster. Report on mission to Bangladesh in the case of the spectrum factory disaster June 5–8, Brussels: ITGLWF.

23 Section 85(3) Bangladesh Labour Act 2006.

24 http://www.cleanclothes.org/urgent-actions/compensation-deceased-garib-workers-still-inadequate (Last accessed April 25 2011).

25 Report of the multi-stakeholder meeting on compensation, fire prevention and other issues arising from the fire on 21 February 2010 at Garib and Garib held at the Best Western La Vinci Hotel, Dhaka, 4th December 2010.

26 ITGLWF 2011 Report of Multi-Stakeholder Meeting on Fire Safety in Bangladesh, 4th–5th of December, Dhaka, unpublished report, Brussels: International Textile Garment and Leather Workers' Federation.

27 International Labour Rights Forum, United Students Against Sweatshops, Maquila Solidarity Network, Worker Rights Consortium were the authors of the joint communiqué issued December 21 along with the Clean Clothes Campaign.

28 Multi-stakeholder round-table meeting on Compensation for victims of the That's it Sportswear (Hameem group) fire Dhaka, 16 and 18 April 2011, demands on compensation. Brussels: ITGLWF.

Chapter 8

1 http://www.ethicaltrade.org/.

2 http://www.etiskhandel.no/English/index.html.

3 http://en.fairwear.nl/.

4 http://www.coc-runder-tisch.de/coc-runder-tisch/rt/f_intro_E.htm (Last accessed 1 July 2009).

5 http://www.bsci-eu.com/index.php?id=2008 (Last accessed 1 July 2009).

6 Multiline had been an earlier client of Shahriyar Fabrics.

7 Document in Bangla shown to the author and translated and witnessed by an interpreter.

8 The evidence regarding cracks as reported by survivors proved to be contradictory. Cf. CCC(2005a) and Klawitter *op.cit.*

9 'Deviations from Rajuk-Approved Designs – 3000 buildings identified', The Daily Star 23.06.2009 http://www.thedailystar.net/new/Design/news-details.php?nid=93820 (Last accessed 20 May 2011).

10 Lukac J.(2006) Zara, Inditex and Amancio Ortega – the Responsibility of Success http://www.triplepundit.com/pages/zara-inditex-an.php (Last accessed 20 May 2011).

11 Interview with Javier Chercolés, 06.09.2009.

12 Inditex Annual Reports 2005–6 (€72,542), 2006–7 (€94,908), 2007–8 there was no expenditure because of the State of Emergency in Bangladesh. During 2008–9 a further €77,000 was allocated. Subsequent annual reports no longer detail Spectrum expenditures.

13 Correspondence between KarstadtQuelle (Far East) & Co.Shanghai Representative Office and Javier Chercolés cited by Javier Chercolés.

14 KarstadtQuelle – Friendship Projekt zur Rehabilitation für die Opfer des Spectrum-Unglückes Status Report by Maren Böhm 14.09.2006. Author's translation from the German.

15 Friendship 2005 Brief proposal "Friendship Survey Report on possible intervention for the victims of the disaster of the Spectrum Sweater Collapse on 11 April 2005 dated 14.4.2005.

16 Interview with Runa Khan, *op.cit.*

17 Inditex 2009 Impact Assessment of the Friendship Initiatives. Unpublished report, Inditex/Bangladesh.

18 Interview with A. K. Masud Ali, INCIDIN offices 09.06.2009.

19 Interview with Neil Kearney, 29.06.2009.

20 Interview with Runa Khan, *op.cit.* There were indeed subsequent disasters following Spectrum and in one case this involved a fire in a building housing Sayem Fashions, an Inditex supplier in March 2008 as reported in an email from Ineke Zeldenrust to Javier Chercolés, 28.3.2008.

21 INCIDIN 2006 Bangladesh RMG Workers Strategic Proposition to MFA Forum, Dhaka: INCIDIN http://www.bgw-info.net/MFA/TU%20paper%20on%20MFA%20forum.pdf, (Last accessed July 15 2009).

22 Interview with K. Masud Ali, *op.cit.*

23 In Palashbari, on the old site, trial production started again in winter 2009 after 4 years. The parent company Shahriyar Fabric Industries Limited received planning permission for this new facility in the middle of 2006. The building is now five storey and built using beamed, instead of 'flat slab' construction. All activities in sweater production have ceased and all dyeing, finishing and circular knitting machines are now located in a single storey mill built out on reclaimed land to the rear of the factory. The factory now has an extended mosque as a mark of respect for the victims.